T0316311

Getting to Know Schools in a Democracy

The Politics and
Process of Evaluation

Social Research and Educational Studies Series

Series Editor
Robert G. Burgess,
Senior Lecturer in Sociology,
University of Warwick

Social Research and Education Studies Series: 5

Getting to Know Schools in a Democracy

The Politics and
Process of Evaluation

Helen Simons

Routledge
Taylor & Francis Group

LONDON AND NEW YORK

First published 1987
by Routledge
2 Park Square, Milton Park, Abingdon, Oxon, OX14 4RN
711 Third Avenue, New York, NY 10017, USA

First issued in hardback 2017

Routledge is an imprint of the Taylor & Francis Group, an informa business

Library of Congress Cataloging in Publication Data

Simons, Helen.
    Getting to know schools in a democracy.

    (Social research and educational studies series; 5)
    1. Educational evaluation—Great Britain.   I. Title.
II. Series.
LB2822.75.S56   1986   379.1′54   86-29376

ISBN 13: 978-1-138-42095-3 (hbk)
ISBN 13: 978-1-85000-148-5 (pbk)

Jacket design by Caroline Archer

Typeset in 11/13 Garamond by
Imago Publishing Ltd, Thame, Oxon

Contents

Acknowledgements

The generation of ideas is a social rather than a solitary process. That being the case I have more people to thank for their contribution to this book than I can possibly acknowledge. Some of my debts will be obvious, some less so. Over the years and sometimes at crucial points in the development of my work, conversations with the following people have helped me to understand my research experience and to shape my practice: Clem Adelman, Mike Atkin, Tony Becher, John Elliott, David Hamilton, Tom Hastings, Ernie House, Stephen Humble, David Jenkins, Barry MacDonald, Malcolm Parlett, Richard Pring, Lou Smith, Bob Stake and Rob Walker. More recently I have appreciated discussions with Tom Fox, Peter Mitchell, Nigel Norris, Desmond Nuttall and Ian Stronach.

There are many more, too numerous to name, to whom I am equally grateful. To all those teachers, pupils, administrators and students with whom I have had the pleasure to work over the years and who may not even know the contribution they have made to the ideas reported here, I owe a special debt and thanks. Research of the particular kind described in this book is a communal enterprise. I want to formally acknowledge that what follows would not have been possible without the collaboration of innumerable practitioners of, and aspirants to, educational practice and curriculum improvement.

I would also like to thank Bob Burgess for his encouragement and very helpful editorial suggestions and Lynn Cairns whose understanding and support was as important to me in seeing the project through as her expert typing of the manuscript.

Series Editor's Preface

The purpose of the *Social Research and Educational Studies* series is to provide authoritative guides to key issues in educational research. The series includes overviews of fields, guidance on good practice and discussions of the practical implications of social and educational research. In particular, the series deals with a variety of approaches to conducting social and educational research. Contributors to this series review recent work, raise critical concerns that are particular to the field of education, and reflect on the implications of research for educational policy and practice.

Each volume in the series draws on material that will be relevant for an international audience. The contributors to this series all have wide experience of teaching, conducting and using educational research. The volumes are written so that they will appeal to a wide audience of students, teachers and researchers. Altogether, the volumes in the *Social Research and Educational Studies* series provide a comprehensive guide for anyone concerned with contemporary educational research.

The series will include individually-authored books and edited volumes on a range of themes in education including: qualitative research, survey research, the interpretation of data, self-evaluation, research and social policy, analyzing data, action research, the politics and ethics of research.

For some years the study of educational evaluation has been dominated by abstract articles that can be found in dense American tomes which claim to review the field. Yet these reviews have rarely provided a concise account of the way in which practising evaluators work. In this book Helen Simons carefully examines the theory and practice of democratic evaluation with special reference to Britain. She explores the practice of evaluation through detailed case studies which give her scope to examine questions relating to the conduct and dissemination of educational evaluation. Finally, she considers the move to school self-evaluation. Throughout this book Helen Simons provides a discussion of evaluation that is linked to the politics of education and the study of the curriculum which will be of interest to researchers, curriculum evaluators, policy makers and teachers.

Robert Burgess
University of Warwick

Author's Preface

In September 1969 I came across an article in *New Society* titled
'Open-minded teaching'. It was written by Lawrence Stenhouse,
Director of the Humanities Curriculum Project, one of the national
curriculum development projects sponsored by the Schools Council
in England in preparation for the raising of the school leaving age,
scheduled for 1970. I was working in Melbourne for the Victoria
Education Department as an educational psychologist, and thinking
about a change of scenery and a change of job. I had been four years
in the job, handling 'miscreants' referred by the ten schools under my
wing. Much of my work involved visits to the schools, either to find
out more about the nature of the problem or to discuss the
reintegration of the adolescent. As with any other role in circumstances of flexibility, I had gradually reconstructed mine to place more
emphasis on prevention rather than repair. Some of the problems
referred to me seemed to be more the result of institutional than
individual deficiency and I found myself getting more and more
interested in schools as a focus for resolving what were clearly not
isolated problem cases. I was not impressed by the curriculum of the
secondary schools, which was typically of the traditional academic
variety, watered down for the less able and unresponsive to either
parental needs or changing social and cultural conditions. In Victoria
syllabuses were centrally prescribed for all state schools.

In 1968, a year before I read Lawrence's article, a radical change
of curriculum policy by the state led to an experiment in one of 'my'
ten schools that changed my thinking about what I wanted to do. In
that year the State Department of Education changed its policy and
allowed the schools for the first time in history to devise their own
syllabuses. One of the schools in my area saw the change as an opportunity to experiment with the total structure and curriculum for the

first and fourth year. Overnight almost they dismantled classroom walls to facilitate open plan learning, regrouped pupils, vertically in some cases, mixed ability in others, dispensed with formal timetables, restructured the curriculum on a topic/issue basis, and decided to teach in teams. For the teachers this meant deciding on relevant themes and translating these into curricular possibilities, working into the night preparing materials and resources which did not in many cases exist, daily forward planning, discussing effects with each other and, in some instances, recording the experience for teachers in other schools. For the pupils it meant learning how to work without direction, how to manage their time, how to research topics, and when and how to use the resources available, including the teacher.

It was an exciting proposal, a full-scale implementation of an innovation that developed in action. It was fascinating to watch. The teachers were totally committed, excited and tired in turn. They had more ideas than they could immediately handle — but their confidence did not pall nor their commitment flag. Of course there was some chaos, uncertainty about appropriate assessment criteria for pupil performance and worry over resources and time, but enough commitment to sustain the challenge.

Pupils were excited too, and, able and less able alike, flourished in the open environment. They were free to express ideas, plan their own work and support their classmates, for team teaching was extended to pupils. Those who found it difficult to initiate work or sustain it without direction were given encouragement by their classmates who sometimes worked alongside or with them. Teachers alternated between the roles of consultants, providers of ideas and resources, and group discussion leaders.

Only the head felt somewhat disphased. His role in this process was less well-defined and his former role of running the school had almost disappeared. Rules of self-government were being generated by teachers and pupils as they went along. But he was content to watch and learn. It was a cooperative experiment.

This experiment was a very stimulating experience for me also. Although the spread of my case load over ten schools restricted my flexibility, I found myself more and more involved with this particular school, struck by the impact of release from prescription on the creativity and energy of the teachers, and by the response of the pupils — the freedom they felt, the confidence they displayed, and the initiatives they took. I spent as much time as I could spare sitting in on staff meetings, talking to teachers and pupils about their plans, aspirations, anxieties, problems. To some extent I became a collaborator in the enterprise feeding back perceptions and offering advice but increasingly conscious that I had no real knowledge base to underpin advice on how to develop new curricular arrangements or how to assess progress. The experiment had, however, opened my eyes to both the possibility and desirability of changing the institutional experience of schooling, and by the end of 1969 I was thinking of looking for a job, perhaps in research, that might give me the opportunity to pursue this interest.

I was thinking of going to England anyway, and when I read Lawrence's article it seemed to me that what the Humanities Project was attempting was to create relationships between teachers and students that would release both from the assumptions of instructional transmission and cultural dominance. I wrote to Lawrence, pointing out similarities between his curriculum aspirations and aspects of the school development with which I had been associated. I asked if there was any possibility of a job with the team when I arrived in 1970. To my surprise he replied, not exactly offering a job, but expressing interest in my observations and concluding with 'if you are prepared to come we will interview you when you arrive'.

That was how I turned up the following summer at a teacher training college in South London, where the Project, then in its third year, was located in two mobile offices and a few small college rooms. The Project was preparing for a dissemination phase and publication of its teacher guides to group discussion of controversial issues and its thematic collections of documentary evidence. It was also preparing to move to Norwich, to the University of East Anglia, which had agreed to incorporate four members of the team at the Centre for Applied Research in Education (CARE). There was no place for me in the development team, but I was fortunate in arriving at a point when Barry MacDonald, the Project evaluator, was staffing a four-person team to carry out the second phase of the evaluation. Evaluation was a new word to me, but it turned out that MacDonald, who was looking for someone to assist with the case study approach to evaluation he had been developing, had been impressed by the observations on school development I had included in my letter to Lawrence. I got the job, and started a new professional life.

The Humanities Curriculum Project was the vehicle through which Stenhouse and his colleagues pursued the ideal of an emancipatory schooling — for all. As an evaluator I found myself committed to a parallel aspiration — understanding the obstacle course which, at all levels of the system, would act to contain, assimilate and neutralize the emancipatory goal. Out of our experience of development and evaluation evolved diverging theories of action. The project development team, taking the view that teacher development was a prerequisite of significant change in the curricular experience of school pupils, evolved varying patterns of collaborative work with teachers, stimulating and supporting investigative and reflective dimensions of the teacher role, creating networks and associations of teachers and teacher educators. We evaluators, on the other hand, beginning with case studies of the immediate, local contexts of new classroom practices but increasingly conscious of the opportunities afforded by their relationship to programmes linking such practice to distant but powerful sources of influence, evolved our own theory and practice of emancipatory action. That theory and practice is the subject of this book.

Helen Simons
October, 1986

Introduction

About the Book

This book is intended to fill a gap in the literature of post-war social research. It is an account of the development of educational evaluation in Britain from the late sixties to the present day. It is a personal account, both in the sense that it is organized around an argument, and in the sense that it is a biography of my experience as a practitioner of evaluation and as a member of a particular evaluation community. Interest in the evaluation of schooling has never been more widespread than it is now, much of it prompted by an accountability movement that has focussed increasingly upon the issue of whether schools are doing as well as they might. This is not for the most part a 'friendly' interest, despite the prominence of the notion of self-evaluation in the strategic advocacies of those who want a data base for political administrative or consumer judgment. My concern in this book is with finding ways of getting to know schools that will enable them to become more democratic institutions offering a more educational service. To the extent that the school is, at least in part, a 'frozen institution' (House, 1974) this means that I have also to be concerned with policy and programme evaluation, with how democratic and educational possibilities are made more or less viable by options and choices made by other institutions and individuals. Evaluators are not alone in this concern, of course, but the context in which evaluation theory and practice have thrived — post-war curriculum reform — has given us better access to the processes of curriculum formation and the problems of change than are generally afforded to other interested parties. A theme of this book is how we have defined and used that opportunity.

The book will, I hope, be of interest for a number of reasons. It offers an introduction to evaluation theory, with a particular focus on the political implications of theoretical formulations, and a detailed exposition of MacDonald's (1974) democratic theory of evaluation. It tells how the case study approach to evaluation evolved, and something about the community of 'naturalistic' evaluators, American as well as British, who made a concerted effort from the early seventies to influence the forms and values of inquiry related to curriculum development. It also reports in detail evaluations I have carried out at different points in time and understanding, against a changing background of curriculum politics.

It is an account of the process of doing evaluations, of researching the problematics of that process, and of reflecting upon the experience. I hope my story will help people to understand that evaluation is a very difficult business to do well and that the transition of the school system from a largely private world in professional hands to a largely public sphere of informed deliberation is a project that calls for imagination, caution and patient determination.

About the Context

'What's the title of your book?'
'Getting to know schools in a democracy.'
'You mean you have found one?'

This exchange took place in June 1986, during a coffee break in one of those frustrating interprofessional discussions that seemed to be convened once a week in those days to discuss the implications of the latest government initiative in education. I can't recall precisely the topic of discussion — it might have been the Technical and Vocational Education Initiative (TVEI), or pupil records of achievement, or teacher appraisal, or the new GCSE examinations, or school self-evaluation, or the latest cuts in university finance, or, or, or. The agenda of the debate in the eighties was dominated by the thrust of political initiatives at the national level. The bid for political control of the curriculum was in full swing, and many of us in the education business were engaged in what we saw to be damage limitation. The sardonic response to my book title was, in this context, a cry of protest about a government that appeared to be increasingly impervious to any reasoning other than its own, and that seemed determined to impose its will and its massive parliamentary majority on a supposedly decentralized system.

That fact alone makes it more difficult than it normally is to describe, for those readers unfamiliar with it, the distribution of power that characterizes the educational system in England and Wales. Normally, the issue of description revolves around an old chestnut. Is the British system best described as a national system locally administered or as a local system nationally administered?

There is certainly a large central administration, the Department of Education and Science (DES), staffed by career civil servants accountable to the Secretary of State, who is a member of the Cabinet. Then there are 104 local administrations, staffed almost exclusively by people whose careers began with classroom teaching and will end with local service. There is, in other words, no mobility between central and local administrations. At the local level officers are accountable to the elected members of the local education authority, usually through an Education Committee. These are local elections, so there is a democratic political authority at two levels in the system. Then there are the schools, each under a headteacher and a governing body of local appointees. Teachers are appointed and paid locally, but according to collectively negotiated salary scales which have to be ratified nationally. Local government can and does raise revenue through rates, but is substantially dependent on the centrally provided rate support grant for the financing of its schools. Then there is Her Majesty's Inspectorate (HMI), a formally independent group of some 500 ex-teachers, located in the DES and often referred to as the Ministry's 'eyes and ears'. They are constituted as an advisory body to central and local administrations, and to schools, which they 'inspect' individually and survey from time to time.

The relationship of these various parties to the business of schooling, ie curriculum, is anything but clear cut, and has always been a matter of dispute between descriptive theorists, but there is, or at least was until quite recently, a consensual rhetoric that captured its spirit:

> For thirty years after 1944, the development of the service was managed by a partnership. The terms of the partnership were that the Secretary of State determined broad national policy and the allocation of resources, the LEA implemented national policy with substantial local discretion, and the individual establishment was responsible for the curriculum and how it was taught. (Hall, 1985, p. 4)

You will not have missed the implication that at some point in the mid-seventies this basically tri-partite arrangement came under some strain, and my earlier remarks give some indication of the nature and source of that strain.

As we move into the late 1980s interventionism in the work of teachers has reached a level whereby the control of the curriculum is being fundamentally restructured in England and Wales. At the time of writing the future pattern is far from clear. The Conservative government in Britain is in two minds and talks with two voices. One voice suggests that the future will reflect a devolution of power to the clientele of the schools. By one means or another parents, both individually and through representation, will have much more say in the service that schools provide than they have enjoyed in the past. The other voice says that curriculum control will be more centralized. Government will employ teachers and shape their work in ways that are not encumbered by the complexities of the local education authority role. Both voices agree on one thing; the professional autonomy of teachers that has for so long been a hallmark of the rhetoric of curriculum control will be curtailed.

Other reforms in the offing, reforms which command an increasing consensus, include the integration of education and training within a single Whitehall department. This at least will have the benefit of unifying the confusing range of interventionist sources that are currently taking the curriculum apart but leaving it to teachers to stitch together again into a coherent form. Prominent among these sources are, of course, the Department of Employment (DoE) through its ad hoc agency, the Manpower Services Commission (MSC), the demoted but still influential Department of Education and Science (DES) and the new politically centralized Secondary Examinations Council (SEC) and the School Curriculum Development Committee (SCDC) (see the notes to chapter 2) whose formal separateness adds to the confusion. The major mechanism of interventionism in direct curriculum control is categorical central funding whilst the parallel mechanism for control of teachers is prescriptive accreditation of teacher training, with teacher appraisal just around the corner. If there is a single overall aim of these various strong arm initiatives it appears to be to make schooling subject to the primacy of centrally defined economic and political goals.

That education is a political issue is in little doubt in 1987. Can we therefore say any less of the array of evaluation enterprises which accompany curriculum interventions? No one should be surprised to learn, if they did not assume, that the evaluation of curriculum development is now subject to a greater degree of control by its powerful sponsors than was the case when educational development was conceived as primarily a matter for the professional judgment of teachers. When curriculum policy is government policy there is little tolerance of evaluators who raise awkward questions about decisions that are seen to be economically imperative and politically irreversible. Neither should one be surprised, in these circumstances, to find that those evaluators, both practitioners and theorists, who developed their concept of evaluation as an information service independent of factional control find it more difficult to work with the executive agencies charged with policy implementation. Bureaucratic evaluation has now assumed the absolute predominance predicted by MacDonald in the early seventies (MacDonald, 1974). The question, for those who see some value in an activity which has at least aspired to bear fair witness to issues in dispute, is whether and how evaluation can overcome an imminent crisis of public credibility. This book basically explores, and attempts to explicate, an approach to the evaluation of educational programmes that seeks to be both useful and fair to all those who have a legitimate interest in what schools do.

The Organization of the Book

The book begins with an introduction to the literature of evaluation theory. This is a voluminous literature and in order to select from it in ways that correspond to my interests I have focussed in chapter 1 on exploring the characteristics of evaluation that demarcate the field of my methodological interest in naturalistic inquiry. In chapter 2 I have used three framing questions — who should carry out evaluation in education?, who should judge the value of curricula, organizational and institutional arrangements?, who should have access to evaluation findings? to examine the political implications of evaluation theory in the work of key evaluation theorists. Chapter 2 ends with an outline of democratic evaluation theory which guides the empirical case studies reported in later chapters. In chapter 3 I document the evolution of the case study approach to evaluation in the context of the Humanities Curriculum Project Evaluation and explore the development in the seventies of the growing field of naturalistic evaluation. Chapter 4 reports the first of two case studies exploring the democratic model of evaluation in practice; it describes the process of engaging teachers in a study of curriculum innovation in their own comprehensive school. The conflicts of principle which arose in the case are discussed in chapter 5 and compared with other interpretations of the aspirations in theory and practice. Chapter 6 reports a second case study examining the democratic model beyond the boundaries of the school. It documents a dispute about control of an evaluation report of a controversial innovative programme in one local education authority in England. Chapter 7 examines the conflicts of interest which arose in that study and explores possible resolutions for evaluation practice in terms of a clarification of the rights of dissemination and fair agreements.

Chapters 8 and 9 report a major shift in the focus of evaluation to school self-evaluation where the control of the process and of the product of evaluation lie outside the jurisdiction of the external evaluator. In the context of a changing political climate chapter 8 explores the adaptation of the case study approach in the naturalistic tradition to the context of school self-evaluation. It describes the process model of school self-evaluation I articulated at that time and examines the experience of this model in practice with a group of teachers conducting curriculum policy evaluations in their own schools. Chapter 9 details further the growth and scope of the school self-evaluation movement in the primary context of accountability demands. It examines and offers a critique of LEA and Project-inspired forms of school self-evaluation and concludes by suggesting a reformulation of the concept of school self-evaluation that entails a fundamental change in the organizational values of the school. Chapter 10 summarizes the main argument of the book and locates future possibilities within the framework of contemporary politics.

1 The Nature and Development of Evaluative Inquiry

> Sorting out the good from the bad has long been a human activity, and one that is essential to society itself. Although institutions have often been accorded authority for making certain value judgments, only in recent times has the evaluation of public programs become so formalized as to constitute a recognizably separate activity — and even a new discipline. (House, 1980, p. 15)

Evaluation may or may not be a new discipline as House suggests but it certainly has emerged over the past twenty-five years as a substantial field of activity with a wide range of models and approaches and its own criteria, principles and standards. The field has developed extremely quickly in response initially to the need to monitor large scale social programmes and more latterly to the need to inform policy deliberations at different levels of educational action and accountability.

Although the field is still proliferating, sufficient agreement has accumulated over this period to enable us to identify some theoretical features of educational evaluation. Evaluation is a practical activity (Stake, 1978; Glass, 1972), a particularistic activity (Stake, 1967a; Guba and Lincoln, 1981) and a political activity (House, 1973a; MacDonald, 1974; Weiss, 1975a). The notion of evaluation as a service activity was established early (Cronbach, 1963), the client initially being defined as the curriculum developer and the purpose as 'formative' (Scriven, 1967), enabling improvements in the curriculum to be made while it was still under development. Scriven distinguished this formative role from 'summative' evaluation, designed to assist choices between alternative curricula. 'Service to whom' became a more and more troublesome question for theorists as the evaluation industry grew apace in the sixties and rather slowly developed a political consciousness. While Stufflebeam developed a concept of evaluation as a service to administrative managers (Stufflebeam *et al*, 1971), Stake was busy enlarging the audience possibilities to multiple constituencies (Stake, 1967b). In this country MacDonald first saw service to decision-makers in terms of locally-based individual buyers of curricula (MacDonald, 1971) and later in terms of a brokerage role (MacDonald, 1974). Consciousness of the role of evaluators in influencing the distribution of resources, and increasing sensitivity to the personal and institutional consequences for those subjected to evaluative scrutiny, also led to acknowledgement of evaluation as an ethical activity (House, 1980; Adelman, 1984).

That evaluation is 'fundamentally and inextricably part of a *public* situation, a collective decision' has been firmly declared by House (1980, p. 18) and reaffirmed by many other evaluators pointing to the significance of the evaluation process in the macro politics of change. It is to House, too, that we owe a clarification of the extent and nature of knowledge that we can expect from evaluation in his conception of evaluation as a persuasive activity (*Ibid*, p. 72). Finally, and more recently, taking account of the need to communicate more effectively to achieve the function of evaluation identified above, evaluation has been overtly recognized as an educative activity (Cronbach, 1982).

So we now have a contemporary profile of evaluation, based on the arguments of its leading theorists, that characterizes evaluation as a practical, particularistic, political, persuasive, educative service. Abstracted from the contexts of evaluative action such a profile does not immediately suggest an idiosyncratic discipline of inquiry. One has to understand why these characteristics were thought worthy of emphasis, what arguments these emphases were trying to counteract, what implications for evaluation practice were intended by their proponents, in order to judge such a claim. In the course of this book I hope to contextualize most of the issues that have shaped the development of evaluation theory, but to pay particular attention to those which bear upon my own evaluation experience and my interest in evaluation as a means of assisting professional self-direction in the improvement of schooling. So, rather than explore in detail all these defining characteristics I wish at this point to concentrate on three — the particular, the political and the persuasive — that constitute the most pertinent framework for the accounts of my experience as an evaluator that follow.

Evaluation of the Particular

Most descriptions of evaluation now refer to the fact that evaluation focusses on the *particular,* whether that be a new curriculum programme or major policy initiative, and the impact of such initiatives within affected settings such as classrooms, schools and regions. Extrapolation or generalization beyond the particular initiative may be regarded as a secondary concern or as a responsibility of the audience rather than the evaluator. This emphasis on the *particular* marked an important change in thinking about programme evaluation, as a brief reference to its history will illustrate.

Seen as a modern industry staffed by specialists, and as an industry that arose first in the USA in the context of massive federal interventionism (see Atkin and House, 1981) one has to remember that the requirement for evaluation was met almost exclusively by experimental psychologists steeped in the null hypothesis. It called for little modification of that tradition to conceive of curriculum innovations as treatment variations designed to elicit new behaviours on the part of students. The new curricula were in this sense seen as 'made to measure' (Hamilton *et al,* 1977) and the psychometrist/evaluators proceeded to measure learning gains, greatly assisted by the technological approach to social interventionism favoured at the time.

Misgivings about this whole approach to curriculum development were first expressed by Myron Atkin (1963) but it was Stake who first suggested that evaluators needed to rethink the nature of their enterprise. When he wrote, in his introduction to the inaugural issue of AERA Monographs on Evaluation (Stake, 1967a) of the need for evaluators to tell the programme 'story' and to 'Let the buyer beware' he set in motion a reconceptualization of the evaluation task in terms of more idiographic traditions of research, and away from the idea of curriculum developments as poorly designed experiments in student learning. 'Let the buyer beware' was a phrase that invoked the commodity market and the need for consumer guidance rather than market research. 'Story-telling' suggested that consumers needed to know a lot more about prestigious innovations than merely whether they survived the unidimensional null hypothesis. Stake's message was one that had little appeal to the institutions of American behaviourism, but one that struck a sympathetic cord across the Atlantic where MacDonald, Hamilton and Parlett were also trying to make sense and utility out of the new role. The development of what I call the Anglo-American alliance of break-away evaluators, described in some detail in chapter 3, was a response to the problem of establishing a bridgehead for a new direction.

In the late sixties, when Stake first called for more detailed attention to the particularities and complexities of curriculum reform initiatives, the context, on both sides of the Atlantic, was a dawning realization that curriculum change was much more difficult than a simple matter of social engineering backed by big money and big science. This realization yielded some support and a great deal of interest on the part of curriculum sponsors for those evaluators, few in number, whose deviations from the output model began to generate a better data base for understanding why projects and programmes were failing to deliver. By the end of the sixties Stake was moving towards the notion of evaluation as 'portrayal' (Stake, 1972b), MacDonald was using case studies for consumer guidance (MacDonald, 1971) and Smith was advocating the need for innovators to pay attention to the contexts of implementation (Smith and Keith, 1971). The baseline for the shift (though we must bear in mind that we are talking of parallel rather than sequential invention) was Stake's early definition of the purpose of evaluation:

> The purpose of educational evaluation is expository: to acquaint the audience with the workings of certain educators and their learners. It differs from educational research in its orientation to a *specific* programme rather than to variables common to many programs. A full evaluation results in a story, supported perhaps by statistics and profiles. It tells what happened. It reveals perceptions and judgments that different groups and individuals hold — obtained, I hope, by objective means. It tells of merit and shortcoming. As a bonus, it may offer generalizations ('The moral of the story is . . .') for the guidance of subsequent educational programs. (Stake, 1967a, p. 5, my emphasis)

Although this movement received support from those who were increasingly dissatisfied with what they saw to be meagre returns for large curriculum investments, it was not until 1975 that 'scientific' legitimation came from an unexpected quarter. In that year Lee Cronbach, the doyen of educational psychology, published a paper in which he argued that the two disciplines of scientific psychology (experimental and correlational research) were inadequate to meet contemporary needs for knowledge of social programmes. Suggesting a need for descriptive studies, Cronbach wrote:

Instead of making generalization the ruling consideration in our research, I suggest that we reverse our priorities. An observer collecting data in one particular situation is in a position to appraise a practice or proposition in that setting, observing effects in context.... As he goes from situation to situation, his first task is to describe and interpret the effect anew in each locale, perhaps taking into account factors that were unique to that locale... As results accumulate, a person who seeks understanding will do his best to trace how the uncontrolled factors could have caused departures from the modal effect. That is, generalization comes late, and the exception is taken as seriously as the rule. (Cronbach, 1975, pp 124–5)

Cronbach might have been describing the design of MacDonald's multi-site case study evaluation of computer-assisted learning (MacDonald *et al*, 1975), then in its second year in England, but his words were more broadly aimed at the over-focalized and insular tradition of applied psychological research and its preoccupation with enduring theories of universal application.

Cronbach's point about generalization echoed a concern of evaluators trying to defend the study of the particular against the criticism that, at least at some levels of decision making, generalization was essential. It was all very well to argue, as Stake did with his concept of 'naturalistic generalization' (Stake, 1978) that many important audiences could generalize from a given case to their own, taking account of the idiosyncracies of each. Without dismantling the whole power structure of curriculum decision-making, this did not meet the needs of policymakers who made decisions affecting a range of cases. Stake responded to this with the 'executive summary' (Stake and Easley, 1978), MacDonald with his list of generalizations for policymakers (MacDonald and Jenkins, 1980), both based on case study programmes.

In exploring the utility of case study as a form of inquiry Stake reaffirmed his commitment to the particular in a slightly different sense by drawing a distinction between academic research (the pursuit of formal knowledge) and evaluation (the pursuit of practical knowledge), the latter appealing to the audience's 'tacit knowledge' (Polyani, 1958) and capacity to reach understanding through vicarious experience (Stake, 1978). In fact he deliberately, and unfortunately, he says, overstates the distinction between formal and practical inquiry 'as a step toward improving and legitimizing inquiries that are needed for understanding and problem-solving but which are unlikely to produce vouchsafed generalizations.' (*Ibid*, p. 7). Stake was very much concerned to extend opportunities to engage in evaluation beyond the confines of the scientific community, a concern that involved him initially with confronting the behavioural psychologists and later the ethnographers who increasingly moved into the space he had created. MacDonald (1982a) tells the story of how, when Harry Wolcott announced from the platform at the AERA convention of 1981[1] that he had come to rescue ethnography from its imposters, Stake stood up from the floor and told him he was talking like a trade unionist.

Although evaluators vary in the degree to which they should contribute to general theories of education and change, or even more broadly to social theory, there is now agreement that their primary task is to elucidate the values and/or effects of a particular project, programme, or policy at a particular point in time in a particular place. Evaluation is, in other words, a study of the idiosyncratic.

Another way of understanding these issues in evaluation is to set them within a discussion of 'scientism' — what Robert Nisbet has called 'science with the spirit of discovery and creation left out' (Nisbet, 1976, p. 4). While Nisbet is attacking a particular sociological research tradition what he has to say is not without significance for educational research and evaluation, especially as many of the early educational evaluators were trained in an educational research tradition dominated by imitation of the natural sciences.

Of course not all educational research is 'scientistic' but those forms of research which slavishly follow what has come to be called the 'scientific method' strongly emphasizing problem design, statistical analyses, hypothesis verification, replication and theory construction (*Ibid*) run that risk. In exploring the connections between art and science Nisbet suggests that the poverty of the social sciences has arisen from a failure to distinguish between *the logic of discovery* and *the logic of demonstration*:

> The second is properly subject to rules and prescriptions; the first isn't. Of all sins against the Muse, however, the greatest is the assertion, or strong implication, in textbooks on methodology and theory construction that the first (and utterly vital) logic can somehow be summoned by obeying the rules of the second. Only intellectual drouth and barrenness can result from that misconception. (*Ibid*, p. 5)

Evaluation theory over the past twenty-five years has increasing-ly emphasized the logic of discovery, arguably at the expense of the logic of demonstration. Nisbet's distinctions are reflected in evalua-tion in the distinction between 'vindicative' and 'indicative' data, the former testifying to policy deeds, the latter to policy needs (Mac-Donald, 1982a, p. 14).

Evaluation as a Political Activity

Evaluation entails a view of society. People differ about evaluation because they differ about what society is, what it can be and what it ought to be. Much of the debate about evaluation is ideology disguised as technology. (Hamilton *et al*, 1977, p. 25)

That evaluation is a political activity is now widely recognized (House, 1973a and 1980; Apple, 1974; MacDonald, 1974; Weiss, 1975a). This recognition was belated and its importance and signi-ficance are still contested. But few would disagree with Cronbach's statement that:

... a theory of evaluation must be as much a theory of political interaction as it is a theory of how knowledge is constructed. (Cronbach *et al*, 1980, p. 52)

House (1973a) was one of the first US evaluators to recognize its importance when he noted what he called the 'context of valuation':

Contrary to common belief, evaluation is not the ultimate arbiter, delivered from pure objectivity and accepted as the final judgment. Evaluation is always derived from biased origins ... Likewise, the way in which the results of an evaluation are accepted depends on whether they help or hinder the person receiving them. Evaluation is an integral part of the political processes of our society. (*Ibid*, p. 3)

Weiss (1975a), well-known for her contribution to policy re-search, makes a similar point when she describes evaluation as a 'rational enterprise that takes place in a political context' (p. 13). Political considerations intrude in evaluation, she says, in three major ways. First, the policies and programs of evaluation with which evaluation deals are the creatures of political decisions, 'proposed, defined, debated, enacted and funded through political processes'. Secondly, because evaluation is undertaken *in order* to feed into decision-making, evaluation reports enter the political arena and 'compete there for attention with other factors that carry weight in the political process'. And thirdly, and 'perhaps least recognized', she intimates, evaluation itself has a political stance:

> By its very nature, it makes implicit political statements about such issues as the problematic nature of some programs and the unassailableness of others, the legitimacy of program goals, the legitimacy of program strategies, the utility of strategies of incremental reform, and even the appropriate role of the social scientist in policy and program formation. (*Ibid*, pp. 13–14)

But the first to give absolute priority to the political nature of evaluation was MacDonald (1974) when he made implicit political leanings the basis of his typology of evaluation approaches. Introducing his classification, he wrote:

> Evaluators do not only live in the real world of educational politics; they actually influence its changing power relationships. Their work produces information which functions as a resource for the promotion of particular interests and values. (*Ibid*, p. 16).

It was partly recognition of this fact and the experience of conducting evaluations that led him to draw a distinction between evaluation and research, a distinction related as much to the role of evaluation as to the inevitable involvement of the evaluator in the political process. MacDonald uses a dramatic metaphor to make his point likening the evaluation enterprise to a piece of street theatre where the evaluator's:

> script of educational issues, actions and consequences is being acted out in a socio-political street theatre which affects not just the performance, but the play itself. He finds he can make few assumptions about what has happened, what is happening, or what is going to happen. He is faced with competing interest groups, with divergent definitions of the situation and conflicting informational needs. If he has accepted narrowly stipulative terms of reference, he may find that his options have been pre-empted by contractual restraints that are subsequently difficult to justify. If, on the other hand, he has freedom of action, he faces acute problems. He has to decide which decision-makers he will serve, what information will be of most use, when it is needed and how it can be obtained.

I am suggesting that the resolution of these issues commits the evaluator to a political stance, an attitude to the government of education.... No such commitment is required of the researcher. He stands outside the political process, and values his detachment from it. For him the production of new knowledge and the social use of that knowledge are rigorously separated. The evaluator is embroiled in the action, ie, the allocation of resources and the determination of goals, roles and tasks. (*Ibid*, pp. 14–15)

Cronbach *et al* (1980) reassert the difference between evaluation and research in a comparison with experimental research:

The scientist gazes at a colony of experimental subjects from the remote end of a microscope. In the reality of a program evaluation, the evaluator swims in the same ocean as his subjects and is buffeted by the same cross currents. (*Ibid*, p. 52)

Although these distinctions between research and evaluation accurately capture the embroilment of the evaluator, they stereotype scientific detachment from society in a way which does not make historical or political sense (Karier *et al*, 1973). It needs to be made clear that the distinction, in so far as it is valid, refers to the conduct of evaluation, the continuous involvement of the evaluator in political and value-laden processes which impinge at every stage upon her activity. In the 'socio-political street theatre' the evaluator is not insulated against interference by the respect shown for the scientific methods of the researcher, whose powers of demonstration are rooted in hallowed conditions of practice. This is no less true of the social as of the natural scientist, although the more flexible and less replicable modes of social science lend themselves to political co-optation in less detectable forms than those we associate with post-war links between the 'hard' sciences and military-industrial complexes. In his 1974 article MacDonald forecast the imminent demise of the 'detached' social scientist in the context of technocratic centrism, and it is certainly true today that almost all social research that is funded by government or quasi-government agencies is constrained by relatively closed definitions of the problems it is required to address.

Some social scientists have characterized the political context of their work as one which calls upon the investigator to decide whose side s/he is on (Becker, 1967). Becker's own response, partisan sociology, was subsequently denounced in a lengthy reply by Gouldner as 'underdog sociology' (Gouldner, 1973). Similarly, in evaluation, political consciousness has made some evaluators think about their responsibilities with respect to societies marked by gross inequalities which are embodied in educational provision. It is one thing to recognize that evaluation is a political activity, quite another to do something about it. House contends that all the major evaluation approaches are based on variations in the assumptions of liberalism (House, 1980, p. 45). While this would seem to limit the choices, there are quite sharp, though theoretically elusive differences in practice. House himself advocates Rawls' (1971) theory of justice as a moral framework for evaluative commitment (House, 1976) and has even advocated that moral criteria be incorporated into the technical concept of validity (House, 1980, p. 257).

Cronbach rejects House's position as partisan and politically impracticable, preferring the concept of the evaluator as the multipartisan 'public scientist' (Cronbach *et al*, 1980, p. 210). MacDonald has sought to make his democratic evaluation model (which I shall discuss in some detail later) the means of gaining purchase on power relationships and enfranchising disadvantaged groups. Since introducing the model he has increasingly sought and obtained evaluation contracts which give him access to high level power groups, and has argued that evaluators must extend their case boundaries to include the sources of social policy (MacDonald and Norris, 1981). His notion that sponsors have no special claim on the evaluation service, and that all parties, irrespective of their power relationships are entitled to the service, imposes a power-equalizing set of procedures on the conduct of the evaluation. Something approximating to this principle was explored recently in the USA under the label of 'stakeholder evaluation', but the reports of this experiment by Weiss and House suggest that its apparently half-hearted and compromised form yielded little satisfaction to anyone (Weiss, 1986; House, 1986).

Most of the views I have referred to so far in dealing with the political dimension of evaluation have had as their context large-scale educational programmes. When we come to consider evaluation at the level of local initiatives I shall revisit some of these issues. The various perspectives different theorists take on the political dimension are dealt with in some detail in the next chapter.

Evaluation as Persuasion

> Evaluations themselves, I would contend, can be no more
> than acts of persuasion.... Evaluative argument is at once
> less certain, more particularized, more personalized, and
> more conducive to action than is research information.
> (House, 1980, pp. 72–3)

Stake, in drawing a distinction between formal inquiry and practical
inquiry, and MacDonald between research and evaluation, both
imply that the criteria for valuing evaluative inquiry must be different
from those which circumscribe research. MacDonald is quite explicit
in fact in warning of the danger of conceptualizing evaluation as a
branch of research in case evaluators become trapped in the 'restrictive tentacles of research respectability', where 'purity may be
substituted for utility, trivial proofs for clumsy attempts to grasp
complex significance' (MacDonald, 1974, p. 15). In positing such a
warning he is also pointing to two important criteria of evaluation,
utility and comprehensiveness.

Several other evaluators have made the same point. Immediate
utility may not be a requirement for research but it is defining of
evaluation (Weiss, 1972; Stake, 1978; House, 1980; Patton, 1978). To
ignore this criterion is to risk being considered irrelevant just as to
ignore the 'vocabulary of action'[2] is to fail to communicate. Both are
intimately connected to the nature of evaluation as a service activity.
If 'vouchsafed generalizations' are impossible, and 'trivial proofs' to
be rejected for their failure to illuminate complex significance by
what kind of knowledge, through what kind of process, does
evaluation hope to influence practice?

In one of the most illuminating accounts in the literature of the
nature of evaluative activity, House (1980) provides an answer that at
once characterizes the nature of evaluative activity, separates it from
research, and highlights the criteria by which it should be valued.
In a pluralist society, House argues, we have to have different expectations of evaluation than we may entertain of research. In a
context of multiple audiences diverse in values and interests evaluation cannot produce necessary propositions for action. In such a
context evaluation 'persuades rather than convinces, argues rather
than demonstrates, is credible rather than certain, is variably accepted
rather than compelling' (*Ibid*, p. 73). Presumably, in House's case,
this would mean being a persuasive advocate of the interests of the
disadvantaged, according to Rawls' concept of social justice. But his

analysis of the logic of evaluative argument (House, 1977) has implications beyond such considerations. In his view it frees the evaluator from the restrictions of deductive and inductive reasoning and enables her to employ a greater range of persuasive modes. 'Once the burden of certainty is lifted', he writes, 'the possibilities for informed action are increased rather than decreased' (p. 7).

By the time House came to formulate this persuasive case for evaluation as persuasion, practising evaluators had already engaged in a wide variety of forms of reporting, including the narrative case study, the photographic essay, the dialogue, even the radio play (Pick and Walker, 1976). And many had drawn on artistic traditions as sources of metaphor and reportage (Brauner, 1974; MacDonald and Walker, 1975; Stake, 1975). Elliot Eisner had also been developing the concept of evaluation as educational criticism for the previous decade (Eisner, 1984).

The notion of evaluation as persuasion is somewhat different, at the very least in emphasis, from MacDonald's view that evaluation should enhance the possibility of the widest possible debate about matters of common interest and consequence. 'In this sense an evaluation report can be seen as fulfilling the function of fore-shadowing (rather than preempting or concluding) a debate about what should happen next. That is the justification for evaluation reports being inconclusive accounts of programmes' (MacDonald and Sanger, 1982, p. 182).

Evaluation and Decision-Making

In this brief review of theorizing about evaluation as a particularistic, political and persuasive activity, we can see how the familiar idea of evaluation as a service to decision-makers, an idea that has been central to evaluation designs for twenty-five years, has not provided a simple solution to the evaluator seeking a form of social service in a liberal democratic society. Since the mid-sixties evaluation has come to be linked with providing information for decision-makers. Prior to this, evaluation was frequently equated with testing of pupil perform-ance or a comparison of a programme's goals with its outcomes to determine how well the goals were met (House, 1973a, p. 3).

It was Cronbach (1963) who first broadened the scope of evaluation to provide information for decision-making:

To draw attention to its full range of functions, we may define

'evaluation' broadly as the collection and use of information
to make decisions about an educational programme. (*Ibid*,
p. 672)

A similar approach differing primarily in the emphasis given to
the *taking* of specific decisions is that adopted by Stufflebeam *et al*
(1971):

Evaluation is the process of delineating, obtaining and providing useful information for judging decision alternatives.
(p. xxv)

Stufflebeam's model was fairly directly tied to serving administrators'
decisions in a rational sequence of stages, built as it was, upon a
rational theory of decision-making. In Britain, the concept of providing information for decision-making was interpreted more as a 'users'
concept, administrators being only one of a range of possible users of
the evaluation (MacDonald, 1971 and 1973).

The notion of informing decision-makers or informing judgments decision-makers may take, rests on the assumption that it is
not the role of the person collecting the information to make the
specific decision about a particular programme, this being subject
to a whole range of influences over which evaluation has no control.
But more than that, it is not the 'right' of evaluators to usurp the
responsibilities of those with legitimate professional positions and
political accountability in a democratic state. These are roles evaluators simply cannot assume, nor, some argue, should presume.

Cronbach *et al* (1980) make the point nicely:

We are defining a professional role in which evaluators
consider themselves responsible to the larger social interest.
They should exercise independent judgment as best they can
but should not attempt to substitute that judgment for the
political process. (*Ibid*, p. 72)

Later descriptions of evaluation still focus on evaluation as a
process of collecting information for the purpose of informing
decision-making but the emphasis has shifted slightly away from the
aspiration to inform immediate decisions to informing policy-making
or informing judgment in the long term (*Ibid*; MacDonald and
Norris, 1981) and several, implicitly or explicitly, emphasize the need
to communicate such learnings as part of that evaluation process
(Stake, 1975; Cronbach *et al*, 1980).

Specific decisions may result from an evaluation but this is not necessary or always the case. Cronbach *et al* (1980) maintain that 'a social agenda almost never calls for a choice between fixed alternatives. Only rarely are "go/no-go" decisions made'; (p. 62) and House (1980) has pointed out that some forms of evaluation 'strive toward understanding rather than judgment' (p. 19). These less direct interpretations of providing information for decision-making have arisen perhaps from three factors: the realization of the difficulty of informing particular decisions, evaluation forming only one small part of the data that is taken into account in coming to a decision; over-reliance on a model of decision-making that has little correspondence with reality; and a reassessment of the responsibilities of evaluation.

An analysis of the lack of utilization of evaluation studies (Weiss, 1977; Patton, 1978) and the dissatisfaction experienced by both evaluators and clients in conducting and receiving evaluations has led Cronbach *et al* (1980) to suggest that we modify our expectations and give evaluation an altogether more humble but at the same time more important educative role. The task of evaluation should not be to decide definitely on the merits of a case, 'Evaluation does not and cannot end political dispute by reducing the merits and demerits of a proposal to "facts"', (p. 61) but rather, to ask what can we learn about the programme in question (p. 35). The task of evaluation should not be to help people decide between alternatives but rather to contribute to dialogue and help shape understanding of social programmes and policy, 'The process is not one of choosing among a few alternatives but of negotiating a next forward step' (p. 66). The role of evaluation, in short, is 'not to produce authoritative truths but to clarify, to document, to raise new questions, and to create new perceptions' (Lindblom and Cohen, 1979, quoted by Cronbach *et al*, 1980, p. 53).

With this realization and the observation that 'evaluative investigation ought to serve those who are discussing or regulating social actions' (Cronbach *et al*, 1980, p. 54), evaluation is much closer to pluralistic policy research than experimental research from where it stemmed.

Naturalistic Evaluation

So far, in presenting an overview of evaluation theory, I have selectively focussed on a small number of writers to represent a densely populated literature. Partly the choice reflects my view of which theorists have been most influential in shaping contemporary evaluation thinking — Stake, House and Cronbach in the USA, and MacDonald in the UK. It is no coincidence, I believe, that these writers have been influential because, more than other evaluators they have focussed critical attention on the technocratic managerialism implicit in post-war curriculum reform movements, recognized a threat to some of the most valued dimensions of liberal democratic societies (such as discourse, dissent and diversity) and created at least some theoretical space for evaluation practices to evolve more communal forms. The title of my book, *Getting to Know Schools in a Democracy,* is intended to convey my own allegiance to such forms, and my preoccupation with the problem of how to construe evaluation in ways which reconcile the publicizing of knowledge about schooling with its healthy professional development. In many ways the rise of what Campbell has called 'the experimenting society' (Campbell, 1977), the notion of society as one great laboratory in which social scientists can help governments determine 'best buys' among competing social programmes, represents the delusion of system quality control that has been so evident in post-war programme-based interventionism (see Apple, 1979). In the past twenty years particularly the history of programme and policy evaluation is a history of co-optation of large numbers of social scientists, with the ad hoc label of 'evaluator' pinned to their lapels, to serve the technocratic ambition. Although I have focussed on the words of those who have, to greater or lesser extent questioned both the feasibility and desirability of such a social 'service' role for evaluators, it would be far from the truth to claim that they have in any substantial way dismantled it. This is by way of a preamble to paying some detailed attention to an overview of the break-away, non-technicist wing of evaluation, which has come to be known as the 'naturalistic school' (Guba, 1978; Guba and Lincoln, 1981 and 1985).

The Concept of Naturalistic Evaluation

Naturalistic inquiry is the generic term that came to be used to describe many of the alternative approaches to evaluation that gained prominence in the seventies as a reaction to more traditional forms of evaluation when these proved inappropriate for understanding the complexity of curriculum reforms. These alternative approaches include holistic evaluation (MacDonald, 1971, 1973 and 1978a);

illuminative evaluation (Parlett and Hamilton, 1972); democratic evaluation (MacDonald, 1974); responsive evaluation (Stake, 1975); evaluation as literary criticism (Kelly, 1975); transactional evaluation (Rippey, 1973); educational connoisseurship (Eisner, 1975) and quasi-legal evaluation (Wolf, 1974) though it has been argued that the last two fit rather better perhaps within a judgmental paradigm and an adversarial paradigm respectively (Guba and Lincoln, 1981).

All these approaches stem from a recognition of the inadequacies of an experimental model of educational research for evaluating complex broad aims programmes that develop in action and have different effects in different contexts. They have been characterized by Hamilton and House as pluralistic evaluation models (that is, models that take account of the value positions of multiple audiences), and House (1980) has also explicated their underlying political assumptions. Hamilton (1977) offers a useful summary of the characteristics of this emerging group of evaluation models:[3]

> Compared with the classical models, they tend to be more extensive (not necessarily centred on numerical data), more naturalistic (based on program activity rather than program intent), and more adaptable (not constrained by experimental or preordinate designs). In turn they are likely to be sensitive to the different values of program participants, to endorse empirical methods which incorporate ethnographic field-work, to develop feed back materials which are couched in the natural language of the recipients, and to shift the locus of formal judgement from the evaluator to the participants. (Hamilton, 1977, p. 30).

As one might expect, it takes a large umbrella to cover a diverse range of alternatives and to impose a unity upon them, even in the carefully 'likely to' terminology employed by Hamilton. The term 'naturalistic' did not emerge as an acceptable banner until the late seventies, but even then the degree to which different theorists within the school emphasized methodological, epistemological or political change in their conceptions varied considerably. I myself would say that naturalistic inquiry signifies a commitment to studying programmes in their social contexts, the use of qualitative methods of inquiry such as unstructured interviewing, direct observation and historical/dramatic reconstruction, and forms of reporting that allow readers to generalize for themselves, utilizing 'naturalistic generalization' (Stake, 1978, p. 6). In his summary House (1980) draws similar attention to naturalistic generalization aimed at non-technical audiences highlighting the use of ordinary language, informal everyday reasoning and the use of arguments attempting to establish the structure of reality (p. 279).

The kind of qualitative arguments House suggests are useful to establish a structure of reality include example, metaphor, illustration and analogy, forms of argumentation that he does not see as inconsistent with the way scientists learn their discipline or the form of evaluative argument he advances for evaluation:

> According to Kuhn, a scientist learns his discipline through a set of exemplars — concrete problems permitting solutions that enable the novice to make comparisons with other disparate problems. The shared meaning is transferred through these experiences and not only through rules. (*Ibid*, p. 282)

Guba and Lincoln (1981) prefer Wolf and Tymitz's description which aims to understand:

> actualities, social realities, and human perceptions that exist untainted by the obtrusiveness of formal measurement or preconceived questions ... Naturalistic inquiry attempts to present 'slice-of-life' episodes documented through natural language and representing as closely as possible how people feel, what they know, and what their concerns, beliefs, perceptions, and understandings are. (p. 78)

MacDonald *et al* (1975) stick with a simpler metaphor: 'Ours is the task of the naturalist who wants to understand the variety and coherence of life in the pond, and its links with the world beyond' (p. 2).

More important than definitions perhaps are the underlying assumptions and postures of naturalistic inquirers. Guba and Lincoln centre their analysis on a comparison with the scientific paradigm which has acquired a 'patina of orthodoxy' even in the social-behavioural sciences (Guba and Lincoln, 1981, p. 56). Both paradigms rest, they suggest, on three assumptions, about reality, about the inquirer-subject relationship, and about the nature of 'truth' statements (see table 1 below).

Table 1:   Basic Assumptions of the Scientific and Naturalistic Paradigms

Assumptions about	Paradigm	
	Scientific	*Naturalistic*
Reality	Singular, convergent fragmentable	Multiple, divergent, inter-related
Inquirer/subject relationship	Independent	Inter-related
Nature of truth statements	Generalizations — nomothetic statements — focus on similarities	Working hypotheses — idiographic statements — focus on differences

Source: Guba and Lincoln, (1981, p. 57)[4]

Descriptions of responsive evaluation (Stake, 1975), case study (MacDonald and Walker, 1975) and illuminative evaluation (Parlett and Hamilton, 1972), three of the modes of evaluation which fall within the naturalistic paradigm tend to support Guba and Lincoln's analysis that naturalistic inquiry is about portraying multiple realities and truths, seeks divergence rather than convergence, is a highly interactive process and generates 'thick descriptions' (Geertz, 1973) and 'working hypotheses' (Cronbach, 1975) rather than generalizations (Guba and Lincoln, 1981, p. 58).

In terms of process and focus House likens naturalistic evaluation to naturalistic sociology, using Denzin (1971) for reference, but then contrasts their interests and roles in this way:

> Of course, the sociologist is interested in constructing a generalizable theory. The naturalistic evaluator is interested only in the case he is evaluating. The sociologist will try to justify his conclusions to a universal audience. The naturalistic evaluator must adjust his work to a particular audience, who may be the participants of the program he is evaluating. In presenting their studies both will rely heavily on examples and illustrations drawn from the field. The evaluator may or may not draw specific conclusions from the examples. If the examples are collected and presented systematically, their logic will resemble that of inductive reasoning. However, in naturalistic evaluation the audience always has the choice of

how to interpret the findings and of how much credibility to assign them. (House, 1980, p. 280)

Validity in Naturalistic Evaluation

It is not enough for the evaluation to be true and credible; it must also be normatively correct ... (*Ibid*, p. 250)

The problem of validity bedevils most researchers, evaluation researchers even more so as the claims to validity can be met in so many different ways. Not all formal research criteria, for instance, are relevant in any particular evaluation, though in the early days of evaluation they were seen to be paramount, and different evaluation approaches embrace their own validity criteria. With the growth of the evaluation movement practical criteria came to be taken into account as much as scientific criteria. Stufflebeam *et al* (1971) offer an extensive list: internal and external validity, reliability, objectivity (scientific criteria); relevance, importance, credibility, timeliness, pervasiveness and efficiency (practical criteria) (pp. 27–30).

House takes validity to mean something like 'worthiness of being recognized' though he also quotes a dictionary definition:

... the quality of being well founded on fact, or established on sound principles, and thoroughly applicable to the case or circumstances; soundness and strength (or argument, proof, authority, etc.) (House, 1980, p. 249)

But as the quotation with which this section began implies he also brings a moral dimension to the concept of validity removing it from purely technical concerns around which most of the debate on validity has taken place. In the modern concept of evaluation as a public decision procedure, an evaluation has obligations to the larger society and 'the concept of validity must be extended to apply to such a significant social practice' (*Ibid*, p. 257).

House does not fall into the trap of oversimplifying claims to validity. While he categorizes evaluation approaches into those which have an objectivist epistemology (systems analysis, behavioural objectives, decision-making) and those which have a subjectivist epistemology (art criticism, professional review, quasi-legal and case study approaches), he recognizes that each has a validity claim of its own. His main criticism lies with the objectivist approaches which rely primarily on explicated methods for their claim to validity, emphasizing replication and reliability in measurement and focussing on the truth aspect of validity to the exclusion of the credibility and normative aspects. 'If this is a weakness in the conduct of science', House comments, 'in evaluation it is a fatal flaw' (p. 251). It is only credible to those who believe in the methodology. More often than not this does not include the evaluated. His second major criticism is that objectivist approaches harbour implicit values built into the instruments of which the investigators themselves are unaware but which have implications for indicating how wants and interests are to be determined. These are simply taken for granted (*Ibid*, p. 252).

MacDonald and Norris (1981) make a similar point about the objectivization of field work traditions in social research:

> It seems clear from the tomes of social research cookbooks that political and ethical issues have become, through successive historical transformations, technical problems. Thus the political discourse that in a democratic community should be attendant upon such issues, was foreclosed almost before it had begun. (p. 21)

The approaches which House labels subjectivist, as they base their claim on an appeal to experience rather than to scientific method, also have their strengths and weaknesses on each validity criterion. In the case study approach, for example, one of the subjectivist approaches House considers:

> Validity depends on the match between the evaluation and the experience of the participants and the audience.
>
> The subjectivists, of course, also claim that their evaluations are true, but they attempt to achieve insights within the frame of reference of the audience and the participants themselves. Meaningfulness is important. The evaluation must be capable of being understood. (House, 1980, p. 253)

For any evaluation to be valid House concludes it must be true, credible and normatively correct — all three. Whilst most commonly validity is taken to be identical to truth (and certainly an evaluation would be invalid if untrue) this is insufficient, he claims, for the evaluation of a social programme. This has to be communicated to an external audience for whom it must be credible, so the audience can trust it. Credibility, he maintains, is as much a function of the evaluator (which can be judged by an understanding of, and belief in, the evaluator's intentions and demonstration of the consistency of his actions) as of the evaluation (which may be judged by the evaluation report itself, whether it is coherent, authentic and so on). A further obligation is to multiple audiences. In the evaluation of a public programme it is not sufficient to provide a service or utility to a particular group. 'A public evaluation must be normatively correct' (p. 256).

The second distinctive contribution House makes to the validity debate is his concept of impartiality. Evaluators working either within a positivistic or phenomenological paradigm, he says, aspire in their role of investigator to be 'disinterested', removed from the interests and concerns of the everyday world. Such a role he regards as 'morally deficient':

> Being indifferent to whose interests are advanced is not the same as advancing the interests of all. (*Ibid*, p. 255)

In his critique of the Follow Through Evaluation (House, 1979a) he cites an example of what he means in commenting that the major error of the systems analysis approach adopted in that evaluation was to mistake objectivity for impartiality:

> The analysts thought objectivity was sufficient to ensure superiority and influence. More often it means irrelevance. Objectivity sought to deal with interests by excluding them. What is needed is impartiality which deals with interests by including and balancing them. (House, 1980, p. 224)

Other authors have been concerned to point out the ways in which claims to validity on these criteria are met differently in naturalistic inquiry compared with scientific inquiry (see, for instance, Dawson, 1977; Guba and Lincoln, 1981 and 1985). And with the more recent recognition of evaluation's kinship with pluralistic policy research (Cronbach *et al*, 1980) has come a modification of traditional validity claims. The most notable example of this is the emphasis given to external validity compared with internal validity. The significance of this shift in emphasis is underlined, imply Cronbach *et al* (1980, p. 74) by the recognition that some authors (Cook and Campbell, 1979, for example) now give to external validity vis-à-vis internal validity. Campbell's recognition of the importance of external validity in applied science may be as significant for defining and legitimizing evaluation as Cronbach's observation that generalizations decay over time was in 1975 (Hamilton, 1980c). Cronbach *et al* (1980) go further in pointing out that internal validity is not of salient importance in an evaluation (p. 314). '"External validity" — validity of inferences that go beyond the data

— is the crux in social action, not "internal validity"' (p. 231), a point of view that is consistent with the modification of the function of evaluation outlined in the concluding part of the previous section of this chapter.

'Democratic evaluation' is in some of its values and postures similar to Cronbach's notion of the evaluator as 'public scientist' serving a pluralist constituency. Indeed Nilsson and Hogben place Cronbach and MacDonald together in a denunciation of their 'value-free', 'deferential' theory of political evaluation (Nilsson and Hogben, 1983). But neither Cronbach nor MacDonald would surely disagree with House when he declares, in the context of discussing the issue of validity, 'Public evaluation should be democratic, fair, and ultimately based upon the moral values of equality, autonomy, impartiality, and reciprocity' (House, 1980, p. 256).

Nevertheless, it should be noted that, of those theorists favouring subjectivist epistemologies, MacDonald retains an objectivist concept of internal validity, and a view that external and internal validity are interdependent. As we shall see, his procedural model of the evaluation process is as much concerned to establish the technical validity of the outcome as it is to embody the values espoused in the House declaration.

Since an important aspect of the reconceptualization of relationships in democratic evaluation seeks 'to dissolve the line that both conceptually and procedurally separates the objects of evaluation from its audiences' (MacDonald and Norris, 1981, p. 24) this must logically mean that the separation of internal and external validity is, within the democratic model, at least questionable. In this sense it is not unreasonable to argue that within a more democratic process of generating accounts of programmes, projects, schools or classrooms, the internal validity of the case becomes more rather than less important. MacDonald and Sanger (1982) quote aptly from a passage in a novel to support this view:

> 'Does the literal truth matter?'
> She thought about that. 'To the person to whom it happened'.
> (p. 176)

As the article goes on to argue, within a more participatory process in which control is shared between evaluator and evaluated, there is a tension between participant attention to internal validity and the evaluator's obligation to persuade what Cronbach *et al* (1980) calls the 'policy-shaping community' in the broader social sphere.

Summary

In summary, this chapter has examined the essential characteristics of evaluative inquiry as it has come to be defined over the past twenty-five years. It notes its evolution away from an aims-achievement model of assessment to the broader framework of informing decision-makers and finally to the broader political purpose of informing and improving the operations of the social system. It examines a number of assumptions about evaluation itself; that it is a particularized, political and persuasive activity.

The concept of naturalistic inquiry is introduced as one way to further certain political aspirations; its claims to validity are examined and are seen, following House, to include a moral dimension. It is with this concept of evaluation that this book explores the possibilities for democratizing knowledge and improving schooling through the process of conducting and disseminating evaluations.

The intention of this chapter was to introduce rather than to settle an ongoing debate about the role of evaluation in society. It will be clear, I hope, from this brief survey that evaluation has begged as many questions as it has resolved. You may have noted, for instance, some tension, if not contradiction, between the evaluative focus on the idiosyncratic and evaluator interest in contributing to a broader notion of public learning and reflection. You may also have noted, with respect to the discussion of validity, that the reconciliation of moral action with a pluralist constituency is rather more problematic than my citations on this issue suggest. Finally, what may not be too clear is how respect for legitimate political authority on the part of evaluators is distinguished from docility to substantive power relationships, or even whether such a distinction is evident in theory, and more importantly, in practice. These are very important issues, and not just for evaluation. But in evaluation there is no escape from such questions. When an evaluator acts, she answers them.

Notes

1 HARRY WOLCOTT presented a paper to the annual meeting of the American Educational Research Association in 1981 titled 'How to look like an anthropologist without really trying'.
2 This is a phrase coined by HOUSE (1972) to refer to the fact that only when evaluation data roughly correspond to the internal vocabulary of action a person has in his mind does he respond to them.

3 Stake (1981) has pointed out that while the literature of programme evaluation contains many references to general models which do represent different approaches, it is a mistake to call them models. He prefers, following HOUSE (1980), the word persuasion to the more contentious and arguably precise concept of model. I'm inclined to agree. I have, nevertheless, used the word model throughout as it is the word most commonly used by the theorists I discuss.

4 GUBA and LINCOLN are aware of the oversimplification this analysis presents but nevertheless use it to indicate the critical features of naturalistic inquiry and the direction of its epistemological stance. In a later book they appear to have extended the categories and substituted positivistic for scientific (GUBA and LINCOLN, 1985).

2 The Political Implications of Evaluation Theory: A Closer Look

In the last chapter I offered a selective overview of evaluation theory, emphasizing aspects of special pertinence to my own work and concerns in this field. The focus of the first part of that overview was on those theorists most conscious of the need to define evaluation in relation to political structures, policy-making processes and scientific traditions. In the second part the focus was on evaluation as naturalistic inquiry, an epistemological shift that opens up a wider range of political options for evaluators seeking a defensible social service role. The relationship between the naturalistic movement in evaluation and the concept of evaluation as political action is one I intend to revisit in chapter 3, employing there a biographical/historical approach to the evolution of the case study approach in Britain and the United States of America. My own work developed in the context of an Anglo-American community of evaluators whose thinking and practice was largely concerned with working out the relationships between politics, knowledge, and methods within such a purview, and I hope that this biography will help the reader to understand more clearly some of the differences between theorists and practitioners whose commonality is generally overstated.

But in the present chapter I wish to pursue in more detail the political implications of evaluation theory, and to include in this overview some of those in this country whose arguments have been directed, not at large scale social programmes, but at individual schools, their development needs in a context of demands for public accountability. Let me remind you, before I begin, of the three questions I posed in the introduction to the book, questions I consider to be particularly crucial to issues of quality in schooling:

Who should carry out evaluation in education?
Who should judge the value of curricula, organizational and

institutional arrangements?
Who should have access to evaluation findings?

One of the problems of theoretical overviews of this kind is the decontextualization of arguments, a problem that a case study practitioner like myself could hardly fail to note. To reduce this problem I have decided in this chapter to deal with American theorists first, followed by British theorists. This has the advantage of keeping the comparative contexts separate, and also allows me to manage the shift of focus in Britain from programme evaluation to school self-evaluation, a phenomenon that had no parallel in the USA.[1] Included in my selection of American theorists is Ralph Tyler, whom I did not mention in chapter 1, although his seminal influence is universally recognized. 'All subsequent approaches to curriculum evaluation have either evolved or recoiled from Tyler's proposals' (Hamilton *et al*, 1977 p. 26).

His inclusion now allows me to make another point. The growth of evaluation as a field of theory and practice in the past twenty-five years might not have taken place, at least on such a scale, had it not been for the legislative enactment in the USA of a mandatory evaluation requirement attached to federal investment in social programmes. The Elementary and Secondary Education Act of 1965 gave an immense impetus to evaluation.[2] Tyler and the early Cronbach made their significant contributions to the field before the passage of this act, and almost everyone else mentioned by me after it. Readers may care to note that the context of investment before 1965 was much more modest than that which followed, and was arguably much more like the context of investment in which much later and in a different country, some of us considered evaluation as an instrument of school self-development. Evaluation has, of course, a much longer history than the period covered in this book might suggest, and I do not mean to imply that earlier traditions can be neglected. But the early history has been well documented (Hamilton, 1976c and 1977; Cronbach *et al*, 1980; Guba and Lincoln, 1981; Norris, 1984) and I feel no need to recapitulate it here.

USA Theorists

Explicit in the writings of several theorists is the assumption that the one with the greatest knowledge, skill and freedom from bias — the evaluation specialist — should do the evaluation. Such a commitment to specialist evaluation is a function of three factors: the rapid growth of this 'new' professional field; the scale of the evaluation industry in the USA; and the specialist backgrounds of those who became evaluators. In a context of massive investment in large scale curriculum programmes, outsiders were needed to independently assess the worth of the programmes. Sponsors had a clear vested interest, developers were too close to the action to judge objectively (Scriven, 1967, p. 45 and 1974, p. 36) and participant teachers too unskilled to do a professional job (Scriven, 1967, p. 47). The demand for evaluation set off by the 1965 mandatory reporting requirement accelerated the growth of the field and consolidated the position of the expert. The complexity of numerous evaluation models which proliferated was such that *only* the specialist evaluator could carry them out. Practitioners shared, and still share, this assumption and so the need for the specialist evaluator has not been seriously questioned in the USA, although Stake, I suggest, is somewhat ambivalent.

The clearest statement of the need for the specialist evaluator comes from Scriven when he writes:

> The very idea that every school system, or every teacher, can today be regarded as capable of meaningful evaluation of his own performance is as absurd as the view that every psychotherapist today is capable of evaluating his work with his own patients. Trivially, they can learn something very important from carefully studying their own work, indeed they can identify some good and bad features about it. But if they or someone else need to know the answers to the important questions, whether process or outcome, they need skills and resources which are conspicuous by their rarity even at the *national* level. (*Ibid*, p. 53)

From a different standpoint Eisner (1984) in his notion of educational criticism and connoisseurship infers that it should be the expert, the outside critic who should do the evaluation. And Stufflebeam *et al* (1971) with his Context, Input, Process Product (CIPP) Model, linked to a rational theory of decision-making, place it beyond the scope of anyone else.

The position of Tyler is much more complex. His main concern in his classical exposition of the behavioural objectives model is to describe how the curriculum can be planned (Tyler, 1949, p. 1), evaluation being but one part of this process. His highly structured theoretical model suggests a task for the specialist. Yet Guba and Lincoln (1981, p. 6) maintain that Tyler was writing primarily for classroom teachers — those who have responsibility for curriculum development and change.

For the most part Tyler is examining the school. His concern is with curriculum improvement and the process he describes, though undoubtedly a very detailed one, does not exclude teachers (see, for example, Tyler, 1949, pp. 107 and 109). But the references he makes to the 'curriculum constructor' (p. 114), the 'curriculum worker' (p. 111), the construction of special evaluation instruments (p. 118) and the large scale of curriculum construction (p. 87), suggest a role for the expert outside the school.

In the event with the rise of the centre-periphery curriculum development projects in the sixties, the model proved a ready-made approach for development and evaluation and it was used primarily by expert 'curriculum makers' as Hamilton has denoted them (Hamilton, 1977).

By the time we get from Tyler to Cronbach (1963) the context of educational development had changed to include a proliferation of national high-school subject projects, given impetus by post-Sputnik alarm (Guba and Lincoln, 1981). Evaluation models, like Tyler's, focussing as it did on decentralized curriculum-making and classroom instruction, were seen to be ill-suited. The role of the expert evaluator in this process of curriculum reform, however, was even more secure. With Stake (1967b) and House (1973a) we begin to move away from consensus models of evaluation but not from the role of the expert evaluator. Specialist expertise is still needed.

There is an element of divergence when we come to my second question — who should judge the value of curricula and institutional arrangements? For several, notably Scriven and Eisner, the answer is the same as that to the first question. Scriven is unequivocal on this point. It is the expert evaluator who should judge the worth of the programme. This is as true of his earlier work (Scriven, 1967) as it is of his later goal-free evaluation (Scriven, 1974). Eisner does not address this question directly but it is implicit, if not explicit, in his notion of educational connoisseurship that it is the expert who should judge. In noting the 'implicit elitism built into a "high culture" notion like connoisseurship' (Hamilton *et al*, 1977) and that it is 'not for the masses' (Guba and Lincoln, 1981), others confirm this view.

Those theorists who work within a framework of providing information for decision-makers (Stake, Stufflebeam, Tyler, Cronbach) while accepting responsibility for collecting judgments of value about the programme do not see it as part of their role to authoritatively judge the programme. That is properly the role of others with professional responsibilities in the system, though precisely who these groups are differs from theorist to theorist.

For Stufflebeam the decision-makers are definitely the administrators (Stufflebeam *et al*, 1971, p. 96). 'The evaluator should neither make nor implement program decisions' (p. 93). Tyler exhibits the same tension as before. While he is basically speaking to teachers who ultimately choose the objectives (Tyler, 1949, p. 4), prior selection of objectives is conceded to curriculum experts (p. 86) and, in the way the model was adopted in the sixties, to curriculum developers.

In Cronbach's early work (Cronbach, 1963) he is clearly addressing the curriculum programme developer and in his later work, noted in the first chapter as similar to pluralistic social research, to all those in the polity who have a right to influence and affect curricula (Cronbach *et al*, 1980, p. 66). The role of evaluation is to offer information for scrutiny and independent interpretation (p. 17), to 'illuminate, not to dictate, the decision' (p. 155). With this formulation of evaluation Cronbach *et al* point out that they have more in common with the alternative tradition (MacDonald and Parlett, 1973) in England, than with the notion that the evaluator, as Scriven suggests, should tell the public whether the programme is good enough (Cronbach *et al*, 1980, p. 154).

Stake takes the broadest view, assuming that many groups, including parents, teachers and taxpayers have a right to judge the value of curricula. While he does not deny that the evaluator by virtue of his training may be qualified to judge, he questions the wisdom of doing so on the grounds that it might be counterproductive to evaluation by others, and argues for a facilitating role for the evaluation: 'A responsibility for processing judgments is much more acceptable to the evaluation specialist than one for rendering judgments himself' (Stake, 1967b, in Hamilton *et al*, 1977, p. 149). At the same time he does not abrogate entirely the ideal of specialist judgments. This is as evident in his earlier work (Stake, 1967b) as in his later work (Stake and Easley, 1978) in the use of expert panels, for instance, even though his basic position had moved considerably by then towards democratic pluralism.

The third question — who should have access to evaluation findings? is, with the exception of Stake, House and the later Cronbach, addressed only indirectly by these theorists and by some (Eisner and Scriven, for example) not at all, although one can make some assumptions, given the specialist dominance of these theorists, that findings will be primarily accessible to colleagues, curriculum developers and sponsors. Stufflebeam, of course, consistent with his rational decision-making loop model, believes that administrators are a sufficient audience and that they, moreover, speak for other interest or reference groups (Stufflebeam *et al*, 1971, pp. 112–3). This is a not dissimilar position to the one Scriven takes when he speaks for the 'welfare of society as a whole' (Scriven, 1967, p. 81).

On this issue Stake and House are most explicit of all. Stake argues in several places but especially in his concept of responsive evaluation, that it is the responsibility of evaluation to report diverse perspectives in language that is accessible to a wide range of people (Stake, 1972a, 1972b and 1975) to give them more of a purchase on the system or at least help them to understand it better. Hamilton *et al* (1977) sum up his position thus:

> Responsive evaluation is 'responsive' to the questions of non-specialist audiences. It is consequently democratic, avoiding jargon and having a preference for 'natural' com- munication. It is focussed on activities rather than intentions, and offers interpretations and descriptions. It is issue-centred, using issues as a way in to the understanding of complex phenomena. (p. 145)

House is the most overtly political of the US theorists as has already been noted. His position is slightly more difficult to discern as his work ranges so widely. Not only is he a practitioner of evaluation (House, *et al*, 1971; House and Gjerde, 1973) and an evaluation theorist (House, 1972, 1976, 1977 and 1979b) but a meta evaluator (House *et al*, 1978 and 1979) and a meta theorist as well (House, 1978 and 1980). These last two roles sometimes make it difficult to know whether House is analyzing or advocating a particular theory.

But two particular contributions by House are relevant to the issue of who the evaluation is for. The first is his early reminder that if evaluations are to be used they need to match the 'vocabulary of action' of the decision-maker (House, 1973, p. 135). The second is his exposition much later (House, 1980) of the politics of democratizing evaluation (pp. 139–57). Here he states his own position on the politics of choice, which is significantly different, he argues, from the purely liberal position from which much policy and evaluation now tacitly proceed:

> The liberal democratic principle of equality of choice requires not only that choice be maximized but that it be distributed somewhat equally. Liberal democracy becomes not only the

politics of maximizing choice but the politics of distributing it. (*Ibid*, p. 141)

It will be clear from this brief account that, with the possible exception of Stake, the work of the American theorists discussed here offered little guidance when I began the work reported in later chapters and even less help in meeting the problems I encountered. This is primarily because my three questions were not seen as particularly problematic by these theorists at that time.

Other reference groups featured little in evaluation deliberations, a situation Hamilton (1977) attributes to the assumption of goal consensus which characterized many of the early evaluation models:

> Throughout, this vision of consensus has been well formulated, overtly rational and immensely powerful. (p. 27)

Such consensus was strengthened by the tendency of 'experts', ie, 'professional competent evaluators' in Scriven's terms (Scriven, 1967, p. 53) or 'curriculum constructors' in Tyler's (1949, p. 114) to speak for the 'welfare of society as a whole' (Scriven, 1967, p. 81). In the late sixties this assumed consensus of values and interests began to be questioned (Atkin, 1967–68; Stake, 1967b), but it was only in the seventies that the issue of value pluralism began to be addressed in evaluation models.

UK Evaluators

The UK evaluation scene was markedly different. Formal, systematic curriculum evaluation, though also attached to a curriculum reform movement, started later than in the USA and did not have such a powerful behaviourist tradition constraining it (Hamilton *et al*, 1977). Spawned largely by the quasi-independent Schools Council[3] to evaluate their national curriculum projects, evaluators came from different sectors of the education system — schools, colleges, universities, LEAs, and had widely differing backgrounds. Though most had a university degree in the social sciences, sciences or the arts, few had any formal research training, and there was no formal training for evaluators in this country nor tradition of specialist evaluation inquiry.[4] Evaluators had to work with what skills they had articulating and developing theory in relation to the problems with which they were faced. Unlike the US theorists, most UK theorists were, first and foremost, *practitioners* of evaluation. British theory was grounded in practice.

These differences in evolution of a field of professional evaluators may partly explain why the preordinate objectives model of curriculum evaluation so predominant in the USA in the fifties and sixties never received such acclaim here (MacDonald, 1974; Hamilton *et al*, 1977) and why alternatives had room to flourish. Hamilton *et al* (1977) also posit a cultural difference between the two countries contrasting the rationalist social-engineering flair of the USA with a distrust of rationality and belief in pragmatism characteristic of the English system.

There was, then, relatively little UK evaluation theory of a political nature to consider when I began the first of the studies reported in this book and much of the USA theory was limited in its applicability. Early efforts to evaluate curriculum reform projects had indicated that attention needed to be paid to classroom and school contexts of implementation and the concept of case study and of holistic evaluation had already been invoked to explore this impact (Simons, 1971; MacDonald, 1971). Unlike the USA, quite early on in the evaluation movement in this country there was some evidence of a shift in the locus of evaluation from programme to school level. For this reason, I have included writers like Eraut and Elliott, who stem more from an in-service teacher education tradition than from programme evaluation, in the following discussion. Given this context, the position evaluators took on the three framing questions was quite different from those identified in the work of the USA theorists.

Two quite different key papers by UK evaluators prior to 1976 were significant. In 1972 Parlett and Hamilton first circulated their paper on 'Illuminative evaluation' which argued the case for a shift from the agricultural-botany to a social-anthropological model of evaluation (Parlett and Hamilton, 1972). This paper was immediately influential in the UK. It was widely read and welcomed by the growing community of curriculum specialists as offering a potentially helpful alternative to evaluation based on outcome measures.

Parlett and Hamilton do not address the first question — who should carry out evaluation? — directly in this paper. Though the methodology they advocate is potentially accessible to non-specialists, they rather assume, like the USA theorists, that the specialist should conduct the evaluation (p. 20). On the second question they clearly have affinities with Stake. No one group should judge the value of curricula:

Clearly, if the evaluator is to acknowledge the interests of all these groups, he cannot, even if requested, provide a simple 'yes' or 'no' on the innovation's future. A decision based on one group's evaluative criteria would almost certainly be disputed by another group's with different priorities ...
(Parlett and Hamilton, 1972, p. 19)

On the third question they are most explicit in advocating that many different groups of decision-makers need to be informed (p. 19). This is supported by the attention they give to communicability and accessibility of reports (p. 20).

Like Stake (1975), Parlett and Hamilton do not address the political dimension directly, nor do they recognize the political context in which evaluations are conducted. In this respect the argument is similar in kind to that of many USA theorists who see evaluation primarily as methodology. That this was the major focus of illuminative evaluation is affirmed by the aspiration in some of Parlett's other writing to establish the illuminative approach as a new research paradigm (Parlett, 1976).

In subsequent papers on illuminative evaluation Parlett[5] begins to address the political dimension in two respects: first in emphasizing that illuminative evaluation is not simply a switch in methodology but a redefinition of evaluation that defines a responsive role for the evaluator to constituent interests (Parlett and Dearden, 1977, p. 33); and secondly, in recognizing the need to achieve a balance between the 'public's right to know' and the 'individual's right to choose what they wish to disclose' (*Ibid*, p. 34) though he does not address the procedural political question of how precisely to achieve this. This move to take account of the political factors in evaluation may be partly a result of the experience of conducting evaluation — the undoubtedly political nature of the field demands such attention — but the very terms in which the issues are conceived and addressed are clearly influenced by MacDonald's political theory, which I will explore at greater length at the end of this chapter.

The second key paper which had a seminal influence on evaluation theory and practice in the UK, MacDonald's 'Evaluation and the control of education' (1974) addresses the political dimension directly. In it MacDonald posits a political classification of evaluation in terms of ideal types, bureaucratic evaluation, autocratic evaluation and democratic evaluation. The concept of democratic evaluation was in part a reaction to and rejection of technocratic forms of evaluation.

Democratic evaluation by contrast recognizes the essentially pluralistic nature of society and asserts 'the evaluator's obligation to democratize his knowledge' (*Ibid*, p. 12).

Recognition of the political nature of evaluation is also to be seen in many of MacDonald's other contributions to evaluation theory which fall into four main areas: the conceptualization and development of democratic evaluation (MacDonald, 1974, 1975 *et al*, and 1984a; MacDonald and Norris, 1981); the development of case study theory and methodology (MacDonald and Parlett, 1973; MacDonald, 1971, 1976, 1980a and 1981; MacDonald and Walker, 1975); the role of evaluation within accountability (MacDonald, 1978b and 1979); and the articulation and development of evaluation policy issues at national and international levels (MacDonald *et al*, 1977, 1981 and 1982; MacDonald and Jenkins, 1980; MacDonald, 1982a).

On the first question — who should do the evaluation? — MacDonald's position is the same as other theorists — it is the professional evaluator — but his reason is slightly different. In democratic evaluation an external evaluator is needed to take an independent brokerage role in the exchange of information (MacDonald, 1974). In other writings, however, he clearly sees a role for practitioners. This is most manifest in his advocacy of the process model of self-report in school evaluation as the appropriate way to render accountability of individual schools (MacDonald, 1978b).

On the second and third questions, concerning judgment and access, MacDonald argues that in a pluralist society:

> The evaluator ... has no right to use his position to promote his personal values, or to choose which particular ideologies he shall regard as legitimate. His job is to identify those who will have to make judgments and decisions about the programme and lay before them those facts of the case that are recognized by them as relevant to their concerns. (MacDonald *et al*, 1975, p. 74)

The next three evaluators, Harlen, Eraut and Elliott focus to varying degrees on school evaluation and in so doing they offer a very different response than the USA theorists to all three questions. On the first each shows a strong commitment, not indicated by any of the USA theorists, to the teacher carrying out evaluation. Though Harlen initially started out as a project evaluator (Harlen, 1973 and 1975), her later work on assessment of pupil progress (Harlen 1976, 1977a and 1977b) and school self-assessment and accountability (Harlen, 1979a and 1979b) clearly demonstrate a concern to improve teacher evaluation by giving teachers a dominant role in the process. This extends to articulating the purposes of evaluation and translating methods into language and schema that teachers can use.

Eraut does not comment directly on the question of who should evaluate but it is evident from his commitment to helping teachers (Eraut, 1976, 1978 and 1984b) that he believes, in many instances, that schools should incorporate evaluation roles. But the theorist who has perhaps most strongly promoted evaluation by teachers is John Elliott. At first (Elliott, 1976) this was stated more in terms of teachers researching their own performance following the concept of 'teacher-as-researcher' first advocated by Stenhouse (1975) but subsequently it was interpreted in terms of evaluating curriculum practice (Elliott, 1979b) and, later still, in terms of rendering accountability (Elliott, J, 1981b).

With all three the focus is very much on assisting *individuals* to evaluate, to improve *classroom processes*. While in some instances the importance of linking process studies into the structure of the school is recognized (Elliott, J, 1980b and 1982; Eraut, 1984b), relatively little attention is given to studying the school as a whole. The strongest advocate for the focus on the classroom is Elliott when he states his conviction that 'self-evaluation in the classroom should be the foundation stone of the total evaluation process in a school' (Elliott, 1979b, p. 6). Eraut and Harlen place their emphasis more on the benefit such self-evaluation processes should have for pupils (Harlen, 1979b; Eraut, 1984b). These three evaluators still see a role for the specialist to help teachers build up appropriate skills (Harlen, 1979b), as an assistant or 'co-evaluator' in the inquiry (Eraut, 1984a), and in clarifying criteria, teacher constructs and offering support (Elliott, 1976). But this is a long way from the evaluator as specialist actually doing the evaluation.

The answer to the question of who should judge is slightly broader. While teachers are clearly one group who should judge the value of curricula, schools need to communicate to parents, tax-payers, employers, all the information that is necessary for them to make appropriate judgments about school curricula (Harlen, 1979b).

Eraut's position is more complex. While he finds Scriven's position quite unacceptable, he also finds the alternative posed by 'illuminative evaluation' unsatisfactory on the grounds of conflict avoidance and conservatism (Eraut, 1984a, p. 31). He proposes a compromise which recognizes the evaluator's accountability to his immediate clients and the wider public *and* the standards and values of the education specialist:

> The process which I like to call *divergent evaluation* recognizes that there are likely to be several different value positions and that some of them are potentially conflicting, and then attempts to relate the empirical evidence to these value positions without according priority to any of them. (*Ibid*, p. 32)

In this way the evaluator can avoid making the summative, simplistic recommendatory statement herself and confront the value conflicts likely to be present in any one evaluation. The question of who should judge is thus left somewhat open for the audiences to whom the evaluation is disseminated to decide but in including a range of value positions within the evaluation related to the empirical evidence or criteria, Eraut indicates that no one group should have a monopoly on judging the value of the programme. This argument of Eraut's sounds identical to that of MacDonald, the main difference being that Eraut believes the value position of the evaluator should be included. In this respect his position is closer to that of Stake.

Elliott's answer is straightforward. The individual teacher is the primary judge or teacher colleagues when reports are shared (Elliott, 1979b). External auditors have a meta-judgment role. In the papers on school self-accountability (Elliott, J, 1981a; Elliott *et al*, 1981) the right of judgment is extended to include governors of schools, parents, LEAs and the wider local community.

Not surprisingly perhaps given the emphasis on teacher evaluation, classroom process and pupil assessment, these three evaluators have little to say on the issue of access which is not distinguished from the issue of judgment. The audiences in the main are local clienteles where accountability is the context but otherwise self-evaluation is seen as an intra-institutional activity serving professional self-improvement.

Elliott offers the strongest justification for restriction to local audiences in maintaining that transactional evaluation has prime utility for interest groups operating in local contexts where 'the transactions they effect with teachers are governed by trust and mutual respect' (Elliott, J, 1981b, p. 242). He goes further in maintaining that 'in order to protect the utility of an evaluation for local audiences an evaluator may have to deny equal access to bureaucratic agencies' (p. 242). This is based on his assumption that 'educational evaluation cannot be procedurally neutral with respect to different audiences, and possess equal utility for them, when the kinds of influence they are in a position to exert radically conflict' (p. 242).

I want now to return to pre-1975 and make two summary points. First it is clear from this review that the focus of evaluation theory has shifted historically from the classroom, with the formulations of Tyler, to the big programme, with the rise of the curriculum reform movement, and finally to the institution when the need to understand resistance to innovation generated a commitment to case study and other forms of evaluation responsive to the developmental process and complexity of change. The Humanities Curriculum Project (HCP) evaluation (1968–72) was one of the first in the UK to recognize the need for a methodological shift from the 'logic of demonstration' to the 'logic of discovery' (Nisbet, 1976). In the USA the shift was manifest in Stake's concept of portrayal (Stake, 1972b). Such a shift in methodology and focus brought its own complexities and a growing awareness of the political and ethical implications of evaluation, the full impact of which did not emerge until much later.

Secondly, it is clear that at this time evaluation theorists, with the exception of MacDonald and House, did not explicitly address the political dimension of evaluation. The search for technical designs and methodologies dominated evaluation practice. While value pluralism began to be addressed in evaluation models in the early seventies in both countries, and there was some move towards democratizing findings, the political implications of a change in methodology and indeed the differing political stances within the alternative methodologies had not yet surfaced. Evaluation theorists of a pluralistic persuasion were, at that time, united by their commonalities. This was as true of the first Cambridge conference of UK and USA evaluators held to discuss the emerging tradition (MacDonald and Parlett, 1973) as it was of the second (Adelman, Kemmis and Jenkins, 1976).

By 1979, however, the context of the debate was quite different and at a third conference to examine the efforts of naturalistic inquirers in practice the consensus was broken. Conflicts in trying to realize the pluralistic models and aspirations in practice had been encountered and revealed not only political differences within the 'new wave' evaluators but also that, if evaluation was to survive, it had to strengthen its procedural response (Jenkins *et al*, 1981; MacDonald and Norris, 1981).

By the early eighties we can note a further shift in the UK within the 'naturalistic school' from specialist evaluation to practitioner evaluation as teachers and schools, in an increasingly politicized climate, began to respond to the need to evaluate their own policies and practice. The methodological and political assumptions of the 'naturalistic school', by then more firmly based, provided an approach that was adaptive to this purpose.

In the next chapter I intend to revisit some of this history in explicating the community context in which case study and naturalistic methodology evolved. First, however, I want to elaborate a little further the theory of democratic evaluation. By so doing I hope to do two things. I hope in the first place to provide the reader with a broad-ranging political framework of problems and issues within which my own work has developed. Secondly, I wish to draw attention to a difference in the rationale of naturalistic evaluation and that of investigative social sciences.

Democratic Evaluation Theory

In 1974 MacDonald wrote three influential papers, the first of which 'Evaluation and the control of education', has already been mentioned. The second paper, 'Case study and the social philosophy of educational research' (co-authored with Rob Walker) grounded the case study tradition which MacDonald had established at CARE in the principles of the democratic model and made a more general case for sharing control of studies of schooling with those studied (MacDonald and Walker, 1974). The third paper, 'Confidentiality: Procedure and principles of the UNCAL evaluation with respect to information about projects in the National Development Programme in Computer Assisted Learning' (co-authored with Bob Stake), spelt out a set of procedures for evaluative data management in the particular context of an attempt to impose a democratic evaluation process on a programme structured in terms of bureaucratic rationality (MacDonald and Stake, 1974).

The first of these papers is one of the most widely quoted but least understood in the literature of evaluation possibly because it is rarely considered in relation to other theoretical statements of its purposes or contexts of application. It is part of my purpose here to offer a fuller understanding.

Let me begin with his well-known typology of evaluation. The typology is, interestingly, based on a review of American theory and practice, at a time when British theory was more embryonic and British practice much thinner on the ground. Almost all American evaluation, he contends, falls into the first two of his three categories. Briefly, he defines as 'bureaucratic' evaluations which play an instrumental role in maintaining and extending managerial power. The 'reality of power' is the implicit rationale of bureaucratic evaluation, which amounts to evaluation for hire. He defines as 'autocratic' evaluations which maintain and extend academic power by offering scientific legitimacy to public policy in exchange for compliance with the evaluator's recommendations. Here the underlying rationale is the 'responsibility of office', with the evaluator as guarantor of executive integrity. It is not difficult to see, and MacDonald has many times confirmed it, that he considered Stufflebeam's model as the prototype of bureaucratic evaluation and Scriven as an example of the autocratic evaluator. Democratic evaluation he describes in the following terms:

> Democratic evaluation is an information service to the community about the characteristics of an educational programme. It recognizes value pluralism and seeks to represent a range of interests in its issue formulation. The basic value is an informed citizenry, and the evaluator acts as broker in exchanges of information between differing groups. His techniques of data gathering and presentation must be accessible to non-specialist audiences. His main activity is the collection of definitions of, and reactions to, the programme. He offers confidentiality to informants and gives them control over his use of information. The report is non recommendatory, and the evaluator has no concept of information misuse. The evaluator engages in periodic negotiation of his relationships with sponsors and programme participants. The criterion of success is the range of audiences served. The report aspires to 'best seller' status. The key concepts of democratic evaluation are 'confidentiality', 'negotiation' and 'accessibility'. The key justificatory concept is the 'right to know'. (MacDonald, 1974, p. 18)

This concept of democratic evaluation has attracted a great deal of comment from other evaluation theorists, not all of it complimentary. House claimed it was, in its political assumptions, close to 'classic liberalism', viewing society as an association of self-determined individuals co-operating for self-interested ends (House, 1980, p. 62). Others have described it as 'facile' (Eraut, 1984a, p. 27), 'manipulative' (Jenkins, 1980), 'humanistic' (Cronbach, 1982) and, as we noted in chapter 1, 'value-free' and 'deferential' (Nilsson and Hogben, 1983).

The most damning criticism has been aimed at the procedural guidelines evolved as an interpretation of the model (MacDonald and Stake, 1974; MacDonald and Walker, 1974) to deal with one of the central issues '... the public "right to know" must always be balanced against the individual's "right to be discreet" ... the boundaries of public knowledge should be negotiated between these two "rights"' (MacDonald *et al*, 1975, p. 12). Since I shall be dealing with the issues and problems arising from such negotiations in the context of my own work, I will not elaborate further on these at this point, but rather pursue a little MacDonald's 'liberal' politics, which became clearer in subsequent papers. 'It is a sufficient condition for democracy if the distribution and exercise of power in a social system is in principle referable to its citizens. Such systems assume the corollary principle of an informed citizenry' (Jenkins *et al*, 1977, p. 25). At the end of this paper, confirming House's (1980) view that the broker role is related to a referee theory of government, MacDonald and his co-authors cite approvingly Smith's 1976 definition of the role of the state in a pluralist society: '... a neutral set of institutions adjudicating between conflicting social and economic interests' (Jenkins *et al*, 1977, p. 35). They then add, crucially in my view, 'It is up to evaluators to find the means of realizing this "fair" aspiration not by assuming the state's neutrality, but by taking its rhetoric as a self-imposed criterion of justification' (p. 35). Later still, in a paper delivered at the University of Illinois, MacDonald writes:

> I start from an attitude to the society I live and work in. That's a liberal democratic society, imperfectly realized but requiring for its political survival reasonable efforts to eliminate *demonstrably disqualifying practices*. The rhetoric of this society (its qualifying values) constitute for me a source of leverage on an unacceptable reality. Liberalism I take to be about maximizing individual powers, democracy I take to be about holding delegated power to informed, collective account. (MacDonald, 1980b, p. 1)

Since MacDonald and his associates at the Centre for Applied Research in Education (CARE) have had a number of opportunities to work out his politics of evaluation in practice, and increasingly in contexts involving access to powerful central policymakers, it is possible to get some idea of what all these statements add up to in practice. The following extract is from a paper delivered in 1982, in which he summarized an early attempt to implement the principles of democratic evaluation. The context was an evaluation of the National Development Programme in Computer Assisted Learning, for which he was commissioned by a funding Committee on which seven government departments were represented (MacDonald *et al*, 1975; MacDonald and Jenkins, 1980). This is a summary of an argument with his sponsors that lasted five years.

1   They wanted an aims/achievement model of evaluation. The funded projects were required to state their objectives before they got any money. They wanted an evaluation focus on whether those objectives were achieved.

    We said no — that was unfair. None of the projects would achieve all their objectives — so they would all fail on that criterion. We would portray their efforts to achieve those objectives so that the Committee could judge whether they were engaged in worthwhile activities, given their constraints and opportunities.

2   They wanted us to make recommendations about which projects should be supported, which terminated.

    We said no — it was their task and responsibility to make such judgments, not ours. They would have to read the evaluation reports, and make up their minds. We are just brokers of information — go-betweens linking people and institutions who want to trade knowledge of each other.

3   They wanted us to add to the written reports — to tell them things about the projects we could not put in the reports.

    We said no — no secret reporting. Our reports were all negotiated with the people whose work we commented on, and not given to the Committee until those people agreed they were accurate, relevant and fair. We would not add to them.

4   They said the reports were too long and too complex for a busy Committee to deal with. Could we not summarize them?

    We said they were as short as we could make them and still negotiate them with the people whose work was being evaluated. We serve the judgment, not the judge.

    They said — but we cannot handle all this complexity —

are you saying we should not be making these decisions?

We said — that is for you to say, and for others who read the evaluation report on the work of this Committee.

5   They said — what do you mean, the evaluation of this Committee? We don't want you to evaluate us, only the projects.

We said — we're afraid we must — it would not be fair only to gather information about the projects. They want to know about how you do your work, whether you reached your objectives, whether you are doing a good job.

6   They said — who do you think you are? We are paying you to do as we say.

We said — we are your democratic independent evaluators. Simply because you pay for the evaluation does not mean that you have any special claim on its services, or exemption from its focus.

You cannot buy an evaluation, you can only sponsor one. Anyone has a right to raise questions and issues for inclusion on the agenda of the evaluation, and no-one has the right to ask for information without being prepared to give it.

These arguments with the bureaucracy were bitter and prolonged. They went on for five years. I raise them here only to indicate the lines of a counter-argument to bureaucratic assumptions based on power and custom rather than responsibility and reasonableness. (MacDonald, 1982b, pp. 8–10)

It will be clear enough from this account, even allowing for its entertaining form, that MacDonald derives from a negotiable rhetoric of liberal democracy a strategy which he employs as a means of equalizing the power relationships in which programmes are embedded. A recent quotation confirms this view, and also links it to naturalistic evaluation. These are his closing remarks in a presentation of democratic evaluation to a conference in Australia:

The fundamental issue, of course, is the impact of evaluation on the distribution of power, and this may come down in the end to the choice of discourse — a question of language. Evaluators who choose the discourse of technocratic management will empower the managers. Evaluators who choose the language of social science will empower themselves and their sector. Evaluators who choose a widely shared language may empower all of us. I'm a common language evaluator, how about you? (MacDonald, 1984a).

Up to this point I have been exploring the logic of the democratic model as a counter to the power relationships encountered in centrally funded programmes of social intervention. In this setting the problem is seen in terms of unequal relationships between sponsors and programme executives on the one hand and those further down the line whose continuity of support depends upon gaining and keeping the approval of those who control funding. It is a context of command. The democratic evaluator in such settings seeks to establish her independence of these relationships, to reject an instrumental role conceived in terms of docility to such a power structure, and to substitute for this role that of a broker in what MacDonald calls the 'exchange of a trading commodity' (MacDonald and Sanger, 1982). That commodity is, of course, programme knowledge, a commodity that is much more equally distributed than the power relationships. The principle which underlies this rationale is 'people own the facts of their lives' (Walker and MacDonald, 1975), an ethical principle which MacDonald converts into a political strategy.

But let me now shift the context of application to that in which the problem of power lies much less in the relationships actualized through political structures than in the relationships between the scientific community and the lay community that constitutes its field of inquiry. Democratic evaluation can also be seen as an attack on the authority of science, and as a strategy for reducing the power inequalities that characterize investigative inquiry in the applied social sciences. It is notable that some of those who found the 'bureaucratic' and 'democratic' models broadly acceptable baulked at the 'autocratic' label. Cronbach, for instance, suggested 'authoritative' as a substitute (Cronbach, 1982), Adelman and Alexander (1982) substituted 'autonomous'. The key to the logic of democratic inquiry in such contexts is to be found in the second paper mentioned at the start of this subsection 'Case study and the social philosophy of educational research'. Taking democratic evaluation as their starting point, MacDonald and Walker attack what they call the 'autocratic tradition' in case study research, which they see as a theory-oriented tradition directed to academic audiences which accords to the researcher the unimpeded right to interpret the social world. They list some critical issues as a basis for questioning this tradition:

> — to whose needs and interests does the research respond?
> — who owns the data (the researcher, the subject, the sponsor)?
> — who has access to the data? (Who is excluded or denied?)
> — what is the status of the researcher's interpretation of events, vis-à-vis the interpretations made by others? (Who decides who tells the truth?)
> — what obligations does the researcher owe to his subjects, his sponsors, his fellow professionals, others?
> — who is the research for? (MacDonald and Walker, 1975, p. 6)

They go on later in the paper to suggest guidelines for a democratic alternative:

> It seems to us feasible to contemplate a form of educational research that would be practice-based in a way research has not been previously. We see this as a form of research which responds actively to practitioners' definitions of situations, conceptual structures and language. Constrained by these the researcher would act as the representative of the various groups involved, exploring their hypotheses, using their language and conceptual structures, both as starting points and as a continuous reference. The aim would not be to create alternative realities for practitioners but to find ways of encouraging them to develop insight into their existing realities, and to understand the realities of other inhabitants. (*Ibid*, p. 9)

And they conclude with this statement: 'The real prize is the prospect of developing techniques and procedures which can be used by schools and ancillary agencies. A specialist research profession will always be a poor substitute for a self-monitoring educational community' (p. 11).

The crux of this paper, as far as the research community was concerned, was the following proposal in relation to confidentiality:

> Confidentiality should be accorded to informants for the term of the study and, thereafter, release of material for publication negotiated with them ... This sharing of control over data with participants does mean that the researcher

often has to face the fact that some of his finest data is lost, diluted or permanently consigned to the files. (*Ibid*, p. 10)

According to one observer (Elliott, 1984) this last proposal, when put to the 1975 annual conference of the British Educational Research Association, caused an uproar of hostility. Put to the 1975 Cambridge conference, Becker's response was that it would hardly do as a procedure for studying a corrupt police department. MacDonald replied that that depended upon how widely you drew the boundaries of the case. Recalling this exchange now it is interesting to note that MacDonald has recently completed an evaluation of police training (MacDonald *et al*, 1987).

We can now see that the logic of action derived from the democratic model varies with the context of application. This is hardly surprising given the commitment to the case study approach in evaluation. Perhaps, though, we can begin to understand how some critics saw in the flexibility of the model, and in the strategies employed in its name, the 'manipulative' possibilities it might afford. Other equally interesting questions arise, such as the relationship between democratic case study and educational ethnography and anthropology, also very lively developments in the seventies.

It is evident from an examination of MacDonald's work that a change of methodology without a change of power relationships is irrelevant in his terms. For instance, in a paper with colleagues arguing for a political change in research:

In establishing a defensible alternative for evaluation it is not simply a matter of choosing between the merits of, say, a psychometric or an anthropological orientation, although alternatives in evaluation have been much debated in such terms ... The relationship between evaluation and educational systems is not a function of the adoption of a disciplinary model. But the choice of political stances does have consequences for the subsequent choice of appropriate tools. (Jenkins *et al*, 1977, p. 24)

He has also strongly criticized sociological case studies such as those of Nash (1973) and Sharp and Green (1975) as examples of what he calls the 'social and ethical inadequacy' of the case study tradition in the social sciences (MacDonald, 1980a). In more general terms he has criticized fieldwork traditions which, even at best, he and Norris contend, promise only to be harmless to their anonymized subjects. 'The fieldworker as evaluator implicitly or explicitly has the responsibility for promoting or denying benefit to the people he studies' (MacDonald and Norris, 1981, p. 19). They conclude:

> ...when the people we study are disenfranchised from the process of issue formulation, data control and information utilization ... we help reproduce the belief and the objective conditions for its persistence, that the powerless are politically docile and uninterested. (*Ibid*, p. 23)

Concluding Comments on the Politics of Evaluation Theory

Contexts matter. In the mid-sixties federal concern about the curriculum of the American public school switched from the promotion of achievement by the most able (the 'catching up with the Russians' syndrome) to improving learning opportunities for disadvantaged social groups (the compensatory education drive). This focus on the 'have nots' of society was increasingly reflected in the consciousness of evaluation theorists, the more so as efforts at compensation did more to reveal than to resolve the entrenched nature of the position of winners and losers in so-called 'open' societies. In this sense House (1974) wrote of education as a 'frozen institution' (p. 5), and MacDonald *et al*, (1982) of the 'functional discrimination of sophisticated democracies' (p. 2). In this country, too, the main focus of curriculum development in the sixties was the raising of the school leaving age, planned for 1970 and implemented in 1972, when it rose from 15 to 16. In both countries the context was one of economic expansion, with money available to those who could design more effective and attractive curricula for low achievers, mainly young children of minority groups in the USA and adolescent working class youngsters in the UK. We should not be surprised that in both countries at least some of those charged with monitoring and reporting programmes of redress should have become sensitive to the political realities of educational change, or to their own responsibilities with respect to these realities. And when, in both countries, 'the war on want gave way to the war on welfare' (*Ibid*) and the growth of spending on education gave way to targeted intervention of a more coercive nature, the problem of the evaluator role became acute. It was more difficult to define social programmes as unequivocally benevolent efforts to redistribute the nation's wealth in favour of its worst-off members.

It is the varying responses of evaluators to this issue that I have dwelt upon in this review, but I must immediately qualify that priority by introducing another explanatory dimension that has not so far been explicitly mentioned. Evaluation theorists such as Cronbach, House, Stake and MacDonald are also theorists of planned change, steeped in the history and analysis of thirty years of curriculum reform. Far from being indifferent to the success or failure of reform initiatives, it is clear that much of what they advocate for evaluation is linked to, if not derived from, a view of the conditions of school improvement.

Seen in this light MacDonald's three categories of evaluation may be seen to embody preferences with regard to competing views about how best to improve the quality of schooling. In endorsing the democratic model, he can therefore be seen to favour a view of curriculum development based on community, diversity, and relationships of mutual accountability. Fairness, reasonableness and respect for persons are root values within such a view, just as power-based relationships and instrumental ways of thinking are hostile to it. Clearly he interprets the rhetoric of liberal democracy as embodying these root values rather than as 'a mere mechanism of authorization' (McPherson, quoted in MacDonald and Norris, 1981, p. 5) and seeks to hold that 'mechanism' to account in terms of fidelity to the values, whilst respecting its legitimacy. Just as clearly he sees the need to hold the research community to account in similar terms.

Personally speaking, the attraction of the democratic model for me lies in its educative logic rather than in its politics of opposition. I am in agreement with MacDonald when he writes of the evaluator's primary purpose as 'to reveal educational possibilities' and of the evaluative process as a shared task. In terms of the case study of schools, to which most of my research energy has been directed, I accept as a baseline this statement of process, focus and values:

> When we are negotiating access to the people in the case . . . let us say to them that we assume all social action is a compromise of some kind between values, interests and circumstances, and that our task, and theirs, is not to defend or attack that compromise but to understand its precise structure. This is not a promise, but an invitation to locate the evaluative act where the action is.' (MacDonald, 1981, p. 6)

I interpret that statement as consistent with an educative and emancipatory role for evaluation. For MacDonald that entails facili-

53

tating reflective agency at all levels of the system. For me, it offers a framework for developing knowledge of schooling, and the confidence to share such knowledge, as a basis for justifiable self-direction in educational practice.

Notes

1 Though some forms of school self-evaluation in the UK, ie, of an extensive checklist format (see chapter 9) resemble the checklists developed for accreditation of schools in the USA their location in different historical periods, as well as cultures, makes parallels misleading.

2 For an excellent account of the aspirations of the Elementary and Secondary Education Act (ESEA) and the fortunes of the evaluation/s which accompanied it see McLAUGHLIN, M.W. (1975) *Evaluation and Reform: The Elementary and Secondary Education Act of 1965, Title 1*, a Rand Educational Policy Study, Cambridge, MA, Ballinger Publishing Company.

3 The Schools Council for Curriculum and Examinations in England and Wales was a quasi-governmental national agency funded, jointly by the DES and LEAs, set up in 1964 to stimulate curriculum development and examination reform in schools. For the first ten years of its existence it supported centrally-developed curriculum projects in a range of school subjects and areas of knowledge. Under increasing criticism and a decreasing budget it shifted its focus in the late seventies to general programmes of study supporting for the most part small-scale curriculum and evaluation projects. Further criticism finally led to its demise in 1984, and the setting up of two separate organizations, the Secondary Examinations Council (SEC) and the School Curriculum Development Committee (SCDC). For an account of the rise and fall of the Schools Council see PLASKOW, M. (Ed) (1985) *Life and Death of the Schools Council*, Lewes, Falmer Press.

4 Her Majesty's Inspectorate (HMI), of course, it could be argued, has been formally evaluating the educational system for years through its inspections of schools but until 1983 reports on schools have been confidential and the process still is. Most HMIs have no background in the academic disciplines of social inquiry (see WALKER, 1982).

5 HAMILTON had, by this time, shifted his interests to classroom research (1976a and 1976b), evaluation theory (1976c, 1977 and 1980c) and the history of ideas in curriculum evaluation and research (1977, 1980a and 1980b).

3 The Evolution of the
Case Study Approach

The particular form of educational case study that is exemplified in later chapters of this book is, as I have said, linked to the 'democratic' mode of evaluation. As I shall make clear in this chapter, however, this case study approach to evaluation preceded the articulation of that model which from 1974 onwards, provided the criteria that shaped its further development. The evolution of these inter-linked ideas is important to the understanding of my own work which, since the first of two periods of collaboration with MacDonald, has focussed increasingly on the role of evaluation in school self-development, while he has sought more macro-contexts in which to mediate power relationships through evaluation.

I also want in this chapter to attempt a clarification of relationships between a number of case study practitioners, relationships which, as a teacher of postgraduate courses in educational evaluation, I know to be a source of confusion among students. This confusion is compounded by the occasional attack on the methods and social theory of so-called 'qualitative evaluation', mainly by ethnographic or radical sociologists who typically allege that the evaluators are perversely innocent of both (see, for example, Atkinson and Delamont, 1985; Whitty, 1985). Students of curriculum theory in the eighties have difficulty in sorting out the ferments and arguments of the seventies, when the anti-technocratic 'counter-culture' of evaluative research was paralleled by a revival of ethnographic studies of schooling in sociology and a burgeoning of the 'knowledge and control' school of radical critique (see, for instance, Wolcott, 1973; Delamont, 1976; Young, 1971).

The reconstruction of that period that I offer is one which takes evaluation problems as the beginning and continuing context of case study development, and treats other movements only in so far as they impinge on that development. Others would no doubt reconstruct differently (see Walker, 1982, for a more comprehensive overview) but my primary purpose is to explicate the development of evaluation theory and practice in the 'democratic' case study mode.

Let us take as a starting point, one from which we can go back as well as forward, an event in 1972.

In 1972, at Churchill College, Cambridge, an 'invisible college' of educational evaluators was founded. There a conference was convened of like minds, whose common identity was a shared sense of the inadequacy of product models in a psychometric tradition. It was an international conference of around twenty people, some of whom represented funding agencies, private and public, with an interest in developing more effective theories and strategies of action in the curriculum development field. The inspiration for the conference came from Tony Becher, then Assistant Director of the Nuffield Foundation, and John Banks, then of the Department of Education and Science (DES). They brought together Barry MacDonald at the University of East Anglia, and Malcolm Parlett of the Centre for Educational Sciences at the University of Edinburgh, and invited them to convene a meeting of evaluators like themselves whose work was leading in new directions.

Becher and Banks had in mind the possibility of setting up, with a combination of private and public funds, two new centres for educational evaluation, and had MacDonald and Parlett earmarked as directors. They were familiar with MacDonald's development of a case study approach, and saw a kinship between this and Parlett and Hamilton's 'Illuminative evaluation' paper (1972) which had just made its appearance. The planned new centres did not, in fact, gain the administrative/financial backing necessary to bring them about, but the 'college' would continue to meet every few years in Cambridge, generating a network, as well as a mutual aid programme, that shaped a school of thought and action that spread from evaluation into other contexts of applied educational research.

That first meeting was attended by some of those who would continue to provide the nucleus of continuity — MacDonald, Parlett, his colleague David Hamilton, Bob Stake and Lou Smith from the USA, and myself. I had been working for two years with MacDonald on the case study side of the evaluation of the Humanities Curriculum Project (Humble and Simons, 1978). The initial cull of like minds also netted for the first conference David Jenkins and David Tawney, who would eighteen months later join MacDonald at Norwich to assist in the evaluation of the National Development Programme in

Computer Assisted Learning, a programme that marked in Britain the emergence in the seventies of a more centrally controlled, technocratic approach to the problem of curriculum change. The commission of MacDonald to handle this evaluation arose directly from the conference, which was attended by the Programme's Director-designate, Richard Hooper. Hooper was looking for an approach to evaluation that would be sensitive to the contexts of innovation, and saw such an approach in the case study that Mac-Donald presented to the meeting. MacDonald had not yet formulated his political taxonomy of evaluation, and was still exploring the political implications of his shift away from 'expert' traditions in field-based methodology.

That first conference consolidated and extended pre-existing contacts. MacDonald already had contact with the evaluation centre CIRCE (Centre for Instructional Research and Curriculum Evaluation) at the University of Illinois, where Mike Atkin, the earliest critic of the behavioural objectives model of curriculum development (Atkin, 1963), was Dean of Education. MacDonald had visited CIRCE in 1970, and was encouraged by the sympathetic reaction he got to his case study evaluation from Bob Stake, whose seminal paper, 'The countenance of educational evaluation' (Stake, 1967b) had reconstituted and greatly enlarged the tasks of evaluation. He also met there Ernie House. Their shared interest in the politics of evaluation led to the inclusion in House's first book (House, 1973a) of an account by MacDonald of the evaluation of the Humanities Curriculum Project. From that point on the relationship between CARE and CIRCE was the axis of an Anglo-American network that grew throughout the seventies and that convened in Cambridge from time to time to review progress and try to move forward. Lou Smith, whose 'Complexities of an urban classroom' (Smith and Geoffrey, 1968) was well known in the UK (see Simons, 1971) was another American who accepted an invitation to Cambridge in 1972. He had been developing his ethnographic studies of schooling within the context of an evaluation commission (Smith and Pohland, 1974) and pursuing his search for a cumulative theory of education grounded in educational practice. Although, like Parlett, and like Rob Walker who joined the 'college' later, Smith did not regard himself primarily as an evaluation specialist, he found the company congenial and remained a key figure in the network.

The conference was not all sweetness and light, as a careful reading of its influential 'manifesto' outcome reveals (MacDonald and Parlett, 1973). Those present were pretty much agreed about what they wanted to see de-emphasized in evaluation, but more divergent about alternatives. More emphasis on the processes and contexts of education, certainly, all could agree on that, but on issues concerning relationships between the evaluators, the evaluated, and the paymasters of both, only an agreement to disagree. It is worth reproducing the manifesto and reading it with this in mind:

On December 20, 1972 at Churchill College, Cambridge, the following conference participants[10] concluded a discussion of the aims and procedures of evaluating educational practices and agreed

I. That past efforts to evaluate these practices have, on the whole, not adequately served the needs of those who require evidence of the effects of such practices, because of:

(a) an under-attention to educational processes including those of the learning milieu;

(b) an over-attention to psychometrically measurable changes in student behaviour (that to an extent represent the outcomes of the practice, but which are a misleading oversimplification of the complex changes that occur in students); and

(c) the existence of an educational research climate that rewards accuracy of measurement and generality of theory but overlooks both mismatch between school problems and research issues and tolerates ineffective communication between researchers and those outside the research community.

II. They also agreed that future efforts to evaluate these practices be designed so as to be:

(a) responsive to the needs and perspectives of differing audiences;

(b) illuminative of the complex organisational, teaching and learning processes at issue;

(c) relevant to public and professional decisions forthcoming; and

(d) reported in language which is accessible to their audiences.

III. More specifically they recommended that, increasingly,

(a) observational data, carefully validated, be used

(sometimes in substitute for data from questioning and testing);

(*b*) the evaluation be designed so as to be flexible enough to allow for response to unanticipated events (progressive focussing rather than pre-ordinate design); and that

(*c*) the value positions of the evaluator, whether high-lighted or constrained by the design, be made evident to the sponsors and audiences of the evaluation.

IV. Though without consensus on the issues themselves, it was agreed that considered attention by those who design evaluation studies should be given to such issues as the following:

(*a*) the sometimes conflicting roles of the same eva-luator as expert, scientist, guide, and teacher of decision-makers on the one hand, and as technical specialist, employee, and servant of decision-makers on the other;

(*b*) the degree to which the evaluator, his sponsors, and his subjects, should specify in advance the limits of enquiry, the circulation of findings, and such matters as may become controversial later;

(*c*) the advantages and disadvantages of intervening in educational practices for the purpose of gathering data or of controlling the variability of certain features in order to increase the generalisability of the findings;

(*d*) the complexity of educational decisions which, as a matter of rule, have political, social and econo-mic implications; and the responsibility that the evaluator may or may not have for exploring these implications;

(*e*) the degree to which the evaluator should interpret his observations rather than leave them for diffe-rent audiences to interpret

It was acknowledged that different evaluation designs will serve different purposes and that even for a single educational programme many different designs could be used. (*Ibid*, pp. 79–80)

Rob Walker's comment on the 1972 manifesto draws attention

to its understated but still evident questioning of the politics of research practice:

> The important thing to note about the 'manifesto' is less its advocacy of qualitative research methods than its stance in relation to research and practice. The manifesto was important because it indicated the possibility of a political shift in the power relations between evaluators and practitioners, opening up the opportunity for teachers and administrators to enter into what were often previously considered to be evaluator's (or researcher's) areas of authority. The effect of attempting to implement the manifesto was to establish rights for participants in the evaluation/research process. (Walker, 1982)

In fact the manifesto overstated the degree of agreement. Lou Smith, for instance, is unlikely to have 'read' that priority in the manifesto. Although his opportunities to develop participant observation had, since completion of the 'Complexities' book, occurred largely in evaluation contexts, which had led him (Smith, 1971) to advocate an expanded role for field studies as a component of evaluation designs, his notion of 'cumulating cases (descriptions, concepts, hypotheses and models)' (quoted in Hamilton *et al*, 1977, p. 207) had as its main aim the generation of grounded educational theory. At the same time, Smith's interest in developing a theory of non-standard methodological procedures (Smith and Schumacher, 1972), a new methodological 'genre', as it were, was closely in tune with the interests of others at the conference. Walker's overall comment on the new evaluators (in response to criticism that their eclecticism led to a cul-de-sac for general theory) that they were 'sceptical about the need to put a high priority on theoretical development' (Walker, 1982) points up an intellectual tension in the group between Smith and, say, Stake, who played the role of guardian of the 'particularity' of the evaluation enterprise (see his critique of SAFARI, Stake, 1974). But this was not the only tension.

Parlett and Hamilton (1972) were arguing for a shift of discipline reference from psychology to anthropology, a move with which Smith was clearly in sympathy, but which MacDonald saw as largely irrelevant to his interest in developing a political model free of discipline-based expertise. Stake's thinking was closest to MacDonald's in terms of rejecting a single discipline base, but he wanted to retain a social science claim for evaluation, whilst MacDonald thought 'science' constituted the main obstacle to be overcome. Curiously Stake, whose advocacy of 'portrayal' had stirred a controversy at the American Educational Research Association's annual meeting (Stake, 1972b), considered it viable to enfranchise non-experts in the practice of evaluation without loss to its scientific respectability. MacDonald sought an expert procedural process that would enfranchise through giving access to educational decision-making. Throw into this mix of 'solutions' David Jenkins' (1978) arguments for a more literary model of evaluation, an argument that would later take him closer to Elliot Eisner (1984) and it is not difficult to see that the manifesto embodied a coalition rather than a consensus. My own interest at the conference, having completed two years of case studies of innovating schools, was in developing a more egalitarian relationship between evaluator and teachers in the processes of inquiry. No doubt my own previous experience working with innovating schools in Australia predisposed me to seek a more congenial social process than a technical concept of evaluation had to offer. I had published in 1971 an article explaining the case study approach we were exploring in the evaluation of the Humanities Curriculum Project (Simons, 1971).

Some other key members of the invisible community that grew from that first conference were not at the first meeting. Rob Walker and Clem Adelman, for instance, then working from the Centre for Science Education at Chelsea College, were too late in finding out about the existence and nature of the conference. Their research in science education had adapted the technology of radio microphones and photography to an ethnographic style of classroom study (Walker and Adelman, 1975). They were particularly keen to meet Lou Smith. Both were soon to move to Norwich; Adelman to work with John Elliott on the Ford Teaching Project, which initiated the action research network, and Walker to join MacDonald on the SAFARI[1] evaluation of the curriculum reform policies of the sixties, another multi-site evaluation programme which MacDonald directed simultaneously with the UNCAL[2] evaluation of computer-assisted learning. Walker was to co-convene, with MacDonald, the next Cambridge conference in 1975.

The theme of the 1975 conference — 'Case study methods' — indicated a trend among the group towards a common language. Throughout the seventies it was the term 'case study' which stuck, and gradually assumed the status of a defining characteristic of the 'new' evaluation approach, just as the term 'naturalistic' (Guba, 1978; Guba and Lincoln, 1981) came to be accepted as a broad descriptor of its style and values. Case study was a metaphor that appealed to those who were looking for a way of integrating the comprehensive data requirements that emerged from various critical reviews of the evaluation tradition (Stake, 1967b; MacDonald, 1971; Parlett and Hamilton, 1972). It was not the only one on offer ('portrayal' and 'illumination' were others) but it proved to have more staying power, and was, at least terminologically, better connected to social science traditions with respectable pedigrees.

There was, of course, nothing new in applied social science about the concept of case study, as critics of 'new wave' evaluation were keen to point out (see Parsons, 1976; Shipman, 1981). But in the context of evaluation and its emerging nexus of methodological, epistemological and political convictions, case study was far from being a straight 'lift' from the idiographic traditions of social science (Simons, 1980a, p. 2). In evaluation the line of case study development was a response to the perceived structure of evaluation problems rather than a mode of research inspired by Glaser and Strauss (1973), Becker *et al*, (1968) or the sociological case studies of Hargreaves (1967) and Lacey (1970).

Evaluators did not ignore these traditions (witness Lou Smith's 'membership' of the network and Howard Becker's attendance at the 1975 Cambridge conference) but they had questions to which ethnographers had no satisfactory answers. These questions concerned the time-scales, audiences, and power-relationships characteristic of evaluation contexts.

Let us now turn to the development of case study within this context of evaluation. MacDonald has written (MacDonald, 1978a) of how he arrived at the need for case study when be began in 1968 to evaluate the Humanities Curriculum Project, which was then undergoing trials in some three dozen schools in England and Wales.

The Project, directed by Lawrence Stenhouse (see Stenhouse *et al*, 1970) was one of the national curriculum projects typical of the centre-periphery approach to development sponsored by the Schools Council and the Nuffield Foundation in the sixties. It was a project aiming to develop in secondary schools a discussion-based programme of controversial issues, with issues embodied in packs of documentary materials. Teachers in the trial schools were asked to experiment with a 'procedurally neutral' role in classroom discussion. MacDonald was brought in initially on a two-year secondment to design an evaluation for implementation in 1970, when the Project would go public. It was envisaged by Stenhouse, who persuaded the Schools Council to fund an evaluation and MacDonald to take it on, that the evaluation would consist of tests of student learning gains based on interaction analysis in trial classrooms. MacDonald writes of his early encounters:

> I visit my first trial school, and sit in on HCP discussions using the pilot war pack. Painful. The kids are mute, the teachers stiff as boards and sweating anxiety. The joys of innovation. It takes months to discover that the head has promised these teachers promotion if they achieve significantly improved public examination results then followed this up by committing them heavily to HCP, a non-examined curriculum in this school. But what is obvious immediately is that classroom process cannot be understood without going beyond the classroom.
>
> I visit another trial school, where the HCP teachers are puzzled by my talk of experiment. They hadn't understood what was said at the induction course. They think they can do what they like. And they don't like what they think Stenhouse said.
>
> I begin to get interested in the different understandings and misunderstandings of the Project message, as well as in the institutional settings. I visit another school where the Project is going well, and where the HCP team leader demonstrates a grasp of Project theory at least equal to that of central team members. I have acquired a tape recorder and record interviews with heads, HCP staff, other staff and pupils. Immediate repercussion — I am bearded in a small office by one HCP teacher who threatens to sue me unless I divulge to him immediately the contents of the interview I have had with the head. It takes half an hour to persuade him to let me leave the room. He appears to believe that the other HCP teachers are conspiring with the head against him, and that I am being used to further this conspiracy. Is this relevant to my evaluation, I ask myself on the way home, or just alien noise? The question never goes away. It's with me yet.

And later in the account he writes:

> My field work focusses increasingly on fewer schools. In September I decide to abandon the notion of spreading my visits over all the trial schools; instead I will case study eight. I write to them through Jean Rudduck[3], wildly overestimating the amount of time I will spend at each one because of other demands on my time. But I have a lot of data already on most

of these schools — recorded interviews with headmaster, project staff, pupils, other staff, some parents, the occasional youth service officer, local advisers. I know something of the history of their involvement with the Project, I have images of the schools gathered informally from local pubs, shops and buses, I have spent many hours in the company of some of their key personnel at residential conferences held by the Project. And I have kept everything, notes of casual as well as formal encounters, correspondence, feedback forms, audio and videotapes, transcripts of interviews, summaries of conferences and workshops, copies of school magazines, rules and notices, agendas of staff and PTA meetings, and so on. My case records of these schools already bulge. But I am short of direct observational data, and am to remain so, depending more and more on interviews triangulated through other interviews, and second hand observational data from members of the central team and the occasional visiting adviser, academic or HMI.

Of his conceptualization of what he was doing at this time he comments:

I don't in any scientific sense know what I'm doing when I claim to be case studying the schools. I find myself, as I interview the various actors in this particular street theatre and observe their behaviour in and out of the institutional setting, drawn by two phenomena — 'discrepancy' and 'conflict'. Discrepancies between what people say they are doing or feeling and what they appear to me to be doing or feeling, or what the same people say at different times or in different company, conflicts between different definitions of the same situation, conflicts of interests, values, perceptions. HCP is centrally concerned with the notion of 'authority' in education, and with the consequences for the authority structure of the school of changing the relationship between teacher, pupil and knowledge. My line of investigation seldom strays from exploring the various meanings of authority within the case study schools, looking particularly for evidence of dissonance or consonance between the notion of authority implicit in the Project's experimental form and the notions of authority embodied in institution practice and policy. (MacDonald, 1978a, pp 287–291)

By 1970 MacDonald was using his case studies of trial schools in the dissemination conferences of the Project, inviting potential adopters of the Project to take account of contextual and decision-making factors affecting productive and unproductive experiences of Project use. He also used this approach in overseas dissemination, which began in 1970 with a conference in the United States sponsored by the Ford Foundation. This led to the funding by Ford of the SAFARI project three years later.

The evaluation design which MacDonald produced for the public phase of the Humanities Project was one he called 'holistic'. In a paper submitted to the American Educational Research Association in 1970 (there was no British equivalent until 1974) he summarized the approach as follows:

> The nature and design of the Project is such that its impact appears to be both comprehensive (it affects pupils, teachers, schools and allied agencies) and individual (a specific setting manifests a unique effects profile).
>
> The evaluation is developing a holistic approach, which views the innovative impact as a gestalt, and attempts, by interweaving naturalistic depth studies in a few schools with data obtained by instrumentation over a large sample, to identify some relationships between context, input, process and outcome. Such an evaluation may promote understanding of the bases and consequences of curriculum decision-making.

Seen in retrospect, the evaluation design was more of a mixed metaphor than its holistic title suggests. MacDonald had not yet escaped some of the 'agronomic assumptions' to which he refers in justifying the design (MacDonald, 1971). Thus the basic idea of the design was to combine a substantial programme of pre- and post-testing of student learning with a multi-site case study programme to help local decision-makers to interpret both positive and negative deviations from mean scores on standardized tests. The central decision-making question, however, was seen to be:

> How can I tell whether this Project would work well in my school, and what should I take account of if I decide to implement it?

MacDonald formulated a propositional rationale for the case study element of the design:

1   Human action in educational institutions differs widely because of the number of variable influences that determine it.

2   The impact of an innovation is not a set of discrete effects but an organically related pattern of acts and consequences. To understand fully a single act one must locate it functionally within that pattern.

3   No two schools are sufficiently alike in their circumstances for prescriptions of curricular action to be able adequately to supplant the judgement of the people in them.

4   The goals and purposes of the programme developers are not necessarily shared by its users. (*Ibid*)

MacDonald's ambitious, and ill-fated, design was funded by the Schools Council, and a team formed in 1970 to help him carry it out. Gajendra Verma was responsible for the measurement programme, Stephen Humble for case study of local authorities, and myself for the case study of schools. Our introduction to the evaluation was a national conference of trial school teachers at which we engaged the teachers in composing case presentations of their own institutional contexts. Soon after I tried to summarize our views of the kind of case study that would be called for. Referring to the four propositions, I wrote:

> If these propositions are sound we believe that the best way to advance the practice of innovation is to make available fully documented accounts of individual cases. The problem posed by such studies comes when one tries to reconcile their three indispensable characteristics. These are firstly, they must be true, secondly, they must not omit relevant data, and finally, they must be publishable.
>
> Fictions have low credibility and quite rightly, because our present grasp of the complex reality is far too tentative to permit accurate predictions of what might have been in hypothetical situations. The same is true of composites. Case studies must not only be based on actual schools, they must report authentic situations. The second characteristic of such studies is just as important. Descriptive accounts of what took place in a given situation will provide needed information, but will do little to advance understanding unless there is, alongside such descriptions, sufficient interpretative data. If people are to make judgments about why an innovation took the

course that it did in a particular school, they will need a great deal of contextual information. While it is true that much of the information required raises no problem in terms of publication, some significant areas will present certain difficulties. In order to interpret events in a school the reader needs to have information about the patterns of functional and affective relationships which constitute the organisational and social setting.

This is where the crunch comes. It is a relatively simple matter to protect the school and its personnel against public identification, by employing fictitious names and by not pinpointing its geographical location. But what is not possible, at least without a crippling degree of distortion, is to protect that school from recognition by the people who work in it. One illustration from an actual case-study may serve to crystallize the kind of difficulty that is presented. A Humanities Curriculum Project teacher, discussing the difficulties he was experiencing in the school, commented: 'We can't get anything moving in this school because of the bloody Welsh teachers.' Clearly the view expressed here is relevant to an understanding of the innovation in the school concerned. Equally clearly, the publication of the view could have serious repercussions among the staff.

This is a key problem in the development and publication of case-studies of schools. It will always be a problem, but it could be less of a problem than it is now if certain developments take place.

The first development concerns the way the case studies are carried out and presented. Such studies must depart from the tradition of subjective impressionism that has caused educational researchers to shun them. The case-study must not only be authentic and detailed, as I have already suggested, it must also be rigorously accurate and impartial. The purpose of the case-study is to make the experience of innovation accessible to public and professional judgment, and not to provide a vehicle for the biases or personal judgments of the evaluator. Case study presentations should be basically *inconclusive* accounts of what happens in a particular school and should contain accurate reports of the judgments, convergent or divergent, of those involved in the events. Misinterpretation can be largely avoided by tape-recording all interviews and classroom transactions, and seeking the agreement of those involved to the fairness of the report. Of course there is no escaping the judgment of the evaluator in terms of what to include and what to leave out of the account, but if he is seen to be impartial and to be avoiding, by close consultation, 'rigging' the evidence, then the problems associated both with publication and with research 'respectability' will be significantly reduced. (Simons, 1971, pp. 121–2)

Reading this now I am reminded of how much that is now regarded as part of the commonsense of educational enquiry was at that time thought of as bold, even rash.

In the late sixties critics were just beginning to question the effectiveness of the engineering model of change (Goodlad, 1967) and some were still extolling its transformational potential (Kerr, 1968). Even in the thinking of the Humanities Project, which embodied Stenhouse's notion of the 'teacher as researcher', it was the classroom that was seen as the unit and therefore the target of change. Not until case studies revealed the innovating teacher as one engaged in institutional struggle did the Project begin to treat headteachers and their employers as more than the gatekeepers of access to the classroom (MacDonald 1978a) The dominant mode of evaluation took a 'black box' view of the process and context of implementation, concentrating on the measurement of student learning outcomes. When the inaugural meeting of Schools Council evaluators was held in 1969, it seemed appropriate for the chairperson to open the meeting with, 'I presume we are all familiar with Bloom's taxonomy' (MacDonald and Parlett, 1973).

The evaluation of the dissemination phase of the Humanities Project was the first attempt to systematically incorporate a case study element within an evaluation design. It was also the first to define as its audience the individual buyer of the project package, the 'decision-maker' in its widest professional sense (MacDonald, 1973). But case study was just one element in a complex and demanding programme of tasks, roles, and goals which had to be completed within a relatively short period of time, and this was probably the single most important factor in shaping its particular form within evaluation. In order to set case study development within the evaluation framework I will now give an abbreviated account[4] of that first attempt, paying particular emphasis to the case study element.

In carrying out the evaluation we had several purposes in mind:

1 to ascertain the effects of the project, document the

circumstances in which they occur, and present this information in a form which will help educational decision-makers to evaluate the likely consequences of adopting the programme;

2 to describe the present situation and operations of the schools and local education systems we study so that decision-makers can understand more fully what it is they are trying to change;

3 to describe the work of the project team in terms which will help the sponsors and planners of such ventures to weigh the value of this form of investment, and to determine more precisely the framework of support, guidance and control which is appropriate;

4 to make a contribution to evaluation theory by articulating our problems clearly, recording our experience and, perhaps most important, by publicizing our errors;

5 to contribute to the understanding of the problems of curriculum innovation generally.

The Evaluation Design

The evaluation design began to take shape when the full unit team of one director and three other evaluators had been recruited by the beginning of the diffusion stage (1970). It looked like this:

(a) *In a large sample of schools* (about 100)

(i) Gathering input, contextual and implementation data by questionnaire.

(ii) Gathering judgment data from teachers and pupils.

(iii) Objective testing of teacher and pupil change.

(iv) Tracing variations in teaching practice through the use of specially devised multiple-choice feedback instruments which require minimal effort by the teacher and are monitored by pupils.

(v) Documenting the effect on the school by means of semi-structured teacher diaries.

(b) *In a small sample of schools* (about 10)

(i) Case studies of patterns in decision-making, communication, training and support in local areas.

(ii) Case studies of individual schools within those areas.

(iii) Study of the dynamics of discussion by tape, videotape and observation.

In a large-scale evaluation of an ongoing programme like the project, such a design could only be an aspiration. We made choices within it, given that we had limited staff, resources and time. But the direction was clear: we chose to conduct a national survey of schools by postal questionnaire, which would give an approximate picture of the pattern of the diffusion of the project; to undertake ten case studies of schools and LEAs, which would provide us with the detailed experience of innovation necessary for understanding the process of change; and to mount an objective testing programme of pupil change which explored the effect of the project upon pupils along a large number of personality attitudinal and cognitive dimensions. (In all, 3500 pupils and 21 tests were involved.)

The main threads of the design — the testing programme and the case studies — were interwoven. Case study schools and local areas were chosen primarily in order to explore how decisions made at local area level related to decisions made within the school and to the classroom experience. But these schools were also drawn from schools sampled for the testing programme. The case study schools were in fact asked to provide more pupils than other schools to complete the tests because the case study output was to be used as a means of interpreting variations in pupil change determined by the testing programme. In the event, the case study schools provided too few pupils for testing to allow such interpretation to take place.

The Implementation of the Evaluation Design

Once the large sample had been drawn and the testing programme launched in December 1970, we selected the schools for case study. The testing programme was designed to elicit comparisons between 'trained' and 'untrained' schools and we included both categories in our case study sample. (Trained schools were schools whose teachers had attended a central or local training course; teachers in untrained schools had not.) The variable of training was chosen because the project team considered it a pre-requisite for implementing the project.

We finally selected eleven case study schools — six trained and five untrained — of different sizes (600 to 2000 pupils on roll) and types (comprehensive, secondary modern, and those in the process of becoming comprehensive), and from different regions. The trained schools were in turn selected because their LEAs, according to the project team, had different and interesting dissemination programmes under way.

In the year which followed (1971–72) we continued to study four of the six trained schools; the other two had only one trained teacher each, and in one of them the materials were employed only intermittently. The study of all the untrained schools terminated early because all but one of the five discontinued the project after one term. The experience of these schools did not augur well for survival of the project. In case we were gaining an unfair picture, in the second year we chose two additional schools for case study, where it seemed that the project team's requirements for successful implementation of the project had been met. Their local settings were also studied and they provided pupils for a second stage of the testing programme.

The testing programme had been launched with some difficulty. There were problems with the adequacy of the sampling frame because not all the schools involved in the project had been included, or included correctly, in the lists of trained schools issued by LEAs and in the lists of untrained schools issued by the project publisher. As the year went on, doubts were raised in our minds about the representativeness of the sample against the background of an uncontrollable and changing diffusion population: some schools abandoned the project and others took it up; trained teachers left and untrained teachers became trained; and groups of pupils differing from those included in the original sample were timetabled for the project. There was so much diversity, in fact, that the test results of pupils involved in the psychometric programme were later recoded for analysis according to the kind of training which their project teachers had received.

Problems arose, too, about implementing a testing programme which was both large and administered by teachers. We under-estimated the time it would take to put the tests together and dispatch them to schools. A six-week postal strike caused further delay, so they arrived late. Although the tests were subdivided into three packages to ease administration and ensure that no pupil took more than seven tests, they were still time-consuming and difficult to administer. The whole process was one to tax the credulity of experienced practitioners of testing. But it is perhaps worth pointing out that the testing programme was not employed without some awareness on our part of its defects and limitations. It was not seen to be a means of making definitive statements about effects; it was envisaged as an exploratory measure; as one of the ways open to us to map the potential of the project, not provide unassailable proof of its accomplishments.

As the year went on, we became conscious of the fact that the results of the evaluation would not come in time for many decision-makers. The evaluation had been commissioned by the Schools Council after it had funded the project. We followed in the wake of everyone else's decisions. It was not enough that we were addressing future potential users of this project and of others. We had a responsibility to the people already involved with the programme.

Our response was to begin to distribute semi-processed evaluation data to our immediate audiences. To every purchaser of project materials (over 1000 schools, LEAs and other institutions and individuals) we distributed free evaluation reports. These reports[5] — nine in all — contained accounts of the experience of using the project by teachers, pupils, LEA staff and members of the project team; the use of film in teaching the project; results of the diffusion survey; early results of the testing programme; and advertisements for other evaluation publications which were sold at cost. This last group of publications included articles explaining the evaluation itself and general problems of curriculum innovation; articles describing the experience of schools and teachers; transcribed interviews with editors of the project materials; articles reporting the project experiment in teaching Race; and edited videotapes of classroom discussion (Hamingson 1973). In addition, we presented accounts of our work at project training courses and various conferences and meetings arranged by LEA staff and the project team.

We attempted to distribute information quickly. But the kind of information which could not be presented quickly was that obtained through case study. Case study data, besides being lengthy, raised problems of utilization, which were difficult to deal with in a system of rapid information turnover.

The Case Study Approach

Studies of single cases enabled us to get closer to reflecting the way in which teachers, heads and LEA staff make judgments in the day-to-day process of innovating. The main strategies of our case study work — interviewing and observing — allowed us to maintain flexibility in the design and be responsive to the needs of the programme. We could change direction, probe relevant issues, investigate unanticipated effects and undertake additional studies.

From our point of view the case study was a means of depicting one situation to an individual in another situation. Rather than attempting to produce generalizations, we chose to focus on the single instance on the assumption that individuals operating in highly idiosyncratic situations themselves appreciate descriptions of individual instances in action because they can relate them to their own experience.

Acknowledging the inherent subjectivity of the case study approach, we built in controls for checking the studies. We reported as accurately as possible, by tape-recording interviews and classroom discussions, writing observation notes on the spot and dictating site reports as soon as possible after visits. We checked information by putting the same or similar questions to different interviewees or by separate interviews with the same person; and we checked our perceptions of what we were studying with our colleagues. We looked for many judgments; we sought ambiguity in order to broaden the range of views and so as not to over-simplify the complex real-life situation.

We knew at the time that, in taking these steps, we wanted to minimize our interpretation of what we were studying. We now realize that we were beginning to try to reduce *our* control over gathering and presenting case study data.

The Conduct of the Case Studies

The Case Studies of Schools

The procedures that we employed in case study did not differ markedly between schools and LEAs, but the differences between single institutions (schools) and multiple institutions (LEAs) created some differences in practice that make it worth while to deal with each separately.

First, the schools. The time spent in each school varied a great deal according to its distance from base, the availability of staff for interviewing, the ease or difficulty with which their experience could be understood, the opportunities for observation, the extent of the implementation of the project in the school and our ongoing commitments to other evaluation work. Four visits to each trained school, from one to three days in length, were the norm. Visits to untrained schools were shorter and less frequent. What we did during the visit varied, but in most of the trained case study schools we generally interviewed heads, project teachers (individually and as a group), pupils involved in the project and teachers not involved in it. We observed teachers, pupils and project discussion groups in the classroom, we discussed their experience with them and looked at pupils' project written and art work. We talked informally with members of staff, pupils and heads, mixed with staff in the staff room, observed interactions of staff with heads and with one another, of non-project teachers with project teachers, and of visiting LEA staff with the teachers and heads. We also noted how we were perceived, how the project team were perceived, and how pupils perceived teachers, heads, the school and the project.

Our initial visits and interviews concentrated on gaining information about the schools and their setting, the conditions for experimentation, the prior decisions made by the LEAs and schools about the project, and the prior expectations of it by the people involved. In subsequent interviews and observations we recorded the classroom experience, the response of pupils, teachers and schools as a whole to the project, and the ways in which the effects of the project were perceived by teachers, pupils and heads. In interviews with individual project teachers and heads we sought specific information on how the project was communicated to them and how they, in turn, communicated the project to pupils, the kind of training they had received, how they viewed this in the light of their experience, and how they and the school met the demands of an innovative curriculum. These were all issues cited in the trial stage by teachers and the project team as important for understanding a school's experience with the project. As time went on, other issues emerged and were explored: the problem of the 'silent' pupil in classroom discussion; the difficulty of teachers in adapting to the role of neutral chairman; and the difficulty teachers had in sustaining interest in discussion over long periods. In the last year, as the project became more widely known and understood, early rejection of it became less frequent and we began to focus upon the conditions necessary to sustain the innovation.

The Case Studies of LEAs

The main difference between studies of schools and those of LEAs was that, with LEAs, more than one institution was usually connected with the dissemination of the project. Sometimes only the education office (at the county or town hall) was involved, or the teachers' centre (usually separated from the office and sometimes located in a school), or even just one school, but often it was a mixture of these. We tried to trace the decision-making process behind the local dissemination programme, and to describe the roles of the various people involved in order to discover the framework within which the project case study school operated. These case studies were not studies of the whole LEA — that would have been too large a task for our limited resources, involving the elected local councillors as well as the permanent officers.

The school case study programme had the advantage of the earlier trial school case studies. With the LEA studies we started virtually from scratch. First, the key decision-makers had to be located. It was often possible to do this by referring to the correspondence between the LEA and the project team. (In the diffusion stage the project team corresponded most often with LEA staff, not with teachers.) LEA staffs typically consist of administrators and advisers. If the LEA had a large advisory team, the project would usually be allocated to one of their number, often an arts specialist. (Humanities advisers, though increasing in number in the early 1970s, were rare.) Otherwise the project became the responsibility of an assistant education officer, teachers' centre warden or teachers, or was simply put on file. The project team's contact in the local area was not necessarily the key policy figure. He may have been handed down a policy to implement. It was a case of trying to disentangle the kind of contribution each made to the organization of the project in the local area.

The LEA case studies, then, lacked the definition of the school studies. There was no one place to visit. There was also, in most instances, no 'programme' to investigate. The contribution of LEA staff to dissemination was often regarded by them as one of initial activity and no more. So observation of a lasting exercise was not possible. Most visits to LEAs, usually three or four to each authority, lasting one to three days, were taken up by single, separate interviews when staff were available. Occasionally visits did coincide with the odd follow-up meeting of project teachers, sometimes with LEA staff present, and here observations were made.

Pupils and teachers provide a check on one another. They share the same experience. No such opportunity was afforded in the case studies of LEAs. The nearest candidates in this regard were school staff, but they are not related to the LEA in the same sense that pupils are related to teachers. Teachers mostly work at a distance from the LEA, and often in ignorance of it.

Because the work with LEAs began well after the dissemination programme was initiated (some made definite plans for dissemination even before the evaluation unit team had been recruited), a lot of time was given to reconstructing past events, especially the reasons for deciding to adopt the project. We sought information on how the LEA generally regarded its schools and kept in touch with them; and about the resources available to the LEA for curriculum innovation. We asked about their attitudes to curriculum innovation and for comparisons with other authorities. Finally, we explored the character of the dissemination programme: whether or not the number of schools involved was restricted, what kind of schools were involved and why, who trained whom and how, what support (both financial and advisory) had been given, and what evaluation and follow-up activities, if any, took place. To sum up, the case studies of local authorities were histories of and studies in curriculum decision-making in the locality; the case studies of schools attempted to some extent to convey a portrait of institutional life.

Reflections on the Humanities Project Evaluation

Writing in 1970, on the eve of embarcation on this adventurous evaluation, I had closed by endorsing these words of Derek Morell,

> The first and most important form of support open to human beings who have anxious problems is to draw closer together, and to pool resources, experiences and perspectives. Unless this is done, it is easy for particular groups within the educational service to imagine that they alone are the guardians of important educational values. (Simons, 1971, p. 123)

We took that statement as the criterial value of an evaluation process that would seek to be more collaborative in its relationships both with actual and prospective innovators in the school system, but which at the same time would seek to be more revelatory of its private world. As it turned out, the pursuit of these two, not obviously compatible goals, threw up a problem structure that we were theoretically and procedurally not equipped to cope with. That problem structure constituted the agenda for the fundamental rethinking that followed (MacDonald, 1974; MacDonald and Walker, 1974). I will summarize some of the most important issues.

In the first place it soon became clear that MacDonald's quasi-experimental design assumed, in the absence of a laboratory style of control, a degree of stability in the schools, both in terms of personnel and Project adoption, that had no correspondence in reality, particularly at a time of high mobility. The sampling basis of the test programme was constantly disrupted by category shifts that compounded the already taxing problem of trying to isolate dependent and independent variables. Given that test technology was in any case deficient (both in terms of the validity and reliability of individual tests and the fact that we were using norm-referenced tests for a problem requiring criterion-referencing), even strenuous efforts in categorical reconstitution and reanalysis could not stem an erosion of our own confidence in the psychometric outcomes (Hamingson, 1973). We had, of course, from the start informed Project practitioners of the qualified status of the measurement data, and continued to stress this in issues of our Evaluation Bulletin. But despite these warnings, our experience from 1970 to 1972 suggested that test data still carried an unwarranted authority. At a conference of Project teachers from case study schools, organized by the evaluation to provide an opportunity for teachers to consider test outcomes alongside their own judgments of student learning gains, the problem of authority was made clear. Faced with test data which suggested that their pupils had made significant gains — in vocabulary, in self-esteem, even in IQ, but also told in no uncertain terms that we had a lot of reservations about the trustworthiness of the measurement programme, the teachers set aside their own much more modest, even pessimistic views of benefit in deference to a crude technology. It was this experience more than any other which convinced MacDonald of the need to abandon testing as an instrument of assessment. He also resisted Stenhouse's understandable enthusiasm for giving publicity to the test results, which offered striking support for the hopes and intentions of the Project developers. (This resistance should not be interpreted in any way as demonstrating scepticism on the part of the evaluators about the merits of the Project. Both MacDonald and I were personally great admirers of the Humanities Project curriculum).

So much for experimental design, for testing, and for the hope that our audiences would use test data to augment and refine their professional judgment. Let me turn now to the case studies. I said earlier that the creation of the Evaluation Bulletin enabled us to make selective use of our field data to disseminate partially contextualized experiences and issues to a practitioner network, but that the full cases did not lend themselves to this quick turnover process. Despite the fact that the amount of time we were able to devote to a single case was rarely more than seven days on site, our records in each instance averaged about 400–500 pages of notes, correspondence and interview transcripts. We had problems of management, selection, condensation and, crucially, of clearance. We were working with procedures for data collection and clearance, but with no precedents to go on. MacDonald had operated without control procedures in his earlier work. Indeed, trial school staff had loudly protested that they didn't even know they were the subjects of a case study (MacDonald, 1978a). In the 1970–1972 period most of the data came from unstructured interviews (Simons, 1977a) in which we offered confidentiality to the informants with a view to subsequent agreement to clearance. The problem was that we had no clear idea of how to proceed in situations where some participants favoured circulation or publication of a report while others did not. The negotiation of case studies, in part and in whole, became a major concern with differing interpretations of the 'agreement' in contention.

It was not until late in 1973, by which time both Stephen Humble and myself had left CARE and were well into new research tasks, that we were able to submit our case study based evaluation report to the Schools Council, and it was not until 1978 that the Council published it (Humble and Simons, 1978). Although we could claim that the publication served some of the more general aims of the evaluation — in particular to advance understanding of the school system as a basis for more effective strategies of intervention, the report fell considerably short of some of the aspirations I had expressed in 1970. For instance, one of the case studies included in the report was published despite the opposition of some of the participants, and justified in terms of an overriding 'public interest'. I would not now wish to defend such an action in circumstances where the objectors were led to believe that publication was dependent upon their agreement. Secondly all the cases, profiles, and personnel in that report were anonymized, a practice which I had in 1970 questioned as both unfeasible and inappropriate to the decision-making context of evaluation reports. So the end result of a process which was conceived in terms of feeding the judgment of a particular group of decision-makers at a particular point in time (while the Project was 'hot') ended up as a historical study of innovation with general policy implications. Nothing wrong with that in a sense, of course, but it was less than we hoped for or aspired to.

On the positive side of the balance sheet I would also argue that the involvement of teachers, advisers and administrators in the construction of the cases itself contributed to and stimulated participants' thinking about their circumstances, values and actions. But at the end of the day we were left with the feeling that the new evaluation had generated more problems than it had solved. The notion of 'fairness' to the subjects of evaluations, a notion we had espoused at the outset, obviously involved a lot more than solving the technical problem of producing 'inconclusive' accounts. We were very much aware of the anxieties of institutions and individuals who thought their competence was on public trial, and who were handicapped by the 'deskilling' effects of engaging in innovatory curriculum practice (Hamingson, 1973). We had engaged Morrell's ideal of inter-professional integration, but had not found a way of reconciling the plurality of interests within the professional sector with the needs and rights of its clienteles.

No one reading these case studies of implementation would invoke the term 'ethnography' to characterize either their process or product. They lacked at least three key features of ethnographic research — immersion in the field, direct observation as the dominant technique, and an interpretive theory of the case by the ethnographer. As far as our limited time on site would allow, we were engaged in an exercise closer to oral history than to ethnography, with an almost exclusive reliance on interviews to elicit the experience and judgments of the participants. The boundaries of the case were drawn widely enough to represent multiple perspectives (pupils, teachers, administrators, advisers, Project team members, Teachers' Centre leaders) and our data sources included correspondence, telephone calls, and internal Project reports. In contrast to MacDonald's earlier documentary, narrative cases, ours were less dramatic, less interpretive, more broadly representative of the constituency of the case. His cases revealed the ethical and political issues of exposure, and made problematic the respective rights and obligations of the evaluator and the evaluated. We in a sense took a step back, approaching the case study task in a much more gingerly and cautious way. In terms of presentational form, however, we followed the pattern of 'storytelling' (Stake, 1967a), using the history of Project-related formal events as a temporal framework that focussed attention on the sequence and interrelationship between national, local, institutional and individual curriculum decisions. But the 'characters' in our stories were only personalized in so far as they chose to personalize themselves in interview, and we did not in interview at this time, actively pursue the private experience of public responsibility.

Politics in Action — Post-1972 Developments

More theory, and opportunities to practice, followed the 1972 Cambridge conference, much more than I can do justice to in this account. Since my intention is to restrict my focus to developments of particular relevance to the theme of this book and to the experiences it reports, I shall limit myself to indications of the span of developments in naturalistic evaluation whilst concentrating on the democratic 'persuasion'. Other lines of thinking and action have been well represented elsewhere (for instance, Stake's responsive evaluation is well represented in Guba and Lincoln (1981) while Falmer Press are publishing three volumes of Lou Smith's study of Kensington Revisited).

With respect to democratic theory, I want to keep separate two concepts of the 'case' in evaluative case study. In the foregoing account of the early development of case study in the Humanities Project evaluation, case study is conceived in terms of portraying in some kind of holistic manner the complexities of circumstance and action within units of an innovation programme, such as schools or local districts. Case study in this sense is seen as an element in an evaluation to which only limited resources can be devoted. I have suggested that the logistics of limited resources, both material and temporal, had a lot to do with its non-conformist shape in such a context, where the evaluators had many other functions to attend to. One might go further and argue that the development of a collaborative ethic in evaluation case study had a fundamentally economic rationale, although this would, in my view, be a simplification of what was seen to be at issue. Whatever the reasons, and advocacy of the case study had many different strands, the theory and practice of case study which emerged in the late sixties and developed through the seventies had in common with ethnographic and anthropological traditions a well established context of application — small, bounded social entities. In relation to programme evaluation, these entities usually contained those social actors on whom fell the burden of delivering social policy — the implementers. At least part of the rationale for such studies was the conviction on the part of advocates that strategies of change needed to be based on a better understanding of, and in general a lot more empathy with, those at the chalkface.

In this sense there was in the case study movement in evaluation a clear line of continuity with the Chicago School of Sociology and its focus on disadvantaged social groups. The context was of course different, a difference strikingly illustrated by the anthropologist of education Harry Wolcott when he said to an audience of anthropo-logically-oriented evaluators, referring to the intent of evaluation to guide decision-making, 'How would you feel if your data was used to continue, revise or terminate a culture?' (quoted in MacDonald *et al*, 1977, p. 51). It was awareness of this context that sensitized eva-luators to the consequential nature of the evaluation activity, and led Walker (1982) to say, of the 1972 Cambridge conference, 'The effect of attempting to implement the manifesto was to establish rights for participants in the evaluation/research process'.

For some of those involved in the naturalistic movement, I would say that their main interest was in forging a better ethical and political framework for research in the Chicago tradition, in other words that they were primarily concerned with conducting case studies of educational institutions in ways which were more directly helpful to those studied. We might call this an 'add-on' interest in what evaluation had to offer those interested in close-up descriptive studies of schooling. I would place in this orientation Lou Smith, Rob Walker, and Clem Adelman. They might well disagree, and I know that their interests and work are much broader than this characteriza-tion suggests, but what I am trying to do is to distinguish some differences within a group of writers who were content for almost a decade to travel under one banner.

I will now try to distinguish this concept of the 'case', and of theory and practice related to it, from the concept of the social programme as a case rather than as a framework within which case studies of different parts of the programme might legitimately and usefully be conducted. In this sense of case, it was Stake who pioneered the idea of the evaluation as an account of the whole pro-ject or programme rather than as a study of particular aspects of it, such as student gains on test scores. And it was the 'programme as case' that MacDonald saw as providing the opportunity for getting to grips with the distribution of power reflected in policy initiatives. Let me explain further this link between the democratic model of evaluation and the case study approach.

Lou Smith, never himself tempted very far in the direction of relinquishing control over his case studies, has remarked of the democratic model, 'In an important sense MacDonald is advocating political change in liberal, democratic national states by exposing gaps between the realities of educational settings and the idealism most of us profess in our ideologies' (Smith *et al*, 1981). This is precisely the point. Most ethnographers and anthropologists of education operate with an implicit idealism. The Chicago School, with its focus on society's underdogs, hoped to make a difference by touching the conscience of the nation (Silverman, 1985).

For MacDonald, this is clearly not enough. The problem for him, as it has been for the longer sociological tradition, is how to get access for case study to powerful groups and individuals (studying the 'haves') and how then to influence their actions. Defining social programmes as the 'case' brought within its boundaries actors and agencies at all levels of the power structure. That provided the kind of access the sociologists seldom had. The second problem was how to gain leverage. For this he chose an acceptable political and moral rhetoric, acceptable that is, to those exercising delegated power. He then gave the rhetoric teeth by converting it into procedures, justified in terms of the shared rhetoric, but which cut into the customary practice of power holders by holding them accountable to criteria endorsed by them.

Not all those who were influenced by, or adopted the democratic model, had this agenda in mind but, as we shall see, even those like myself who saw in the model the basis of more collegial relationships with the subjects of study found themselves sometimes in confrontational situations that derived from its logic (see chapter 6). There is no evidence that MacDonald himself sought or welcomed confrontation with those in powerful positions. It is clear, for instance with respect to the UNCAL evaluation, that he regarded the battle with the Programme Committee as a failure of the evaluation (MacDonald *et al*, 1975). On one occasion, responding to an address by Michael Apple on the 'proletarianization' of the teaching force by the bureaucracy he contended that the proletarianization of the bureaucracy by a combination of political pressures and 'bad ideas' was a problem equally in need of address (MacDonald, 1983a). It is also clear, in various of his writings, particularly on interviewing, that he regards 'respect for persons' and the need to separate persons from roles in order to develop their evaluative insight on their own actions, as applying to all levels of action in the system (1981 and 1982a).

Lakomski (1983) has argued, nevertheless, that democratic evaluation is politically 'conservative'. 'It cannot simultaneously accept as legitimate that which it wishes to change'. Popkewitz, another 'radical' critic, has also laid the same charge (Popkewitz, 1984). Lakomski supports the view of House (1976) that democratic evaluation is 'generally strong on the principle of equal liberty, but weaker on issues of social justice' (Lakomski, 1983, p. 273). She goes on to argue, like House, that the voices of those socially and educationally least advantaged must be presented unequally, and that to do that, democratic evaluation must be recast as a moral activity based on a critique of domination. But it is quite clear, to me at least, that democratic evaluation combines a respect for the legitimacy of authorized activities with a moral critique of the way in which legitimate actors discharge their responsibilities. The subtlety of the democratic model lies in the way MacDonald derives the moral code from the rhetoric of liberal democracy, thus establishing evaluation as a service to a society which seeks self-improvement to close the gap between its own rhetoric and its own reality. Some may define this as political sleight-of-hand, but it is the basis of the argument mounted by MacDonald and Norris (1981) as an alternative to 'partisan' eva-luation, which they define as an honourable but short-lived attack on the 'reality of power'. '. . . from our point of view, the partisan will find the gates of the power-house of policy generation firmly closed to his definitionally hostile enquiry . . . it is difficult to change what we have no opportunity to understand' (p. 14).

In terms of my own interpretation, that is to say from an interest in the educative potential of the theory, I find a coherent set of relationships that are essentially emancipatory. An emancipatory intent is based on respect for the autonomy of the individual and a rationale of stimulated self-improvement. I therefore see 'respect for persons' and 'respect for society' as logically consonant and quite consistent with an educative, emancipatory role within both concepts of the case that I have distinguished. I am here arguing that the democratic model provides an educational form of social theory, an argument opposed to that of Fox and Stronach (1986) who claim that the democratic model is a non-educational social theory of schooling.

It may be, of course, that democratic evaluation proves to be no less short-lived than straightforward partisanship. It has certainly had a more troubled experience to date than either the allegation of conservatism or my claim that it is educational would have forecast. I have already referred several times to the problems encountered by the evaluation of the National Development Programme in Compu-ter Assisted Learning. The final report of that evaluation (MacDonald and Jenkins, 1980) has never been published and the Department of Education and Science continues to decline to provide a copy to inquirers. The meta-evaluation of the European Commission's 'Transition from education to working life' met a similar fate. The evaluation of bilingual education in the USA (MacDonald and Kushner, 1982) was self-reportedly controversial. However, at the time of sending this manuscript to press, MacDonald *et al's* con-troversial report on police training in England and Wales, commissioned by the Home Secretary, an evaluation conducted under the auspices of the Official Secrets Act, is about to be published (in full) by the government.

Such a record is, perhaps, hardly reassuring as a record of evaluation designed to deliver an information service to the citizenry at large. At the same time it does represent successive efforts to tackle the hard end of the power spectrum. As my own, more limited experience reported in chapter 6 demonstrates, there is a mountain to climb and a long haul in prospect. In chapter 7 I take up the issue of how to secure the dissemination of evaluation reports.

The mid-seventies, as these comments suggest, was a period of sponsored expansion of naturalistic case study evaluation. This was accompanied by a proliferating literature seeking to clarify the politics, epistemology and methodology of naturalistic approaches and concepts. I have already mentioned the key papers from CARE written by MacDonald, Stake, and Walker in 1974. At the end of that year CARE also published the first set of SAFARI papers (MacDonald and Walker, 1974) and further relevant contributions in that and the following year were written either individually or jointly by members of the 'college' (Smith, 1974 [with Pohland]; Stake, 1974 and 1975; Walker and Adelman, 1975; MacDonald *et al*, 1975; Parlett, 1975). Much of this writing consisted of a conceptual mapping out of the territory, with specialist evaluators like Stake and MacDonald primarily concerned with obligations to multiple constituencies, comparative epistemologists like Hamilton and, increasingly, House focussing on the differences between naturalistic and positivistic traditions, classroom observers like Walker and Adelman exploring consonances and dissonances between the emerging approach and fieldwork traditions in sociology and social anthropology, Jenkins exploring literary and artistic metaphors, Parlett developing his individual model of a short-span, consultancy-based evaluation service, and Smith analyzing case study data in terms of the processes of generating theory.

There was a great deal of interaction between these individuals throughout the seventies, and unchartable mutual influence. Many of them, by 1974, were based at CARE and the links between CARE and CIRCE were strengthened by lengthy visits from Stake, Smith, House and Hamilton, who spent a year there following the second Cambridge conference. Stake and Easley's (1978) 'Case studies in science education' subsequently reversed the traffic flow, with both Smith and Walker undertaking between them three of the eleven case studies, and Hamilton and myself involved in consultancy roles. By this time Adelman had left CARE for Bulmershe College to take up an evaluation commission (Adelman, 1979) and Elliott had moved to the Cambridge Institute, where he also took on project evaluation work (Elliott, 1985). By the late seventies the other permanent members of CARE, Stenhouse and Rudduck, were also involved with case study programmes (Stenhouse *et al*, 1982; Rudduck *et al*, 1983). Naturalistic inquiry, therefore, was best considered during this period as a broad church with a number of sub-divisions, some common inclinations that constitute its centre, but radiating in different directions.

Having now tried to give an admittedly sketchy picture of the movement, let me focus now on my own opportunities and experiences as an individual member of this broad community. I left CARE at the end of 1972 and moved to the Nuffield Foundation, where I worked for the next four years with Malcolm Parlett and others on a project concerned with curriculum development in higher education, directed by Tony Becher (see, for instance, Simons and Parlett, 1976; Parlett and Simons, 1976; Simons, 1974 and 1975). My next contact with CARE was as a case study worker on the SAFARI project, and it is this experience that is reported and discussed in the next two chapters.

The SAFARI Project and the Principle of Participant Control

The principles of democratic evaluation were first explored in practice in the SAFARI Project, which began in 1973 (see MacDonald and Walker, 1974). SAFARI (success and failure and recent innovation) sought to examine the impact of centrally-developed curriculum innovation several years after funding had ceased and central project teams had disbanded. Four national curriculum development projects were chosen for study:

(i) the *Humanities Curriculum Project*
(ii) *Geography for the Young School Leaver*
(iii) *Project Technology*
(iv) *Nuffield Secondary Science*

All four were secondary school curricula. These were studied at three levels — school, local education authority (LEA) and system (MacDonald and Walker, 1976). The LEA case study itself had three strands: a study of LEA administrators, of local advisers and of four schools with a relative density of take-up of at least three of the projects chosen for study. The case study reported in chapter 4 is a description of the research process in one of these four schools.

SAFARI was a complex study with a sometimes perplexing interpenetration of substantive interests, methodological and procedural concerns and political aspirations. It represented the coming together of several ideas in currency at the time: the emerging concept of democratic evaluation, the acknowledgement of participant/consumer rights, the desire for research to be more useful to practitioners and the growth and acceptance of new approaches to enquiry. The SAFARI Project was a coalescence of all these trends.

The adoption of the case study approach was an extension of the approach developed in the evaluation of the Humanities Curriculum Project, which I have already described. The potential of case study to support a more communal mode of research was quite evident, and, at least by the time I was commissioned to do one of the school studies, was underpinned by the democratic model and the 'social philosophy' paper referred to earlier (see pp. 49–51). Besides the substantive focus of the Project therefore, SAFARI had a process aim — to explore a democratic process of research in schools. This aspiration stemmed from the concern noted by MacDonald and Walker (Director and Principal Researcher respectively of the SAFARI study) about the inadequacy of existing research procedures to address the plurality of interests and conflicts of value increasingly at stake in the evaluation of any educational programme.

Though the SAFARI principles were first formulated within an evaluation context they were held to have equal applicability for case study research. The clearest statement of the problem SAFARI was trying to resolve can be seen in this statement from a progress report.

> A primary concern in doing the research has been how to resolve the question of, on the one hand, a commitment to inform ('people have a right to know') and on the other hand, respect for persons ('people own the facts of their lives').
>
> This has led us to develop a (growing) set of procedures to control and direct the research. The aspirations behind the procedures are:
> — the attempt to focus on the collection rather than the validation of different points of view as a primary function of the research; we seek to portray divergence rather than resolve it.

— the construction of multiple points of control at which informants can edit or alter statements before they become established as research data. We share responsibility for the picture that emerges with participants. (Walker and MacDonald, 1975, p. 3)

The exact procedures for the conduct of the school case studies were these:

- interviews would be conducted on the principle of confidentiality;
- use of data would be negotiated with participants;
- interview data would only be used with individuals' consent;
- participants would have ultimate control over how far they allowed the whole study to become public;
- reports would aspire to reflect participants' judgments and perceptions of reality;
- reports would be progressively negotiated for clearance, first with individuals, secondly with departments, thirdly with the school as a whole or representatives of the school.

Procedures were based primarily on the assumption that people owned the data generated about them by the research — it was their property, in fact, only to be released for wider circulation and discussion with their consent. The 'right to know' justification in this formulation of the procedures was, for the purposes of experiment, held to be subsidiary to this principle. Normally, one would argue a stronger case for the 'right to know', in terms of the public interest, than the one SAFARI adopted. SAFARI chose a weaker version in order to focus on the problem of imbalance in power relationships between the researcher and the researched. Given such a departure from autocratic traditions of researcher control, the rules for the case study were clearly hypotheses to be explored. So was the temporal flow-chart for completion of the studies, based as it was on the SAFARI team's notion of 'condensed field work' (MacDonald and Walker, 1974). The time scale for data generation and negotiation was extremely demanding, or optimistic, perhaps both (see next chapter for details).

I had several reservations about the proposals at the outset, reservations which may have influenced the decisions I made in the field. I was not unhappy with the concept of condensed fieldwork. My previous experience of case study had involved me necessarily in exploiting limited opportunities for direct data-gathering, as I have already explained. It was the connection between condensed time scales and democratic aspirations that I found difficult to accept. I could see some sense in it within a long term perspective of trying to construct an approach that ultimately educational professionals themselves might be able to adopt, and I could see in it the possibility of providing for practitioners the kind of quick feedback that might be useful to them as decision-makers, but I still found it difficult to anticipate that a more democratic process of inquiry, with all the checks and balances built in, could result in a shorter period of time. Especially a process that was unfamiliar to schools.

My second reservation, which was at the time a real puzzle, was why the SAFARI team needed both a principle of confidentiality and a principle of participant control. Surely the principle of control was enough to guarantee confidentiality. The answers I got then, which amounted to saying that confidentiality was about quick access and control was about subsequent release, did not clarify the problem for me. Ten years on, my interpretation of democratic evaluation as an educative activity with respect to all its informants makes it clearer to me that a process that was simply interested in generating public learning and therefore primarily in instrumental relationships with its sources, could not claim to have an educative relationship with participants. I now see more clearly than I, or I believe anyone else did then, that both principles are necessary to maintain the aims of private as well as public learning.

At the time I remained confused! My attraction to the democratic model, however, encapsulating many of the concerns we had experienced in the course of the Humanities Project evaluation, was enough to secure my commitment. My task, as I understood it, was to secure the substantive case study if at all possible, but more importantly to document the process of the study in action. The other case study workers were Rob Walker, Lawrence Stenhouse, and John Elliott, and the hope was that at the end of the day we would have a basis of experience for future developments in the direction of collaborative inquiry. I suspended my reservations, accepted the 'rules' as hypotheses, and worked rigorously to them.

Notes

1 SAFARI (Success and Failure and Recent Innovation) was funded by the Ford Foundation in 1973 to explore the medium-term effects of centrally-developed curriculum projects. For further details see MacDonald and Walker, 1974, 1975 and 1976; Norris, 1977.

2 UNCAL (Understanding Computer Assisted Learning) was the independent educational evaluation of the National Development Programme in Computer Assisted Learning, funded, again, in 1973, by the Department of Education and Science (DES). Both were multi-site case-study projects exploring with different emphases a democratic approach to evaluation.

3 Jean Rudduck was the Schools' Liaison Officer in the Humanities Curriculum Project team.

4 For a full account of the Humanities Curriculum Project's evaluation in its dissemination phase see HUMBLE and SIMONS (1978).

5 These reports were formally called Evaluation Bulletins.

4   Democratic Principles in Practice:
A Case Study in a
Comprehensive School

This study was my first attempt to put into practice the new rationale for the conduct of case study at the school level. Not suprisingly it fell short of some of its aims, partly because of the unfamiliarity of the process and partly because of intrinsic difficulties. There were many things I would do differently another time as will become clear in the course of this book. Chapter 5 is mainly concerned with analyzing the experience of this early study. But first I tell the story, what happened and what I, and to some extent the other participants, thought about engaging in a research process that gave them a more influential role than they had any reason to expect from a 'researcher' in defining and evaluating curriculum development in their school. I am concerned here not with presenting the case study product that emerged, but with the process through which that product was sought and shaped. Of course, in so far as the substantive focus on curriculum management and change helped to generate discussion on the research process, the two were intimately connected.

The process data is drawn from my field notes, first and second drafts of sections of the substantive case study, letters from the teachers responding to draft reports and to their involvement in the process, my letters to them, interviews with school staff and reflections on the study written at the time and afterwards. In accordance with the usual convention in research reporting I have anonymized personnel, in this case using neither names nor teaching subjects. The letters from teachers were a problem. I had not negotiated their use for my present purpose. But the research convention of anonymity, a luxury not usually available to evaluators without undermining their utility, eased the dilemma, as did the passage of time — ten years. 'The continuous restriction of information that long ago should have been de-classified helps to discredit the rules that protect justifiable confidentiality' (MacDonald and Stake, 1974). Nonetheless, I have used them sparingly. For evaluators of my persuasion the consequences of disclosure for persons who make it possible, are never far from the forefront of the mind.

The school, one of the first comprehensive secondary schools in the local education authority (LEA), and here called Castle Manor, had 2000 pupils and 100 staff. It was situated some 150 miles from the SAFARI base in Norwich. I myself was based in London and commissioned by the SAFARI team to do one case study, of this school. The design called for a total commitment of one month spread over a year.

In the description which follows heads of department are referred to as HODs, the second in charge of a department as 2-i-C and the four national projects and the departments in which they were located as 1, 2, 3 and 4. Key participants who were party to ad hoc group meetings and who constituted the decision-making group for the 'whole school' clearance of the case study were the Head, the Deputy Head and six HODs — the four in which the projects were located and two others related to Project 3. Six reports were produced, one for each of the four projects (referred to as Report 1, 2, 3 and 4 respectively), one on the Head's view of curriculum development (Report 5) and one on the HODs' collective views (Group Report). In drawing upon letters, transcripts, and fieldnotes, I have replaced identifying names with this code. Brackets around the code names are introduced from time to time to remind the reader of this retroactive artifice.

Breakdown of Time

The SAFARI interest in short time-scales set boundaries for the case workers. In precise terms it meant that each of us was restricted to *seven days* in the field generating data and *twenty-one days* writing up, negotiating clearance and control and completing the study. The twenty-one days were to be spread over a year. What follows is a summary of how the time was spent, and how the time-scale fared.

First One-day Visit — December, Day 1

Introductory to secure access; discussed research procedures; interviewed Head about the general organization and running of the school, legacies of the projects, views on curriculum development; discussed possible participants — HODs in which projects were located, related staff, management (Deputy Head and Head) and pupils; met Deputy Head responsible for timetable who would arrange initial interviews; collected available documentary data on school; became familiar with the school layout; promised to return in January for a three-day visit.

First Three-day Visit — January, Days 2, 3 and 4

Prime data-gathering visit: held group meeting with all key participants (management and subject heads) to discuss research procedures; interviewed Head more precisely about his perspective on curriculum development; interviewed four HODs of subjects in which projects were located, two HODs in related subject areas to Project 3, a lecturer from a local college who had once taught Project 3 in the school; observed two project classrooms, staff room, playground and school; collected more documentary data on school.

Second Three-day Visit (divided into two parts)

One-day visit — May, day 5

Prime task to present and negotiate reports (five in number, a sixth still to be completed).

Two-day visit (one week later) — May, days 6 and 7

Prime task negotiating and further data-gathering; planned to continue negotiating reports left the previous week, interview pupils (four groups of fourth years, two fifth years, one sixth in subject areas of the projects) and possible junior staff in the same subject areas; two-thirds of one day spent on resolving a breach of confidentiality issue which generated an unplanned interview, three informal discussions and a group meeting; in addition to interviewing above groups, interviewed two senior girls.

Final One-day Visit — December, Day 8

Major task to complete arrangements for the final writing up of the case study. In between visits, my time was spent writing reports, corresponding with participants, negotiating by post, revising drafts and writing further sections of the case study. From May to September the correspondence generated almost as much data as the initial data-gathering phase. Given the response to the study negotiations were extended for a time until the momentum faded, unable to be maintained from a distance. This is why a further (ie, beyond the stipulated seven days) visit was made to the school at the end of the year to try to complete arrangements for the final writing up. Final clearances were given by post during the second year. The study never formally ended. Time simply ran out.

First One-day Visit

My work in the school started one day in December with a visit to the Head to secure access. In a telephone call to arrange the visit, the Head had in fact given permission, possibly precipitated by a letter from the SAFARI Director, outlining the scope and intentions of the study and introducing me as the case worker. My task this first day was to explore the implications for the school more fully and, assuming an agreed understanding was reached, get launched into the study.

My field notes recall that the Head granted access for a case study very readily, much as he would, it appeared, welcome any study of the school. Of the focus he commented that it was time the centre-periphery model of curriculum development was investigated, adding 'We are not doing much with these projects here' and, of the procedures, that they were 'sensible and fair'. I had expected that more discussion and perhaps reassurance would be needed. Later experience suggested more discussion was needed, but in field work one cannot force the pace of social relations and understanding. I did not want to labour the points. Given only seven days it seemed important to start the study immediately, which I did with a long interview with the Head on the organization of the school. The Head's ready willingness for the school to be studied is not at all surprising. The school was, and always had been, very much in the public eye. One of the first comprehensive schools in that local education authority it was visited frequently, if not researched.[1] The public image it maintained may have been a significant factor in its response to my work.

I wanted to accomplish two things on this visit. The first was to establish credibility with the Head as a research worker who focussed sharply on curriculum development issues, was sensitive to the process of conducting research in schools and was aware of the history of his particular school. I was aided in this process by having taken part the year before in a policy study in that same Authority and, while Castle Manor had not itself been involved, a comparable local school had. Both this and the SAFARI staff's early discussion with the LEA's advisers and administrators yielded useful background information which I used at several points in my first interview.

The second was to gather as much background on the school as possible, to have a clear understanding of the Head's attitude to curriculum development and to design a plan of action for my next visit to the school. Both aspirations were reasonably fulfilled. But the task I was faced with at the end of the day seemed impossible: how extensive and accurate a representation of the school's response to curriculum development could I gain in seven days' field work given a multi-site school of 2000 pupils and 100 staff which was hierarchically organized and had a favourable public image to defend? The task was daunting.

First Three-day Visit

The three-day visit, six weeks later, was taken up with interviewing the Head, the Deputy Head, the six HODs and the college lecturer referred to in the summary. HODs seemed an obvious starting point for interviews. Any attempt to investigate the four projects would inevitably require their agreement, if not participation. It was an evidently hierarchical school, so it seemed the quickest route to raising curriculum development issues for the school as a whole. The Head had indicated in his initial interview that much of the curriculum development was delegated to HODs.

My reasons for using unstructured interviewing as the main mode of data-gathering reflected both the flexibility of the technique and the design constraints of the study. Unstructured interviews promised the quickest and richest database for representing teachers' perspectives, for engaging them in the process and creating a dialogue. Classroom observation, for instance, takes a long time and is less susceptible to participant involvement, unless triangulation is adopted which is very time-consuming. There was, in any case, little opportunity for direct observation of the projects. Only one of the four was fully operative in the school. Unstructured interviewing was also my preferred mode of data-gathering, the one in which I had had most experience and the one I had found apposite in my previous five years of case study evaluation. Like Denny (1978) I had found that 'frequently after an observation and interview, a teacher would say something in a few sentences that summed up several hours of observing for me' (pp. 1-2). One does not, of course, interview without bringing in observations. All field work in naturalistic inquiry is a combination of both (Smith, 1978; Schatzman and Strauss, 1973). Here observations were background rather than foreground.

Interviews varied in length from two hours (with the Head) to thirty-five minutes (with the 2-i-C), the length of one of the time-tabled periods in the school. The majority lasted an hour to an hour-and-a-half utilizing double periods where possible or two separate periods on successive days. No intentionality should be attributed to the precise distribution of time according to status in the school; it was more a function of the distribution of availability (mainly dictated by the timetable). I would have liked to have interviewed each person for two hours, in order to slow the pace and encourage reflectiveness.

In between interviews I collected other documentation on the school — prospectuses, syllabuses, an article by the Head on comprehensive schools; made general observations of playgrounds, classrooms, staffroom, library, lunchroom and made short specific observations of two department classrooms; talked to other teachers informally in the staffroom including one student teacher; noted the style of interaction between staff and pupils. I kept my eyes and ears continually open, in other words, for whatever might be potentially relevant to the curriculum development story, although I did not, could not, go as far as Denny did, some years later, as a case study specialist on Stake and Easley's (1978) 'Case studies in science education project'. With five weeks on site he had, of course, a lot more time. He was, like me, doing condensed field work, but within a time-scale that allowed immersion. Listen to this, for instance. It's a different process.

> I interviewed teachers in their rooms, hallways and lounges from 7.15am, through to 10pm; in lobbies of restaurants, dermatologists' offices, and hairdressers' salons; on hall duty, on playground duty, on lunchroom duty or bus duty; before school, during lunch, after school, on Saturday and even on Sunday; at board meetings, and PTO Thanksgiving and Christmas concerts.

>After a while I stopped bringing students into rooms
>for interviews and started talking with them after school;
>at a basketball game, for example. I put away the project's
>observation schedule and just 'hung around' school. I ended
>up listening to social studies, science and maths teachers
>talking about themselves, about their own children, their
>students, their dreams, doubts and dilemmas. In the course
>of five weeks I filled twenty spiral hip-pocket notebooks.
>Teachers filled about fifty hours of my cassette tapes. Since
>then I have read and listened to their words again and again. It
>is incredible what I hear the second or third time around. My
>observational notes pale in the strength of their words. So, I
>shall go with the teachers' words: Res ipsit loquiter, more or
>less. (Denny, 1978, pp. 1–2)

This kind of research process has, of course, long roots in
ethnographic traditions. But Denny saw himself modestly as the
teacher's scribe, facilitating their story-telling. The SAFARI aim was
to do that and something more; to get them to 'invent the study'
(Kemmis, 1980).

Establishing a Participatory Ethos

On the first day, before interviewing any staff, I arranged a meeting
with all those HODs selected for the initial interviews, together with
the Deputy Head, to fully explain the purpose and procedures of the
study and to seek their agreement to being a participant. Seeking their
agreement was a formality in the context perhaps, given the previous
agreement of the Head in such a school, but not, in terms of my
process hopes, a cosmetic. Though they may have felt under an
obligation to talk to me, I nevertheless wanted to try to establish the
best possible climate for that discussion — one in which they would
feel able to risk openness, to take part in the formulation of an issues
structure and to criticize the procedures. I had to establish that I was
independent of the Head.

I explained the focus of the study on tracking the impact of the
projects in the context of the school's own curriculum development
processes, the procedures and reasons for them, and our different
roles in the process (mine to initiate and produce reports for
discussion, theirs to initiate issues and check reportage for balance
and bias). I stressed three points in particular. First the participatory

aspiration of the research. Secondly, the opportunity that shared control gave them to shape the study and determine the process and extent of release within and beyond the school. Thirdly, the responsibility I would like them to take in identifying my personal or professional biases, pointing out errors of fact or emphasis, misperceptions of what was going on, poor judgments or interpretations.

I suggested that the sharing of control implied a sharing of the responsibility. It was 'their' study, I argued, as much as mine; their perceptions and judgments I was interested in recording; their constructions of meaning and significance I was seeking; that I was a facilitator in this process, placing a mirror, if they liked, up to the school to reflect itself (Walker, 1974b, p. 97). Like John Berger's 'clerk of their own records' (Berger and Mohr, 1976), though I did not use this analogy. I outlined the three stage process of clearance of data I would adopt within the school: first with individuals; secondly with departments; and thirdly with the whole school. I suggested that for this purpose, given the time-scale, they might constitute a decision-making group on behalf of the school. I also explained the three-stage design of the whole SAFARI study which hoped, eventually, to exchange school case studies, adviser studies and administrator studies; and the experimental nature of the enterprise.

There were few questions (as in the first meeting with the Head) which again I found slightly surprising, though it may have been a lot to take in at one time. It might also have reflected an uncertainty about working together. In the group situation I detected unvoiced doubts. Acceptance was passive. I do not think they grasped the significance of the participatory intention. HODs agreed to take part but not, at that point, to share any responsibility for the study. Nor did they show any interest in taking an *active* part in the process, though they did, in a general sense, welcome the alternative style of research, particularly the commitment to negotiate the relevance, accuracy and fairness of any reports produced. One HOD compared and contrasted this process with a previous research study which had been conducted in the school by a national research agency of which, he said, they had heard nothing after the visits until a book appeared.

One of the few questions centred on their selection. Why this chosen few? My explanation was in terms of the logical starting points in the subjects and allied subjects in which the Projects were located but also in terms of their roles in the development of curriculum within the school, pointing out here the study's aspiration to define the projects from the perspective of the school's own processes of curriculum development. A reversal of centre-periphery thinking, that was the idea. They seemed more comfortable in this role I had cast them in, as spokespeople of the school's curriculum development processes, when I stressed that ultimate control lay with them.

I also stressed again that precisely how the study would proceed was a matter for discussion and negotiation. If there were issues or directions they thought the study should explore they should raise them, if there were pertinent people they thought I should interview to mention them and so on. I also had to stress, of course, the limited time we had. We then discussed the timetable of interviews for the three days.

This meeting was not tape-recorded, a decision taken to encourage discussion of the approach to the study. All interviews, however, were tape-recorded. Permission to tape-record was sought and the procedures for the use of data explained again to participants before each interview. The advantages of tape-recorded interviews have been outlined elsewhere (Weiss, 1975b; Simons, 1977a) and extensively analyzed by MacDonald and Sanger (1982), particularly in relation to the case for democratic evaluation. In that article they not only draw attention to the opportunity tape-recording offers the interviewer to pay full attention to developing an interpersonal dynamic and to evoking interviewee's experience and meanings of events but also to the importance of the record itself: in providing an accurate check of the verbal component of the interview, (a total record of what both participants said), and the basis for subsequent negotiations about its use in a reported context. In the context of condensed fieldwork, tape-recording was essential for practical reasons as well. Previous experience had warned me that given a busy three-day schedule, with many people to interview and observations to record, memory could easily fail and note-taking, even if possible while establishing rapport for a difficult process, become too selective, too soon.

The main disadvantage of tape-recording interviews is the time it takes to listen to them and transcribe. In the context of the SAFARI study tapes were transcribed by secretaries, although this did not diminish the researcher's responsibility for listening to them, both to check the accuracy of the transcription and capture the precise meanings conveyed by tone, emphasis and delivery.

The Process of Clearance at Castle Manor

The SAFARI ethic started from the procedure of offering blanket confidentiality to participants in interview. This freed them from having constantly to monitor what they said. It was the first step in a process of progressively negotiating the data for the construction of a case study that might, if all agreed, become a public record.

To assist in the process of clearance of data for reports in the short time-scale, I adopted two further procedures. The first was to ask each interviewee at the end of the interview if there was anything that struck them immediately they would prefer not to be reported. The second was to offer them the tape recording to take home that evening to check, edit, or re-record. Only one chose to do this and altered nothing.

A further procedure adopted in some studies for the clearance of data (see, for instance, MacDonald *et al*, 1982) is to send the complete transcript of an interview to interviewees for editing or reconstructing before utilizing any of it in a report. This offers individuals the opportunity to delete any information they feel sensitive about, whatever the context, before it becomes signposted as an issue in a report, when it may prove more difficult to edit.

In a seven-day field work, one month study, there was no time, even if considered desirable, to adopt a procedure of clearing transcripts of interviews before proceeding with the next stage of the study. But since clearance of data was obviously going to take some time, the two procedures cited above — of checking for particular vulnerabilities at the end of the interview and offering the tape for editing — offered minimal guidance to the case study worker on possibly sensitive issues. I did not feel confident that these moves were more than a gesture in the direction of clearance, however. It seemed important to me then, and still does, for the use of data to be cleared in the context in which it is eventually to appear. That process was still to come.

By the end of the second day of interviews I was concerned about the strong degree of consensus and convergence I was receiving on the self-image of the school. While I had to accept that this might well be how it was in a well orchestrated school with a useful public image, it nevertheless struck me as odd that in a school of 100 staff there were not some differences of view being expressed. Was I only getting the polite response, the public image? If so, and my assumption, based on experience, of divergence beneath the surface was correct, the problem facing me then was how to get behind the facade to capture more of the reality. Interviews on the third day show evidence of trying to move the interviews beyond the descriptive and the impersonal to engage interviewees in analyzing the state and process of curriculum development in their school. Such a move was essential to my process aims. I tried to encourage interviewees to be more proactive in evaluating their own setting. The case for a style of interviewing that concentrates upon the interviewee as a person rather than as a role incumbent and invites that person to take a personal, evaluative stance towards his/her professional situation was explored later by MacDonald (1981). In a different context, that of exploring individualism and commitment in American life, Bellah *et al* (1985) make a similar point when they write 'Active interviews create the possibility of public conversation and argument' (p. 305). Though in the case reported here that 'publicness' was restricted to the school, Bellah *et al* highlight its significance for published accounts. 'When data from such interviews are well presented, they stimulate the reader to enter the conversation, to argue with what is being said' (*Ibid*).

Back at Base

Loaded with tape-recordings and field notebooks I returned to base. The interview tapes were sent to SAFARI headquarters for transcription along with a dictated account of the three days in the field, describing the events and characteristics of the school and noting initial hunches and interpretive asides (Smith and Pohland, 1974) on the school's curriculum development processes. I began thinking about organizing principles for the report.

I had assumed before I visited that I would probably write one report of approximately ten-twenty pages which I hoped to deliver back to the school for negotiation and clearance by the end of the first term. In the event there was enough data for ten reports. My anxiety about not generating enough data in three days to produce a case study had resulted in too much! The problem was now how to utilize it. Rather than try to condense the issues into one report, I wrote six: one on each of the four projects — a logical focus given SAFARI's concerns and starting points; one on the Head's view of curriculum development (this seemed critical as well as diplomatic given his position in shaping the school — he was the first and only Head — and the consensus of all staff interviewed that the extent of change was effectively controlled by him); and one collective report on management of curriculum within the school based upon the observations and perceptions of the six heads of departments. This was to balance the Head's report and explore the extent to which curriculum decisions were delegated.

The reports took the form of a playback on the interview describing, through narrative and selected quotations, the position of the projects within the curriculum of the school. This was followed by a series of questions seeking further information to round out the account, raising possible interpretations, including alternatives, and probing issues further. Reports varied from ten to twenty pages in length. They were open in the sense of calling for further discussion, verification and refutation. Though the issues were drawn from the interview data they were selected by me for inclusion in the reports. Ideally, in a democratic process of research, issues for inclusion in the report would be negotiated with participants. This was impossible to attempt in the short time-scale. Participants could, of course, reject issues and in several instances in this study they did. In addition to these six reports, two profiles, one on the school and one on the extent of project adoption in the school, were written as contexts for the case study.

These reports became the negotiating currency — the basis on which improvements and clearance were sought. Each was drafted twice and checked for bias by a SAFARI colleague. One particular report was rewritten to take account of the following response from a colleague:

> Throughout, you seem to take it for granted that (the project) is a good thing and to fix on the heads (this refers to the heads of department of relevant subjects) as responsible for its lack of impetus. This seems rather narrow, and a bit unfair in the circumstances as you outline them ...
>
> What was the LEA doing all the time? What advisory support was there? The fact is that an important opportunity for the LEA to support individual teacher initiative seems to have been missed.

I acknowledged and tried to take account of this analysis and rewrote parts of the report to soften the tone, redress the balance, and respond to the context more fairly.

Second Three-day Visit

Preparation of these six reports undoubtedly took longer than the one initially intended would have required. It was early in the second term when I returned to the school to negotiate clearance of the reports with staff. At the outset of the case study 1 had planned to make two, three-day visits to the school. Given the length and nature of the reports (asking critical questions, probing interpretations), I decided to split the second three-day visit into two: first a one-day visit to present the reports and negotiate with individuals; secondly a two-day visit, to negotiate possible further release, to identify issues or themes, to round out the study and to interview pupils. These visits were to be made a week apart to give individuals time to reflect upon the reports. In between I asked HODs to discuss with their departmental colleagues the extent to which the reports were an *accurate, fair and relevant* account (the SAFARI criteria) of curriculum development in the department and so pave the way for departmental clearance.

The One-day Visit

It was a formidable task. Even allowing one hour for each negotiation, all could not be completed in one day. There were six HODs, each of whom had to clear individual comments in a Project Report *and* a Group Report. There was also the Head and Deputy Head. I knew that I would have to seek individuals' help in continuing to check their contributions and the use made of them beyond my visit but I felt it was important to set the tone for negotiation by initiating the process face-to-face. Before beginning I emphasized yet again the procedures of the study; reports were confidential until released by them; ultimate control over the extent to which the data became public lay with them; they had the right to edit, reshape, or refocus on the grounds of accuracy, fairness and relevance. I did manage to speak to all but one Head of Department to clear individual comments. The exception was the one who had implemented a project most extensively, Project 4. With the exception of Report 3 (which I could not leave until parts had been rewritten to take account of my bias, and until some comments had been cleared with a contributor not on site)[2] I left the reports with individual HODs to finish checking and, if feasible, to discuss with their departments.

As with the interviews themselves, negotiation of reports started with the Head. With minor amendments, the Head cleared his report in full. It took two-and-a-half hours, the first forty-five minutes of which were taken up with a discussion of the television film which had been shot on my first three-day visit and broadcast the previous week. For this forty-five minutes the Head sat behind his desk. For the clearance of the report we sat side by side, a practice adopted to signal the change of purpose and engender a collaborative mode for negotiating the account.

The fifteen-page narrative report described, primarily through the Head's own words, the evolution of curriculum development and change in 'his' school, the curriculum management structure, the role of HODs and the presentation of the curriculum and school to the community. The narrative was interspersed with questions inviting further analysis and ended with two alternative interpretations of the Head's role in curriculum development in the school. The edited negotiation below is included to give the reader some idea of the nature of the process, and of what kinds of points the Head chose to challenge.

In the clearance session he pointed out one or two errors of fact, suggested readjustments of tone, asked for explanations of interpretations and offered further elaborations of issues, changing substantially very little.

1   *p 1, para 1*: The whole question of curriculum development has only loomed large in the past five years. When the school was first opened I was thinking more about the structure of the school — offering grammar school opportunities to all pupils and establishing the nature of the school in terms of what parents wanted. We did not think of curriculum development. There were subjects and we taught them.

2   *para 2*: He asked to change the last part of the quote from 'I don't seek to turn them into innovators or maintain them as a set square' to 'have them necessarily maintain the status quo'.

3   From p 2 to 5 he only corrected one or two factual points like dates.

4   *p 5, para 2*: He asked to change the wording in the quote where he distinguished teaching and management activities. He could not remember saying it quite as it was reported. At this point we went back to the original transcript and found an alternative that he was happy with.

5   *p 6*: He emphasized while he was reading that his management team were first rate . . .

7   *p 7, para 2*: He glossed over the questions and I had to bring his attention to them . . .

9   *p 9, para 2*: He agreed to let me have details of the exact

stay of heads of departments. He mused on his metaphor of risk running through a lot of his quotations and attributed it to his background in economics.

10 *p 10*: He emphasized that there was no majority vote and again that the heads of department's opinions carry the most weight.

11 *p 11*: He wanted to change the quotation about the shifting resources from the local authority. This was simply a question of correcting it and updating it ...

12 *p 12, para 3*: 'It's not a question of not exercising the power of imposing change. Change is only going to take successfully if it has the support of the head of department and the consensus of the heads of department as a body.' Playing devil's advocate here to push the point a little further I put the opposite side of the case. If he had a burning desire to introduce some change would he? 'I see my role as a stimulator', he says, 'if I saw something exciting I would bring it to their notice'.

But I said again, pushing it a little further, 'if a head of department came to you with an idea and you did not at that point have confidence in him to carry it through would you support him?'. 'It would be quite wrong to remain neutral. I try to temper my own enthusiasm by what the head of department says about it. I try not to be too overbearing.' What would he do about the head with the exciting idea? 'I would adopt a compromise — and give it a trial.'

13 *p 12, para 3*: He asked me to explain what I meant by 'backing system growth while maintaining system stability'.

14 *p 12, para 4*: He endorsed the whole tone of this paragraph agreeing wholeheartedly with the last sentence 'but in practice, where does the balance lie?'

15 *p 12, para 5*: What happens when initiatives in individual departments involve other departments is less clear. 'There is a good example of this in relation to (HOD 4). He wanted to carry out fieldwork that would interfere with the school as a community. If I were to sanction that it would be to invite conflict from several other departments. I have to see to the overall aims of the school whereas I would expect the head of department to take a limited view.' ... 'The question of timing for

innovation is my decision. But the kind of innovation is the responsibility of the head of department. So it is not, he went on to say, referring to a question in para 3, 'a prescription for stalemate. The evidence is (HOD 4). But it very much depends on the innovation.' ...

I asked him what did he think, of the power-based interpretation of the head running a school? 'That's absolutely right. The question of a balance of power and resolving conflict is what the head's position is all about ... In some respects I have to align myself with (HOD 4) against the management team and some other members of staff who are not entirely in sympathy with what he is doing and say "this is the right thing". When it comes down to certain situations I cannot maintain this regal, non-commital attitude. I really have to show my claws.'

16 *p 13, para 2*: Did the fact that any proposed changes had to be put to the management team mean that they had the power in fact to determine whether or not changes were introduced? 'No', said the Head, 'it is a point but it would not prevent innovation. It is similarly true to say', he went on, 'that the management team is prisoner of heads of departments. We wouldn't drive through something if there was substantial opposition on management things ...'

17 *p 13, para 2*: Emphasizes the importance of innovation through appointments. 'This gives me tremendous power to build up the sort of school I want. You can regard it as authoritarian but equally as a golden opportunity for gathering like-minded people.'

18 *p 13, paras 3 and 4*: He liked the point about examinations in Castle Manor not being seen as a constraint on change and the whole of the discussion on p 14 in terms of risk.

19 *p 15, para 2*: He fully supported the comment that anything which entails the reorganization of the school is a risk for which the headmaster in the final analysis is accountable. 'I fully accept that ... In its purest form I want any changes that take place to have, first of all the full and unequivocal support of the head of department. Secondly, one hopes that the majority of other departments don't view it as too disturbing ... though I cannot

and would not want to disassociate myself from that risk (of change).'

20 *p 15, paras 3 and 4*: Was the involvement with the community seen as a constraint or opportunity? 'It could be a constraint but I think that I am ahead of parental opinion but not so far ahead that I lose their sympathy ...' (Edited five-page Negotiation of Head's Report, Field note, May)

There were other points that I wanted to push him further on but two-and-a-half hours had passed and I had four other reports to clear. He thought it was a very fair and interesting account and asked if it would help proceedings at this stage if he said to all the others involved that he had cleared his report and was happy for them to read it. I deferred a decision about this until I had discussed individual reports with HODs because I knew that there were passages in their reports that they might not so easily clear. I did not want them to feel under pressure to circulate their reports because the Head had taken the first step. But I left it open with the Head to take it up the following week if that seemed desirable. In the meantime I would make the alterations he suggested and bring several copies of the redrafted report when I visited the school again the next week.

For the same reasons as applied to the interviews, the same length of time was not available for all negotiations. And not all were so straightforward. Only a single period was available for each of five HODs, all of whom had comments to clear in two reports.

The first report was cleared totally by the HOD. Nothing was altered but I prevailed upon him to check again after I left, as I felt he was too accepting of my interpretation. A start was made on clearing the second report, on clearing comments in the group report and the third report. The fourth report was deferred, for lack of time, to the following week.

For the next visit, the following week, plans were made to finish negotiations, to interview pupils and to hold a group meeting to decide what else was needed to round out the study.

The Two-day Visit

I arrived the evening before to check individual comments on Report 3 with the person who had taught Project 3 but was no longer in the school. For over an hour she questioned the research approach. She asked what my qualifications were, how I came to be involved, how long it would take to complete the study and what I would be doing next. Her disagreement was with the style of research. Pure, descriptive research, which was how she perceived it, even the best journalism, was totally inadequate. Educational research coming from a mixture of disciplines had no sound theoretical basis. It lacked explanatory power. Because of the authority often attached to research there was a danger, she thought, that people like students would accept inadequate theory without question. The only educational researcher she excepted from this criticism was Elizabeth Richardson (see chapter 8, note 6). She was also unhappy about the fact that researchers move in and out of schools raising questions that might cause teachers some anxiety and yet are not there to follow up and give support.

At the end of an hour-and-a-half, however, she suspended judgment to check the accuracy of the report. She asked for one description to be removed (the same description my colleague said I had given too much weight to), hesitated on one issue, but left it in because it seemed to her crucial to an understanding of the school, offered further explanations, one of which she thought was very pertinent to an understanding of the school at that point in time. She also commented upon perceptions she had not thought of before. In response to my request for help in identifying further issues she indicated two.

Breach of confidentiality incident

This incident dominated my two-day and supposedly final visit, in view of the seven days allocated to the field phase.

At break on the first day I went into the staffroom. HOD 1 greeted me with 'You've created a furore, you have ...' Though the comment sounds hostile in print it was not delivered in a hostile manner. The week before I had briefly, in a thirty-five minute period, discussed the Project 1 Report with the HOD. He had read it through very quickly, nodding at his own comments but not pausing for deliberation. He had been in fact more keen on bringing me up-to-date with what had happened since my previous visit and how he thought another project which had just arrived was more relevant for the level of ability of pupils in Castle Manor. He agreed to go through the report more carefully when I had gone and to discuss it with other members of the department to see how far the views were shared. I was not to know that this would raise an old personality conflict in the department. My field notes record:

> Next period I had a therapy session on my hands while (HOD 1) told me what had happened. When he had shown (Report 1) to (the 2-i-C), head of a different section of the department, he had taken it straight to the head. He said that the 2-i-C objected to the picture that he, the HOD, presented of the school. The 2-i-C thought it was critical of the school and he did not want to be associated with anything that was critical because he had been at Castle Manor for over eleven years and thought that they were doing a good job. He wanted to make sure that the head saw that it was not a consensus of the department. The HOD also thought that the 2-i-C read into the report that he (that is, the HOD) wanted to impose Project 1 on the department. This was an old issue, irresolvable perhaps because of a personality conflict between the HOD and the 2-i-C. The HOD thought that there would be no point in trying to pursue a discussion right now. While two of the younger teachers were keen, another two uncertain, the remaining two (there were seven in the department) definitely agreed with the 2-i-C that there would be no point in discussing old issues again. The HOD was still keen to pursue it, but later perhaps in the term.

At lunchtime I decided to see the Head. Having left him the previous week on good terms after he had cleared his report, I decided to be quite direct. 'I believe there has been some difficulty over a report I wrote and that you are about to throw me out of the school.' He laughed and went on to say that it simply revived an old personality conflict about which there was very little we could do. It was a personality problem with the HOD. 'Intellectually he is concerned to introduce (Project 1) and thinks that the project is right. But the brutal fact is he hasn't the ability to carry it through.' At the same time he said that the 2-i-C, who takes a plausible line in discussion, could be very difficult, even stubborn, at times.

At the centre of the problem was a familiar issue in school politics. The HOD had been brought in and appointed over the 2-i-C. The Head disclaimed responsibility for the appointment over which he said he had had no control. He had been pressurized, he said, by the local authority to take the HOD to help them out with administrative reorganization of the secondary schools. His qualifications were good and he had been previously in charge of a large department in another comprehensive school. But the Head readily admitted in retrospect that it was a bad appointment. I asked him what he thought of the report, 'Was it a fair account in his view?'. 'I didn't read it', he said hastily. Later in our conversation I raised the same question, assuming that he must at least have glanced at it. But he repeated that he had not read it. He had given it to the Deputy Head, though he did not tell me this directly. The HOD 1 had indicated earlier that day that the report was now with the Deputy Head.

I asked the Head how we should resolve the incident. Would it be a good idea if I chaired a department meeting, for instance, or had a discussion with the 2-i-C. Either, he thought, would be a good idea and we decided on the latter. The 2-i-C only agreed to be interviewed on the condition that he did not have to respond to any of the judgments the HOD had made or questions I raised in the report.

I spoke to the 2-i-C next day. He had done his homework and made out a list of points that he wished to say and no more. He also said he had discussed the report with another teacher in his section of the department. The 2-i-C repeated that it was very much a personality issue and there was no point in dragging this up again and that the HOD was ill when he came to Castle Manor. 'He came under a cloud from his previous school and tried to get people very enthusiastic here. But it didn't work ...'

That same day I also spoke to the Deputy Head on the pretext of clearing some comments with him but really to explore the breach of confidentiality issue. I had asked the HOD 1 what the Deputy Head thought of the report and he replied that he had thought it was fair. I told the Deputy Head that I was surprised the report had come into his hands since it was confidential to the HOD and to whoever he wished to show it to in his department. The Deputy Head said he did not know that ... 'In any case he had not read it, only glanced at it.' But he went on to say that he thought it was biased towards a view that the organization of the school prevented development. It was obvious to me he had read further. As we went on to discuss comments arising from his interview on the previous visit he interrupted with other comments like 'You seem to have a view that it is difficult for the school to change because we have successful examination results ...', which tended to confirm my hunch that he had read the report. However, I did not pursue it further. My field notes record: 'The (Project 1) incident rests there. I now have two different perspectives of the fate of Project 1 in Castle Manor.'

I have quoted this incident at length because it raises relevant issues for the implementation of a democratic process of research control. This incident constituted a breach of the procedures as I had understood them and tried to convey them to participants. Reports were confidential to individuals and, in the second instance, departments, until cleared by them for further release. Clearly not all members of the department or school perceived them that way or were committed to them as strongly as I was. Or else, more simply perhaps, the rules of research conflicted with the rules of running the school. The Deputy Head had been in on the discussion of procedures and been interviewed when they were discussed again, but had chosen to read a confidential report. The Head, who had also been through the same procedures, including respecting his own confidentiality, protected the rhetoric and possibly the practice, though he may have been caught in the same bind as the Deputy Head as a senior manager of the school. In other words, the authority/management structure of the school conflicted with the procedural rules.

The incident points to the fact that unfamiliar procedures for internal control of data, intended to protect participants, can easily be overtaken by traditional processes of complaint. No breach of confidentiality may have been intended by the 2-i-C of Department 1. He may not have been aware of the rules of procedure that the lead participants had been reminded of three or four times (at the preliminary meeting, before interview, after interview and before negotiation), or he may not have accepted them. What this suggests is that more time may be needed at the outset to seek the agreement of all possible participants with the rules of procedure.

More importantly, perhaps, such incidents suddenly break the surface of school life, like the tip of the iceberg. The data matrix expands to accommodate a new range of 'public issues', raising the reality level of the enquiry. But, most significantly, it indicates how a responsive process of research can easily get out of logistical control. The aspiration was to complete the research within seven days' fieldwork and a further month spread over a year. It seemed at this point that the process could not be managed within this time-scale. For instance, as an upshot of the breach of confidentiality incident, the planned programme of interviews with pupils and junior staff was interrupted. Instead, I had to discuss the incident with the Head and Deputy Head and, to be fair, I had to interview the 2-i-C of the department. This took two-thirds of one day of my two-day visit, a severe encroachment on the time-scale, but a necessary one, in the event, to ensure that the study could continue, that grievances were dealt with, and the involvement of staff nurtured.

To re-establish procedures I sought a group meeting with 'key' participants the next day.

Group meeting

This was arranged for half-an-hour at lunchtime on the second day. All the HODs involved were there except HOD 4. The Deputy Head and Head were also present. The Head first of all asked me to explain the full context of the study, which I did. He asked how the schools would be named in the final report and how the report might look. I replied that these questions were very open at this stage and I would welcome their suggestions. They were not concerned. I then went on to explain the similarity in the way the reports were written, why they were written in that particular way, re-emphasized the checks and control that they had over the use of the data and that it was their perceptions that should be reflected in the reports. I invited questions and also asked them to point out now or at any stage any biases that they thought I might have. In many respects it was a repeat of the first group meeting.

The meeting was fairly formal. The Head took the initiative, offering comments on his report, which he said was a fair reflection of the position he held in relation to curriculum development. He assured the others that he was not seeking to 'project the image of the school, as I have done on other occasions', and intimated that people who develop projects obviously have a vested interest in them and will tend to see things in a different light. 'It may be', he added, 'that some of you feel Miss Simons has an assumption that change is necessarily a good thing.' And so on . . .

There were few questions. HOD 2 asked when I was coming back since he felt it was important to discuss the rest of his report with me in person. The week before and for one period this visit I had discussed report 2 with him and we had only got to page 4, so held up was he by embarrassment at seeing his words in print. I explained again that we were working within limited time constraints in the school and trying to see what pictures we could get within that time and asked for their cooperation by post. HOD 1, in querying how it was possible to distinguish Project 1 from general project work in the department, repeated part of the interview I had had with him on the previous visit. I explained again that I was there to reflect his perceptions and judgments of what constructions should be placed on Project 1 in the teaching of the department, not to see whether or not they measured up to some standard prescribed by the national project developers, or myself.

We discussed timing, whether it would be preferable to respond to the reports by tape or in writing. We left it that I would be in touch by post and visit again if they saw a need to discuss the next stage with me. Clearly, they all expected that I would be visiting again and that it was necessary. HOD 2 did in fact send off the first half of Report 2 the next week with additions on every page but added that the last part he would like to discuss with me in person when next I visited the school.

I asked HOD 5 after school how he thought the meeting had gone. He, who had not said a word in the meeting but had made notes, said, somewhat cynically I thought:

> that was diplomatic, a gesture. The one thing you can say about the head is that he is a master of diplomacy. But you have to go through these gestures in this school. What I saw of the picture you showed me seems to be the truth. The difficulty is will it be possible to say the truth? ... When I came here I thought my truth was the truth but other people saw it differently. There are several truths ... there are those who have been here a long time who may not wish to change in quite the same way as I do.

I saw the Deputy Head as I was leaving the school and asked him also about the meeting. While he thought it might have cleared the air he still considered the study was 'very very threatening ...'. He was quite pleased when I told him that I had not written a separate report on his views but would like to include some of them in a total school report. He asked if he could see these comments again to reflect upon what he had said as he was concerned about the use of them in context. He was the only member of staff who actually took the tape recording home while I was at the school, listened to it and gave clearance for it next morning. He was constrained then, but seemed concerned now. I knew that he aspired to a headship, and could understand at least that source of his evident anxiety about the possibility of adverse reaction to any public account.

In the time that was left of these two days in the school I interviewed pupils from science, humanities and the sixth form. On return to base I wrote the following concluding comments to my field notes of this second three-day visit:

1   There was not one 35–40 minute period that was not fully used. Even though a lot of time was taken up exploring the (Project 1) incident and checking with each of the six people involved their comments in Reports 2, 3 and the Group Report, I still managed to interview the 2-i-C in Department 1 and five groups of pupils: fourth and fifth year humanities, two groups of Project 2 and one sixth form group of geography and english pupils. The pupil interviews were not wholly satisfactory especially with the fourth years. By the time they got in and got settled down we only had 25 minutes. That was hardly time enough to get their confidence. The mixed interview had the additional problem of sharp differentiations in sex roles.

2   I had difficulty in trying to get the message over that I was not on the side of the projects. Nearly all the teachers tended to assume that I was in some way or another associated with the 'curriculum developer'. This led some of them to adopt a justificatory position.

3   At the end of my second three days in the school it seems to me that the role of negotiation is somewhat at odds with the notion of condensed fieldwork. It seems that my work has just begun. I now have to rewrite parts of Report 3 before I send it to the four people involved for their collective or individual response. I have to do the same with the Group Report which then has to be sent to six people for their collective or individual response. I have two perspectives of the fate of Project 1 which will have to be interwoven and rewritten in another report, no comment on Report 4, and Report 2 still to be completed. Pupil interviews have yet to be integrated and so have the Deputy Head's comments. If the teachers do respond to the questions and issues raised in the six reports at least some of these responses will have to be integrated into any final account.

Back at Base

The seven days' fieldwork had now ended, though there were still a few days left for writing up and negotiating reports. I had interpreted the seven days' fieldwork to mean on-site, in the school, including personal negotiation. Had I thought that negotiation was part of the twenty-one subsequent days — and since it certainly generated more data it could have been — I might have felt less constrained, although the writing up and rewriting time, in fact, consumed most of the twenty-one days.

What transpired over the next six months went beyond the planned time commitment. It was not only the time taken up with rewriting reports that was at a premium but the correspondence which ensued. Adhering strictly to the seven days in the field stipulation I now had to find a way to keep up the momentum from a distance. I sought participants' help in two ways; through letters and through asking HODs to discuss reports departmentally in my absence. In the case of the Group Report I asked one HOD, HOD 5, to convene a meeting with the six HODs to discuss the content of the report.

Negotiation by Post

I first of all wrote to HOD 4. He had been absent on the last day of my second and last visit. I explained the context of the reports and asked him to respond by post to Report 4 and to his comments in the Group Report to enable me to circulate this for discussion amongst the group. Prompted perhaps by the breach of confidentiality incident, I included a warning sentence: 'There may be all sorts of things you feel it would be better not to say or to emphasize in view of how things are going at present and of which I am not aware.'

I indicated that it would be helpful if we could circulate reports in two weeks' time and included a tape in case he found it easier to record comments. I also rewrote parts of Report 3 and sent it to the three HODs in the school and the lecturer at the college. One week later, ie, two weeks after my visit, I received the amended abridged second report with one section deferred for clearance until it could be discussed in person with me on my next visit. Clearly, the expectation here, as on the last visit to the school, was that I would be visiting again. While this was a perfectly reasonable assumption to make given that we were working towards a completed study, and that negotiation at every stage was the procedure, it did not take account of the seven days in the field time limit. What this signalled was that a truly participatory process of research was difficult to accomplish in such a time-scale.

The dilemma this posed was whether to respond strictly to the time-scales and end the study when the time ran out or to explore the participatory possibilities which were just beginning. The SAFARI team encouraged the latter. Given that the research was experimental, it would be important to see just how far the participatory process could be extended, what the structure of the problem was and what might result. (Not all the school case studies took this form. Each case study worker while respecting the SAFARI principles and procedures generated processes of different kinds with different results).

Three weeks after I had written to HOD 4 I wrote him a reminder particularly to request clearance of his comments in the Group Report, so that I could circulate this for discussion. I also wrote to the five other HODs apologizing for the delay. HOD 4 replied as requested to both reports by return post and with sincere apologies. That same day I received a letter from the lecturer giving final clearance of her comments in Report 3:

> Thank you very much for your letter and copy of the report. I don't really think there are any further comments to make except to say that you have very much undermined my prejudices about this kind of research; I found the report stimulating and much more analytical than I had expected when we talked together about the problems of this method . . .

At the same time also (i.e., four weeks after my last visit to the school) I received a three-page foolscap letter from HOD 1 reassuring me about the effect of my report on the department:

> You need have no fears about the effect of your report on the other members of my department. When I circulated it, I was well aware that it would produce reactions — I just did not anticipate that they would be so violent. It has, however, given everyone the chance to think again about the relevance of the project to the work we do — and this must be a good thing!

The letter also contained further comments on the report somewhat more optimistic in tone about the scope for change than his earlier comments in interview, viz:

> Within the bounds of available rooms, equipment and expense there is nothing that *we* cannot do if we so desire — and *we* (his emphasis) would be held responsible for the

consequences ... The opportunity for experiment at Castle Manor is wide open! ...

The present examination system does not preclude this kind of development. It may not actively encourage it.

He also added a number of specific comments on Project 1 itself to explain the level of adoption, including the possibility of lack of effective leadership.

Five weeks after my visit but only two weeks after the receipt of the amended Report 3, I received a long three-page foolscap letter from the three HODs concerned with Report 3, noting two errors of fact and raising a number of points of interpretation and bias including the bias I thought I had removed in the second draft.

I replied twice, once immediately to acknowledge receipt of their response before I went on holiday, the second time on my return, to comment in detail on the substance of their comments on the report. In between I wrote to the SAFARI Director indicating how important I thought it was to negotiate reports in person (in my absence I suspected apprehensiveness had returned and participants had moved to a less critical stance). I also expressed my concern that I had raised issues too sharply. I checked again with a colleague whether Report 3 was still biased. In his view it was. I was at this point beginning to realize how educative this process of case study was for me. I then replied to the school staff concerned with Project 3 as follows:

> ... Perhaps the most important point that you raised for me was that the report seems to be biased not only in favour of the project (it did not escape your notice that given appropriate conditions, I do think it has a lot to offer), but also in terms of organization, structure, and degree of commitment failing to support the project within the school. When I was writing the report, I was very worried that I was not detaching myself sufficiently from what I had learnt of the difficulties of introducing this particular project to fairly represent how you are using the materials. This is something that I have been struggling to avoid for some time, but clearly have not succeeded in achieving. I mentioned my worry to a colleague who agreed that in the context as I described it, I was unfairly asking too many questions of the school, too few of the project and the LEA. I altered it but did not, it seems, change the emphasis ...
>
> The problem I have in reporting on this project (and it may well have spilled over into others) relates to my previous

experience ... For the first two years that the project was on the open market, I studied how it was adopted in different schools and settings all over the country ...

There follows here a description of what I learned about the difficulties of innovation in evaluating this project. My reply continued:

... In the report I was trying to explore the relevance of some of these problems for Castle Manor. But it seems that they have impeded rather than helped me to ask the appropriate questions in your situation. Fortunately, the style of research we are hoping to establish is one that reflects and builds upon how you view events not how we have come to analyze them. It is your views, not mine, which will be most helpful to those considering how to manage curriculum development in the future....

... I take your point about the use of the materials that it would be unfair to convey that the materials were used purely as vehicles of information. In fact, in other places (on page 1 and page 6) of the report, I have referred to their use as a stimulus for discussion. But perhaps I need to bring these points closer together and discuss both in terms of the variation of ways the materials are used.

The issues you raise on page 2, paragraph 2, about differentiating between the organization and the personalities of those occupying leading roles is a very complex one that in the time available I have not been able to deal with adequately. Both this and the question of how the organization affects curriculum change are issues that I feel it would be valuable to discuss further, rather than write about. So may we take them up when next we meet?

You are right that the comment on success (page 3, paragraph 1) begs the question of what one might justifiably view as success. I did not go into this whole question here because I raised it to some extent in the composite group report. However, you did catch my meaning and the question you raise in response to it is the one I think that the curriculum developers and we should be asking.

What you have pointed out very clearly, and it is something I ought to bring out in the re-draft, is that it is the course which the school developed to meet the needs of Castle Manor pupils which is central. The report should describe a little more about this, how it is assessed and how the (Project 3) materials were and are used in this course. It was clear to me when I talked with you that you never intended to introduce the project as a curriculum in its own right, so you are quite right to point out that some of the questions I raised are inappropriate in this context. I did not intend to be critical. I am caught, I think, in my own dilemma. But I will work on it . . . (Detailed three-page reply to the teachers' comments on Report 3 edited to include only discussion on contentious issues crucial to the criteria of fairness and relevance.)

Shortly after I had heard from the HOD 4 clearing his comments in the Group Report, I had forwarded it to the six HODs. On my last visit to the school I had asked HOD 5 to chair a meeting to discuss the report in my absence.

Three weeks later, I received a seven-page letter from HOD 5 commenting generally and specifically on the issues on the Group Report (of twenty pages) up to page 3. The six HODs had met three times, twice after school and once at lunchtime. They reported that the discussions were very lively and of great value as they found themselves realizing not only that they disagreed about the scope for innovation in the school but more and more the reasons for that difference. They also felt that the issues arising were perennial and they did not have time to do justice to their complexity. Respecting my request for feedback within a fortnight, they had had to call a halt to the discussions — they were already a week overdue — but indicated a willingness to continue the discussion if I would find that helpful. The majority of the letter was taken up with specific points on interpretations generated by me but working from issues identified by them, on differences amongst them (the consensus had been broken) and points of agreement and emphasis. The letter concluded with four general points to me: the first indicating a bias they thought I had towards Schools Council materials; the second seeking care in the alignment of interview and commentary; the third seeking clarification of the connection between the fate of the Schools Council materials and my inquiry, focussing on some HODs, into the whole scope for change; the fourth indicating that the discussions had been interesting and valuable — 'more valuable than all the heads of departments' meetings and staff meetings'.

With reference to point three, the letter concluded that here was an opportunity to develop a conversation with me on the rationale of the inquiry. In offering to continue the discussion, I felt that they had entered into the process in more than a formal way. Keen to continue the dialogue, I responded, one week later, as follows:

I found your letter in reply to the group report on the Safari project immensely helpful. It made me realize just how complex each point is and how misleading it can sometimes be to try and summarize. The reality is obviously much less coherent than I had presented it and I am glad that you have pointed out detailed responses to the different issues and questions. Thank you for taking so much time to discuss and report.

If the differences in view apply to other parts of the report I would be pleased if you would continue the discussions. I am trying to work to a fairly tight time restriction which is why I suggested a fortnight initially. But in view of the complexity I think we should extend it a little because I do not want to go ahead with anything which is misleading or does not accurately portray what people feel ...

I shall have to give some careful study to the detailed points you have made, particularly those on which people differed, to ensure that the different views are incorporated and that the Castle Manor which you say is not described in the present account gets a fair hearing. This will almost certainly mean rewriting, and may mean adopting a different framework.

I have noted carefully the additional points you raised especially over the use of quotations interspersed with commentary. You are right. The interview comments do not always fit easily with the commentary. ...

Thank you for pointing out the likely bias in the report. I certainly did not want to convey that I think a school which does not use Schools Council projects must be resisting innovation. My view is that adoption of projects is only one of a variety of ways in which schools might innovate and that when and how they do is the result of a whole complex of factors of local and historical origin — the staffing position, availability of resources, personal interests, pupil ability, growth of the school, local authority support, to name a few. I accept that local innovations may well be more relevant to a particular school's need and that while sometimes less visible than national projects which receive a lot of publicity, they are no less important. However, despite what I say, if you think a bias comes through in the report to the contrary, I must look closely again with a view to changing the tone or emphasis.

It may be easier to discuss the rationale of the enquiry in detail in person when I can answer individual queries. But I can make a start here ...

The next page of the letter details the assumptions of the SAFARI study, the need to understand the use of projects in the social and historical contexts of particular schools, leading up to explaining the importance of the HOD's role in understanding the curriculum processes within their school. The letter continues:

... Finally explanations will fall short if they are not seen from the point of view of the teachers as well as the curriculum developers. It is for this reason that I am most concerned in this study to report your views and judgements. One of the reasons for the lack of sustained use of projects may be because developers have failed in the past to take account of how and why schools change, what teachers think, value and need and the conditions in which they work. The project teams may be working, in other words, on assumptions about teachers, pupils and schools which do not match with reality ...

In my discussions with you the projects have been the focus but, as you intimated, only a focus. I have asked how you view the whole question of change both within your subject and the school because it is your views on these broader questions that will be as helpful to future curriculum planning as precise comments on the projects themselves.

There had to be some limits to the study particularly when we are trying to work to a short time scale. It seemed logical to start with the projects and, in Castle Manor, with heads of departments in related subject areas since both the head and several heads of departments stressed the degree of autonomy heads of departments have to develop the curriculum including the spending of resources. If there had been more time and substantial innovations had been pointed out to me in other departments, I would have attempted to follow these up as well.

I hope this begins to answer your query about the rationale of the enquiry. If you wish to take up these or any other points I shall be happy to continue discussing them with you ... (Edited four-page letter, reply to HODs' comments on Report 6.)

Departmental comments on Report 4 were still outstanding. The day before sending the reply to the Group Report I, had written to the HOD 4 enclosing a redrafted Report 4 taking account of his comments and requesting that he take up the questions with his department. My letter indicated hesitancy at asking anything more of him as he was one of the six involved in the detailed reply I had just received on the Group Report. But I wanted to keep to the same process for all reports extending clearance to departments. This was now two-and-a-half months since my last visit to the school in May and the beginning of the school summer holidays.

There is now a gap in correspondence until the end of October, when I wrote to the Head to indicate that a visit I had been planning early in the autumn to discuss the final version of the case study had been delayed to take account of the 'encouraging response to some of the initial reports' but that I now wished to complete the case study by the end of the year. The letter asked if the school would welcome a further visit to discuss the progress of the study. I also wrote to the Deputy Head requesting clearance of some statements of his I wished to include in the final account. He replied a week later making a number of minor amendments on language, not content. On the last day of that month the HOD 4 replied to my July letter which he had received seven weeks before on his return to school after the holidays (ie, at the beginning of September) with a tape of comments first from him and secondly from other members of the department.

Final Visit

I then arranged a further visit to the school one day in December to discuss the redrafted reports, the structure of the final version of the case study and to pursue any questions staff had. I requested a further group meeting and time for discussion with individuals.

On the day of my visit I spoke to all participants with the exception of the 'lead' HOD who chaired the HOD group meetings to discuss Report 6. He was not in the school that day. By the end of the visit Reports 1, 3 and 4 had been finally cleared departmentally, and the Head's Report had been cleared. All that remained to pursue was the Group Report and Report 2.

The day after my visit I wrote to the 'lead' HOD putting him in the picture and seeking any further comments on the group report. The letter outlined the structure of the final version of the case study, sought his comments on whether HODs would want to be identified or anonymized in a study that went outside the school (raising the relevant issues which impinge on this dilemma), and asked if it would be possible to hold a further group meeting to comment, however quickly, on the other issues raised in Report 6, from page 3 onwards. I also wrote to the other HODs likewise.

That same day I received a letter from HOD 1 asking me again to exercise caution over the use of his forthright remarks, intimating that he had paid insufficient attention to internal politics, and seeking to put on record the beginnings of a new project but with a modified reason for its lack of success rather than the one he had offered the day before. He did not wish to retract the information, rather to have it expressed more moderately or in terms of a question rather than by direct attribution. The letter concluded:

> I am sorry if I seem not to have the courage of my convictions but recent events lead me to believe that peace of mind at Castle Manor depends upon moderation.

I replied as follows:

> Thank you for your letter immediately after my last visit to Castle Manor. I have noted the point you made about the (new) course and will modify the account accordingly. I had decided in fact that catastrophe was perhaps too strong a word and that it might be preferable to say something like 'the course did not work too well with this group of pupils'.
>
> I quite understand your concern not to imply that failure of one venture in the department lies with the school and will take the caution you suggest by raising the point indirectly through a question or series of questions. I appreciate your frankness in discussing the experience of the course and would like to assure you that I shall strive to present the experience in a way which will not revive internal dissension.

Five days later I sent the redrafted version of the first half of Report 2 for final comment. The HOD had yet to return the second half. One month later, now in the year following the year of the study, he replied still concerned about the expression of his views. Instead of amending the reported quotations he deleted those he thought were inaccurate and incoherent and rewrote his updated considered thoughts on the issues. His basic views, he claimed, were the same but his expression of them more coherent and complete.

Earlier that month (January) the lead participant I had selected to chair the group report meetings responded to my December letter requesting a further meeting, indicating that he had not been able to hold the meeing because of pressure of committee work, but he offered some further comments on the structure and content of the report. He left the question of anonymity to my discretion and requested that I take into account two further criteria in putting the final study together; the actual damage to the departments' future attempts to create change and the possibility of noncomprehension by outside readers.

I took this reply as an indication that the momentum for further discussion could not be maintained — at least in my absence — and in the following reply did not ask for more:

> ... Once again your comments are very helpful in furthering my understanding of the Castle Manor context. They reminded me particularly of the importance of individual differences in discussing events in Castle Manor. How people perceive the school, curriculum development, examinations, whatever, will depend, as you point out in several places, on the value position of the person making the judgement. It is a point I subscribe to strongly but one that does not always come across in writing. I am reminded that I should be careful about generalizing ...
>
> One of the assumptions I work on in presenting a case study is that different people come to understand the experience of others by relating it to a reality that is familiar to them. Hence it is important to present a range of perspectives and judgements. But one cannot, of course, foresee exactly how people will perceive these comments, and they may misinterpret. It is here, I think, that I have to exercise the restraint you ask me to consider in allowing for possible incomprehension.
>
> The second major point your comments emphasized is the ethos of individualism in Castle Manor which had not struck me quite so forcibly before ... the ethos is one of 'let individuals get on with the job'. At the same time this is set within a rhetoric of a community enterprise which implies all are working towards the same ends. Individuals who do not

share the objectives and values of the school as you have said, have difficulty pursuing their aims unless they compromise which may defeat their aims. Allowing people to pursue their own interests is a difficult policy to question on democratic grounds, yet it is one which does not encourage the corporate development needed to support innovation.

Once or twice you refer to remarks that you were not sure you actually made. In the instances you cite you did not actually make those comments.[3] Someone else did, but they were close to other comments you did make ...

I take the restraints you ask me to consider seriously and will try to present the issues in a way that will not prejudice the departments' future attempts to create change. This suggests that I should adopt the anonymity stance in places. It may also mean withholding some statements, reporting indirectly or raising questions from them. I respect your decision to act politically in Castle Manor and I think the way in which I report comments you have made should reflect this, even if it means saying a little less of the truth as you see it. There is no guarantee how others will interpret and I would rather err on the side of understatement than risk prejudicing your future either in or outside Castle Manor. (Edited two-page letter on criteria of relevance and fairness.)

It remained for me to complete the study. My time and year had run out. I only had one month free from other commitments to undertake this study. My full-time colleagues were not unaware that it had taken longer. It was now the year following the year designated for the study and I was engaged full-time on two other studies. Nevertheless, because of my interest in bringing the study to completion, I continued to correspond with the school for the clearance of reports.

Negotiations continued by post until October of the second year by which time Report 1 (drafted three times, the third time to include a section from the 2-i-C) had been cleared; Report 2 (drafted three times) had been cleared and declared a 'reasonable and very fair picture'; Report 3 (drafted four times) had been cleared; Report 4 (drafted three times) had been cleared; and the Head's Report (Report 5) drafted three times had been cleared. The only outstanding report to be rewritten was the Group Report to take account of the extensive comments made by the six HODs. It only remained for this to be completed and the whole case study integrated. This was the point at which work with the school ceased. It was with some regret that it had to be left at this point as the process in many respects had just begun, but time had run out. I had started something I could not finish. This book is an attempt to work out the implications. The process begins in the next chapter.

Notes

1 In fact in the course of my study two other studies were made of the school, one by a television company, the other by a university. Both made films of the school, the first on the same two days of my first visit; the second the two days prior to my last visit.
2 Report 3 had to be cleared with three HODs who had used project materials and a college lecturer who had once taught the project in the school.
3 The comments he refers to were not attributed to him or anyone else in the Group Report. This raises a familiar problem with anonymization — how to prevent people attributing comments to themselves or to others they did not in fact make and raising unnecessary anxieties. Anonymity may not always be the most appropriate way to offer individuals assurance or to confer protection.

5 Losing Control: Reflections on the Case

Although it did not seem so at the time, when I look back on my study of Castle Manor it seems a very small step in the direction of democracy. It operated totally within the hierarchy of a traditional school, and in this sense was more 'bureaucratic' than democratic in terms of the typology. Participant control, and to a considerable extent participation itself, was largely confined to managerial levels of the institution, and further extensions of involvement left to the discretion of senior staff.

But I remind myself, and the reader, that this was an experiment, a tentative exploration in the transfer of responsibility from outsider to insider, a test case to see what the problem structure of such an aspiration might look like. I don't mean by this that there was no real intention to publish the cases, because clearly there was, both on my part and on the part of the SAFARI team. But the fact that the substantive goal of the study and commitment to the sponsor was to be met by the publication of a book (MacDonald and Walker, 1976) meant that case workers had a licence within the remaining time span and resources of the project, to take a chance with further studies that might not reach the public. This was known to the case study workers — Stenhouse, Elliott, Walker and myself before we began. When in practice it seemed important to pursue the participatory process, it was not difficult to accord the external product a subordinate status. The case study of Castle Manor in fact was never formally published or disseminated.

Technically the study was difficult to accomplish as it aspired to operationalize and manage several conflicts of principle that were manifest particularly sharply in the time scale prescribed for the research. By the end of the study I had come to the conclusion that democratic case study was simply incompatible with short time-scales. Only later with hindsight and the experience of conducting other evaluation studies using these principles did I come to a working resolution of this conflict, a resolution responsive to the circumstances of each case.

Negotiation, Condensed Fieldwork and Short Time Scales

What the study revealed was just how time-consuming the process of individualized stage-by-stage negotiation is. With ten teachers involved, the number of key participants in this study, it was soon evident that it would take at least four days to negotiate reports at one stage in a process of gradually making reports publicly accessible. Within the seven-day field restriction the time available for personal negotiation was quite insufficient.

In looking at the logistics of the exercise it is important to keep in mind the unfamiliarity and uncertainty that attended each stage. Although it took the participants a long time to see some of the fundamental implications of the logic of the process, and even longer for some of them to begin to actively engage in shaping the product, they were quickly aware of certain consequences. Even at the first stage they were aware that in some sense that the reports 'represented' them as individual thinkers — as historians of their own departments, as theorists of curriculum decision-making, as practitioners whose competence was at stake in such representations. I am not suggesting that their consciousness was articulated in such clear terms, but that it was embryonic. It was only with time, and with my persistent refusal to defend my interpretations in the face of their criticisms, that a transition was effected in their definitions of the situation. The transition was from a definition in which I was responsible for the representation of their views and experience, with them playing a validation role, to one in which they took primary responsibility for the generation and validity of interpretation, with me playing a comparative, synthesizing and responsive role. Such a change, to even the limited extent of its achievement at Castle Manor, inevitably stretched the time-scale.

One must also add that schools are not presently constructed to facilitate this kind of engagement on the part of staff. Timetables make clear that teacher-pupil contact is the teacher's job, and that the notion of the reflective practitioner, if it is to be pursued within the daily five hours of required presence, must be pursued in the limited space available, or by special ad hoc arrangements. Even at the managerial levels of the school, where direct teaching is less all-consuming, the task of curriculum maintenance is a demanding one.

The initial response of participant teachers in this study followed a pattern that has since become familiar. They had no experience of seeing their spoken language in print, of their judgments, memories, curriculum views represented in transcribed form, as an identifiable artefact of a conversation, intended eventually for public reading. Their first concern was to improve their syntax, to render the spoken in more of an essay form suitable for a written report. Their second concern was to polish, rather than develop their positions with respect to the various issues raised, to correct the content. Some were more anxious than others, a few were surprised and impressed with the articulateness of what they had said. I was aware, however, that in many ways the exercise was seen as a one-off rather than as a process of development. The information resource that had been generated was governed by protocols of politeness, of respectability, of prudent self-defence. At this stage, as at all stages of negotiation, the participants had anxieties about sharing their accounts with others in the school, about the implications of such a process for the deprivatization of professional knowledge and values within the institution. This was a stronger anxiety than the prospect, at the end, of publication beyond the boundaries of the school. This is a point, as I have said in an earlier chapter, to be borne in mind by those who see anonymization of case studies as a solution to the obligation to protect participants in case study research from the consequences that might follow identification.

These concerns of participants at the early stage called for detailed negotiation of a point-by-point nature, with an emphasis on correction. Later in the study, when some of the participants began to see the study as an opportunity for internal, collaborative inquiry leading to new insights and a developing sophistication of perspectives, the negotiation problem changed. Then it became a problem not of stimulating this kind of activity, but of containing it. I was tempted at times to shift to an autocratic concept of control in order to foreclose on a study over which I had lost even administrative control. The participants were enthused, and wanted to go on. They had, in effect, taken control of the inquiry and reconstructed it to meet their own needs and interests.

Indirectly, this shortage of time for negotiation adds weight to the arguments of some critics (see, for instance, Jenkins, 1980) who suggest that negotiation gives all the power to the researcher who wants something out of the negotiation process. Unless participants have genuinely entered into the spirit of the research as a partnership, they do not start from the same basis. They need time to experience what participation or 'shared responsibility' means especially in the host-visitor context where desire to please can lead too readily to acceptance of the researcher's interpretations. This was not so in the case of Castle Manor. With one exception participants took the time they thought that they needed within reasonable administrative deadlines for the conduct of the study.

One further constraint on time in negotiation is the repetition of procedures that is necessary. Given the short time-scales, the procedures were invoked to some extent to replace the time required to build up trust that long term studies rely upon (Walker, 1974b, p. 86). They could not replace it, however. Time was still needed to demonstrate what the procedures meant. The rationale and procedures were discussed and received consent at the beginning, but their implications for practice were not fully understood. In the breach of confidentiality incident, for instance, the Head had to be reminded of the procedures and the Deputy Head that he had forgotten them.

Negotiation by Post

Aspiring to keep to the deadline of seven days in the field, I tried to negotiate by post. This was not an altogether satisfactory solution although it did generate much discussion and possibly gave the teachers a freer hand to explore the issues in my absence. They did not have to please — always a worry in interviewing or personal negotiation situations and exacerbated by the politeness of the host-visitor situation. They could always dismiss my interpretations without appearing to be impolite. Negotiation by post, however, is no less time-consuming than negotiating in person. And it has further disadvantages, the main one being loss of administrative control. You cannot pre-determine how long it might take staff to get together to discuss reports or what might be demanded in return. In Castle Manor staff more or less kept to the suggested deadline for return of comments but the issues they raised stretched my deadline. The letter, for instance, from the Heads of Department raised a host of complex points on which different heads disagreed. Having asked for the response I had a responsibility to take account of the differences in rewriting the report. But the dilemma I was faced with at this point was whether to encourage teachers to continue or to foreclose the discussion in the interests of completing the study. This raised the critical question: are these aspirations compatible in practice? The evidence from Castle Manor suggests that they are not.

Participant Control and Public Clearance

What the study also revealed was that giving control to participants is a much more complex process than gaining clearance. Clearance can be accomplished in a relatively short time, often does not entail negotiation — permission to use data is simply sought and right of reply sometimes offered. It is facilitated by the authoritative role customarily granted the researcher and his/her interpretations and, in naturalistic research, by the interpersonal dimension of participant observation and interviewing. While at best this can lead to open and honest negotiation of data with participants, it can also mean that the researcher's personal skills and personality can dominate to get clearance of data that suits the researcher's purpose but which the interviewee would really prefer to keep private. The authority, status, personal skills and time constraints in which researchers and evaluators work exerts pressure for clearance. Moreover, reports prepared by 'experts' are often perceived to be a fait accompli, not open to negotiation (see MacDonald, 1976).

Practically all of the above points are contrary to the logic of giving control to participants. To genuinely meet this aspiration, the outsider has to de-emphasize her research skills and curriculum knowledge to encourage individuals to *actually take control* over data. She must also ensure that the time constraints do not prevent adequate and careful negotiation with participants. The right to 'own the facts of their lives' (Walker and MacDonald, 1975) must mean the right to say no to the use of private and personalized data for publication. People can only effectively exercise that right if they have access to the data, time to consider it, freedom from pressure and a context in which to judge.

The essential issue here again is one of time. Ideally giving participants control over their data means giving them access to the raw data the researcher has so that they can check selective reporting, decide what to restrict and check that subsequently released data is not used out of context. This means more than seeking permission on site for the subsequent use of interview data or offering duplicate tape-recordings or transcripts of their interviews — two procedures adopted by SAFARI case study workers. Control cannot be assumed unless the person interviewed has listened to the tape-recording or read the transcript and considered the content. The researcher has to spend time conferring with the person over the use of the material, discussing the implications of comments, even pointing out prudential considerations.

To meet the control aspiration, in summary, participants need to know the *context* in which data will be presented in order to make judgments in their best interests. It may be, for instance, politically expedient for participants to withhold certain views from the rest of the staff so as not to prejudice productive relationships. But it may be difficult to make judgments of this kind without knowing how other participants are responding to the balance of risks and responsibilities. There was some evidence of this at Castle Manor. Once or twice participants asked that observations negotiated in individual reports, then included in the group report, be modified, though one has to keep in mind here as well that the closer negotiation got to final clearance the more nervous participants may have become.

The question arises, in relation to a context in which participants have full access to the study, what is the role of the case study worker? Is it to represent the outside world, the public 'right to know'? Is it to support and encourage the school to ask its own questions? Yes it is both of these things, but it is something more, which takes us back to the democratic broker role. Schools are hierarchical organizations, institutional contexts of command, despite the fact that many of them have a collegial rhetoric and a strong sense of community. Without the external broker the conduct of the inquiry is likely to assume a form consonant with the school's power relationships and management prerogatives. It is the responsibility of the case study worker to negotiate rules of procedure which impose a more egalitarian structure of participation for the generation of shared knowledge, and to provide conditions in which individuals at different levels of the hierarchy can generate knowledge under protected conditions and make considered judgments about its release through a process of graduated reciprocity. We have seen in Castle Manor how easy it was for individuals to resort to internal traditions of management in the school in certain circumstances.

The issue is a profound one for the future of school-based self evaluation, and I deal with its implications at some length in chapter 9. At this point I content myself by observing that, if this was a problem in the context of a school like Castle Manor where participation was largely restricted to three levels of the hierarchy, how much more of a problem is faced in studies where participation is more comprehensive, transgressing boundaries between teachers, students, parents, and others who may be defined within the boundaries of the case?

The SAFARI School Case Studies — Other Views

There were four studies and four case study workers. I have given an account of my own, and some indication of its strengths and weaknesses. Only one of the four studies was published, that of Rob Walker, which was completed and disseminated within the time-scale. John Elliott completed his study but ran into irresolvable problems in trying to negotiate its dissemination. Lawrence Stenhouse was forced by illness to hand over his incomplete study to Richard Pring. Later a disagreement between Stenhouse and Pring about either the conduct or ownership of the study (I cannot recall which) led to its premature demise. There was a sense in which the LEA study (of which these studies were part) ran into the ground, or petered out. No doubt this was in good part due to intrinsic difficulties to which I have already referred. No doubt also that a contributory factor was the heavy involvement of the SAFARI Director who was supposedly coordinating the studies, in managing the contentious UNCAL evaluation which, as I indicated in chapter 2, was locked in battle with its sponsors. And no doubt that the departure of Rob Walker in 1976 for the USA to undertake two of the case studies in Stake and Easley's (1978) 'Case studies in science education' Programme, left SAFARI short of central manpower in the later stages of the school studies. For all these, and probably other reasons, the individual case workers were left in the end to make the best of the enterprise.

It is interesting to see what others made of the experience. Both Walker and Elliott have written about their reactions. Stenhouse did not, or at least not directly, nor did Pring, although both wrote subsequently about issues rooted in the case study approach (see Pring and Stenhouse in Adelman, 1984). For Stenhouse the SAFARI involvement was his first experience of case study, an approach of which he had earlier been sceptical in the context of the Humanities Project Evaluation. Characteristically, he adopted from the outset his own approach, eschewing confidentiality and dealing only in 'on-the-record' data to produce a public account. Whilst accepting the goal of producing an account which represented the school's view of curriculum development, he did not accept the need to enter into the politics of institutional life, and certainly did not share his colleague

MacDonald's interest in the motivation of educational actors. I hesitate to say more, since I am relying even for these observations on recalling meetings of the SAFARI team at which the approaches of each of the case study workers were discussed. However, my recall does seem consistent with Stenhouse's later writings on case records (Stenhouse, 1977 and 1978).

In Walker's (1986) recent account of his experience of conducting his SAFARI case study, I note some similarities to the problems I experienced in Castle Manor. Like me, he spent an initial three days in the school mainly tape-recording interviews with teachers, then returned to the University and spent several weeks writing up a first draft of a case study. Unlike me he did not write multiple reports. Aware of the difficulty of condensing the interview material, the problems of editing, not to mention his 'penchant for dramatic reconstruction' (p. 107) and the difficulty for the subjects to have any control over this, he duplicated all the tapes and left copies with each of the subjects. As he left the school at the end of the three-day field visit, he said:

> I am taking away with me no more than I have left with you. We have equal access to the data. If you are unhappy with what I write for whatever reason, if you think I have misquoted you, misunderstood or misrepresented you, you and I can both return to the tapes to check what has happened and to correct it. (p. 107)

He also added that he thought it important they they each keep the tapes to themselves, even if they felt happy to share their tapes with their colleagues. 'I would not want a situation to arise where someone who wanted to suppress what they had said found it difficult to resist staff-room pressure to pre-release the data. Everybody accepted this as reasonable and agreed to wait until the written reports were available' (p. 107).

His description of what happened on his return to school strongly accords with aspects of my experience:

> When I returned to the school some four weeks later I knew something was wrong. People who had been friendly during the earlier visit ignored me or paid me the minimum of attention. When I started to show people the written reports they were off-hand and dismissive. They did not seem to want to know anything about them. I was puzzled, but by mid-morning the story broke. One of the teachers took me

on one side and told me that immediately after my previous visit the head had asked each of them to hand over their tapes. Some refused but eventually gave in. Within a few days the Head had all the tapes but one, and locked them in his office.

My response was one of disbelief, followed quickly by confusion. What should I do? Should I confront the Head and demand an explanation? Should I wait and see what happened, pretending I didn't know? How could I best rescue the study? Later that day I managed to talk to the Head, and to let him know that I knew what had happened without actually confronting him with a sense of anger or disappointment. His explanation was a good one. He had been the last person I had interviewed during the previous visit. He claimed it was only when I talked to him that he realized some of the implications of the questions I had asked other teachers. While he did not object to being asked such things he realized that the total set of the data was potentially explosive. 'But I had promised you I would not show it to anyone until you had a chance to see it, as individuals and as a school', I protested. 'I think I trust you', he said, 'but I am not sure I trust everyone else involved'. The way he saw it there were teachers who might get together and share their tapes and find ways of using them that were not in what he saw as the interest of the school. As Head, he did not feel he could take the risk of having such information loose in the school while I was 'away in the university'. If something went wrong, he argued, he had to be in control of the situation. If information was leaked to the local press or to the office, he had to know what was happening. He realized he had broken the procedures of the research, but claimed that he had a greater responsibility for the running of the school, which overrode any agreements he might have with me. (pp. 107–8)

Walker comments:

It was a direct collision between the 'democratic' model built-in to the design of the research, and a bureaucratic model built-in to the organization of the school. It caused me some anguish and loss of sleep. I recovered the situation enough to be able to complete the study. I don't think that any of the teachers suffered as a result of what happened or the school was in any way changed by the events I had precipitated, though whether the school let any later re-

searchers through the door I don't know. I certainly haven't
left any tapes behind anywhere since. (p. 108)

Walker does not describe how he recovered the situation, although
the fact that he completed and published the study suggests that he
was able to repair the damage. What his experience reinforces in my
own is the importance of the external broker in studies of this kind to
sustain the opportunities for individuals to take their own risks while
working towards a public account. While meeting one democratic
aspiration of giving participants equal access to the raw data, he had,
inadvertently, and at the same time, made them vulnerable to the
power structure of the school.

Later in this same paper Walker writes of the conservatism of
case studies in describing practice. 'Once fixed, the case study
changes little, but the situations and the people caught in it have
moved even before the image is available' (p. 113). He cites the
example of having worked hard to portray the state of a number of
curriculum issues in a school, only to be told by the school at the fifth
draft of the report, 'You've got it. That is right. That is an accurate
account of the way things were a year ago. But since then everything
has changed!' (p. 114). In this sense he is clearly using the term
'conservative' to mean 'out-of-date', and in this sense I would agree
that published accounts are always out-of-date. At the same time it
does appear from his last comment that he used the time available to
try to improve his initial account of the school, rather than as a
stimulus to development, as I did. This does tend to suggest that the
SAFARI case study workers were operating with differing interpretations of what the research was essentially about.

Walker's closing comments I find slightly surprising, in view of
the fact that SAFARI was avowedly based on the democratic model
of evaluation. He suggests that future case study research be designed
'such that those with power over the lives of others included in the
scope of the study are required by design to see the nature of their
responsibilities. In particular, to design studies that give those at
different levels of the system equal access to, and control over, the
resources that the research provides' (p. 115). Since this precisely
describes the function of the principles and procedures derived from
the democratic model, and tested by the SAFARI case studies, I can
only assume that by using the word 'required' in this suggestion,
Walker is implying the need for a formal contract of some kind that is
binding upon participants.

While Walker's experience of case study leads towards more

secure controls for the exercise of participant rights, Elliott's experience leads him to more fundamental dissatisfaction with SAFARI's so-called 'ethics' and to advocate a more controlling and judgmental role for the evaluator (Elliott, 1977). In support of his arguments he cites some experiences:

1   some of my interviewees agreed to release interview data to other staff which retrospectively I feel may not have been in their interests as members of staff in the school and which I ought to have kept confidential in spite of their willingness after 'negotiation' to release it.
2   one of my interviewees gave me confidential information which suggested that certain constraints were limiting her freedom to exercise her responsibilities to others within the school. I felt it was in her interests that this information should be released to other staff as soon as possible.

In other words I found myself intuitively making assessments about whether the others had the right to know and whether interviewees had the right to privacy. I realised that I was operating intuitively with certain criteria of information misuse; criteria which MacDonald claims the evaluator should not possess. The fact that SAFARI procedures as I interpreted them restricted my control over use meant in practice that I had to deny my own intuitions. The inner conflict was intensified later by various letters from interviewees suggesting that the release of data I had negotiated between members of the interview group had resulted in harmful consequences for at least some members of that group. (pp. 199–200)

He goes on to argue that SAFARI is a case of 'moral schizophrenia' (p. 197). Participants cannot have the right to privacy and the public the right to know, with respect to the same data. Nor can judgments of private and public interest be left to participants. It is for the evaluator to judge what should be confined to the private domain and what should become public. Elliott makes an interesting distinction between 'educational evaluation', wherein the object is the sharing of knowledge among educational professionals, and 'social evaluation' which would address the public right to know. 'This means that the contents of a case study released for intra-professional inspection should differ from the contents of a case study released for public inspection' (p. 202). In Elliott's subsequent work, as noted in chapter 2, he goes further in questioning educational administrators' rights of access to self-studies carried out by school staffs (Elliott, J, 1981b).

I would counter, in response to this critique, that the SAFARI procedures, through the stage-by-stage negotiation, provide for participants to place limits on the circulation of reports, which could meet the distinction that Elliott posits between public knowledge and knowledge for fellow professionals. The problem I see in the evaluator judging what the public is entitled to know is precisely the problem in the autocratic tradition. It is surprising how often such 'objective' judgments prove to be rewarding for those who make them. Better surely, in a situation where participants will make varied and mutually exclusive judgments about what should be made known, to have a broker who negotiates an outcome that is seen to be reasonably fair to all interests. One point on which all case workers involved in these studies would agree is the unlikelihood of participant control leading to bland accounts. The problem, acutely experienced by Elliott but to some extent by all of us, is more often that of alerting participants to the consequences of the high risks entailed in their decisions. Despite this experience of case study evaluators Elliott goes on to argue that in a situation characterized by mutually exclusive rights the evaluator will inevitably push the 'right to know' and use her negotiating power to 'get the data out' (Elliott, 1977, p. 201). In my view there is no inevitability, though, as I mentioned earlier, it is important to guard against such a tendency deriving from accountability to the outside world. The democratic persuasion is a way of actualizing certain values. It can only serve those values if they are truly held and sustained in situations where there are difficulties and counter pressures, especially the pressure for visible products.

Walker, in his article referred to earlier, also expresses doubts about the use of 'confidentiality' in order to generate data where the intention is to produce public knowledge, and Jenkins has written a trenchant critique (Jenkins, 1980), to which both Walker and Elliott refer, of the joint principles of confidentiality and negotiation. Jenkins argues, in effect, that what this amounts to is a manipulative set of principles guaranteed to gain access by offerring confidentiality and then coerce release through negotiation. (It should be kept in mind that Jenkins' experience of using these principles was in the UNCAL evaluation which worked to a very tight reporting requirement. Nor did UNCAL give participants the degree of control over reports accorded in SAFARI [MacDonald *et al*, 1975].

I would not deny that the combination of principles can be used in this way, any more than a statistician would deny that some of her colleagues manipulate data analysis until they come up with a significant result. The principles are not proof against abuse. But I would come back to my earlier arguments about the educative potential of democratic evaluation. It may be that some case study inquirers see their educative role strongly in terms of advancing public knowledge. 'The right to know' is important, and many researchers have interpreted their public obligation as the duty to tell what they have been able to find out. Given this view, it would be shameful to use a false promise of confidentiality to gather data that might otherwise be withheld. But, as the theory of democratic evaluation makes clear, this is not the only 'right' at issue, and therefore not the only obligation involved.

From an educational point of view, and taking account of the respect for persons that is one of the 'liberal' values of the theory, there is an obligation to develop private knowledge on the part of participants, as well as of the case worker, that goes beyond what may be made public. This is surely what is meant by 'dissolving the line that conceptually and procedurally separates the objects of evaluation from its audiences' (see chapter 1, p. 28). The 'confidential' generation of data is not just a stage in the process of creating a public account. It is the means by which a personal knowledge resource is created and placed at the disposal of the participants, individually and collectively, which will be helpful to them in pursuing many different agendas. One of the common agenda items is the provision of a public account, for which the case study worker bears a greater responsibility than the participants. But I do not assume, either when I am interviewing teachers or when I am negotiating an account, that the only knowledge that matters is public knowledge, or even knowledge shared between people who work together in one place. Nor would I conclude, for instance in the case of Castle Manor, that because no public account emerged that no public benefit accrued. In democratic evaluation 'openness' is seen as a problematic value, a point not understood either by Elliott (1977) or by Pring (1984) both of whom argue that it is an overriding value of the model. Those who see the joint principles of confidentiality and negotiation as cynical manipulation for the purpose of public reporting have, in my view, failed to grasp the complex set of obligations entailed in democratic case study as an educational form of inquiry.

Guidelines for Designing a Democratic Case Study of a School

The SAFARI case studies were carried out in the mid-seventies. It is a long time ago in terms of the development of a literature of case studies in educational settings, a literature of both exemplars and theoretic exposition. Novice practitioners now have available an extensive body of articulated experience, from a range of perspectives, including naturalistic evaluation and research, ethnography, and critical sociology, on which to draw (see, for example, Reid and Walker, 1975; Burgess, 1984a and 1984b; Simons, 1980a; Stake and Easley, 1978; Norris, 1977; Hammersley and Hargreaves, 1983. See also Burgess (1985a) for a useful bibliography of qualitative methodology and empirical studies).

This literature is replete with cautionary tales, problem definitions and advice. There is, of course, also a longer lineage of experience and theory, mainly from sociology, social psychology and anthropology, to which I have already referred. But in these closing comments on school case study, closing in the sense of referring to this particular stage of my experience, my suggestions are related to case studies of schools, initiated and conducted by outsiders, within the democratic 'persuasion'. Stake's distinction between persuasion and model, raised earlier in the book (see chapter 1, note 3), is important in this context. I am not offering a prescription for the precise conduct of a democratic case study, but rather offering a general outline of how to go about it, what important things have to be attended to and in some cases how some difficult problems may be overcome. In offering this outline I am taking account of subsequent experience as well as the experience recounted in the previous chapter.

1 Agree at the outset a contract with the school which is fair to and binding upon all parties, but renegotiable in the light of unanticipated difficulties on either side. The agreement should specify rights, obligations and time-scales. (Try to make sure that the school creates 'reflective' time, built into the timetable for collective discussion of reports).

2 Emphasize the utility of the study to the school and be guided initially by their interests and aspirations.

3 Limit direct data-gathering to a few days (condensed field-work) but allow a lengthy period for the completion of the

139

study (perhaps one year, longer if your contract with the funding body or other commitments permit).

4   Carry out fieldwork early, and report back quickly. (For one day in the field allow one week writing up). Reports are the stimulus, not the end product. The task thereafter is to encourage and develop responses to report/s, to extend the agenda by representing external audience interests, to construct stage reports reflecting the developing inquiry. (Keep intial reports short — 8–10 pages — open in interpretation, questioning, and inviting response).

5   Maintain responsibility for managing the conduct of the inquiry according to agreed democratic principles of participation and access which must involve a suspension of power-based relationships within the institution. Ensure that the sharing of knowledge within the school respects the rights of individuals to decide for themselves at all stages the level of risk they are willing to take. The shift from private to shared knowledge within the institution will have to be carefully graduated.

6   Allow sufficient time (two to three weeks perhaps) for participants to respond to reports but keep to the deadlines established at the outset for movement from one phase to the next.

7   Allow for the time needed by the case worker to increase continuously throughout the study (ideally a shift from part-time to in the end a full-time commitment).

8   When the study reaches a stage where circulation beyond the school is the prime consideration take account of the fact that the hierarchy of vulnerability to consequence changes to reflect contractual and public views of responsibility for the work of the school.

9   Be prepared to cope with threats to the time-scale, shifts in interest and purpose, unanticipated consequences of the spread of responsibility. Democratic case study is about managing a balance between empowering those within the case and empowering those outside who are entitled to know what is going on.

6   *The Right to Know: A Dispute about the Dissemination of an Evaluation Report*

Introduction

Two years later I began an evaluation commission which was to profoundly reveal to me the problems of carrying out the democratic evaluation role in situations where administrators are in the front line of public accountability. The context was very different from Castle Manor, in which my prime concern had been to find ways of reducing the authority of the social scientist in order to stimulate and empower teachers in the study of their work. The new context took me back into the world of programme evaluation, but within a new scenario. In the late seventies the European Commission (EC), based in Brussels, launched two major, policy-related, Community-wide educational programmes. One was the 'Transition from education to working life' programme (for which Stake was the consultant evaluator and MacDonald the meta-evaluator) and the other was the 'Migrant education' programme. My evaluation assignment concerned a pilot project in this latter programme, a project concerned to provide mother tongue teaching to Italian and Asian children in one local education authority (LEA) in England. The LEA was funded directly from Brussels, initially for three years, and it was a requirement for further funding that the LEA commission an external evaluation of the project. The LEA (meaning the executive rather than elected officials) approached their local institute and contracted with them to sub-contract a part-time evaluator. The institute invited me (I was known to them although not on their staff) to undertake the evaluation commission. I did, and the result was one of the most harrowing experiences of my research life. When the project funding was continued for a fourth year I declined to continue, and the evaluation was picked up by a national research agency.

For reasons which will become clear by the end of this account, which itself does not name the institutions involved, let me state now that the LEA was Bedfordshire, the institute was the Cambridge Institute of Education, and the national agency the National Foundation for Educational Research. The evaluation reports referred to in the text are available from the Cambridge Institute to 'bona fide' enquirers. This curious stipulation will be explained in the course of the account, which basically is the story of how a local authority attempted to save itself from possible embarrassment by blocking the circulation of an evaluation report. For those who believe that the 'right to know' is in safe hands, I hope the story is educative.

Setting Up the Evaluation

I was appointed late in the project when it had been underway in fact for more than a year. The appointment was for the remainder of the project's life — at that time twenty months. The evaluation was part-time, one day a week of my time with minimal secretarial help, for eighteen months, five terms of the school year. This was nearly three times as much as that allocated for the Castle Manor study but it had to stretch further over several institutions (there were six schools involved) and several levels of decision-making. I was based in London, some seventy miles from the project site and some seventy miles also from the Institute which provided secretarial help.

There was, crucially, no formal contract, only a letter recording the administrative and financial arrangements between myself, the Institute and the LEA. This letter did, however, state that the Institute would retain copyright of the two evaluation reports I was expected to write. The project was exploring a controversial area and both the Institute and I thought it necessary to assert academic control over the evaluation from the outset. Early English reaction to the EC's policy in this controversial area had not been favourable.

At the same time I took the further step of asking an experienced evaluation colleague to act as consultant adviser for the period of the assignment. Why did I take this step? Well, this was 1978, not 1975. By this time those who had conducted case study evaluations were much more aware of the need to protect such evaluations against threats to their independence of action, particularly in bureaucratic contexts (see Norris, 1977). Principles and procedures for the conduct of such evaluations were beginning to supplement trust and assumption as the basis of conduct. UNCAL had ended; the 'Case studies in science education' Project (Stake and Easley, 1978) was underway in the USA; Adelman was reporting bureaucratic constraints in his institutional evaluation (Adelman, 1979); and the EC initiatives brought into play a new structure of responsibility for innovation. The sponsor was now Europe's largest bureaucracy, the developer for the first time an educational administration. This meant that, in terms of 'telling the story' of the project the LEA officials were unambiguously within the boundary of the case. It did not take a great deal of prescience to anticipate the possibility that a part-time evaluator, working alone on such a story, might at some point need back-up support.

Following a preliminary discussion with the two LEA officials most concerned with the project (a specialist adviser and senior administrator) and before accepting the assignment, I wrote a two-page statement[1] summarizing the approach, purposes and aims of the evaluation. I thought this was important for two reasons, first because the two officials seemed so anxious to secure the evaluation, and secondly, because they declared that they wanted precisely the kind of evaluation I outlined. I was not confident that they fully understood its scope and limitations. I also tried at the preliminary meeting to detail the precise procedures by which the flow of information would be guided.

The principles and procedures of the evaluation were an extension of the procedures adopted in the Castle Manor study and shared the same underlying value structure, but they were modified slightly to take account of the different power structure. Independence, for instance, was underlined to protect the interests of all groups within and beyond the project; negotiation remained a central principle although the wording was changed to consultation to reflect the commitment to negotiate data but nevertheless retain control over the evaluation process; and impartiality was added to secure the credibility and independence of the evaluation in a context where understanding of criteria governing the validity of evaluations could not be assumed.

The LEA officials showed little interest in these principles and procedures. My field notes recall that I thought the evaluation was being treated more as an administrative requirement than a resource to inform policy. The statement was forwarded to the Institute and the LEA and subsequently discussed at a meeting with project personnel, heads of schools involved in the project and LEA officials, at which I offered to discuss its implications. It was accepted without question.

Data Search, Collation and Negotiation

During the next nine months I gradually traced the development of the project and documented its early experience through interviewing key personnel at LEA, project and school level, observing project meetings on and off site (at the LEA's office as distinct from the development project's headquarters) and studying documents relevant to the setting up and development of the project.

Antecedents as Stake (1967b) has emphasized are as important in an evaluation as the transactions and outcomes. Since early difficulties had been signposted (in a preliminary report commissioned by the Institute the year before) it seemed crucial to revisit this period of the programme to trace the background which might offer explanations for the way the programme evolved. This I did concurrent with observations of the programme in action. My preference was to study the prehistory first, but the context required concurrent action. It seemed important to be visible early on to the development team to secure their cooperation and establish credibility of the evaluation (they had the biggest development role and were potentially most at risk in the evaluation). I also wanted to demonstrate the impartiality and independence of the evaluation from the LEA (County Hall) office where the early documents were kept.

Access to both people and documents was negotiated and individuals were told at the time they would have the opportunity to check the fairness, accuracy and relevance of any information that was attributed to them if it was utilized in the evaluation report. The exact procedures followed and the step-by-step process of clearance, discussed at each stage, are detailed in later sections of this case study.

The first nine months were characterized by prolonged conflict, of people and ideas, within the case. Much of this conflict was concerned with managerial rather than classroom decision-making and was not unrelated to early and ill-judged administrative decisions concerning appointments to the development team, roles and responsibilities. The appointment for instance of a teacher of Hindi before the LEA discovered that the majority of the Asian pupils in their schools came from Punjabi-speaking families, may give an indication of early problems.

Examples of some of these conflicts are detailed in the evaluation report. Others were too personal to record even though considered relevant, in the view of both participants and myself, to the precise way in which the programme evolved and the difficulties it encountered. Several of the conflicts related to the hierarchical management structure which became increasingly demanding (with sometimes contrary requests from the two officials in charge of the management of the project), as requests for substantive evidence of accomplishment came from the EC. (Project funding was on a year-by-year basis, so that at least in theory it could be terminated at almost any point).

It was in studying the early documents at County Hall, of which there were three complete files incorporating sixty to seventy items each (letters, policy statements, reports and memos), that I came across the first indication that the kind of evaluation I was pursuing was not the kind sought by the EC, though it had been endorsed by the LEA which commissioned the evaluation.

A letter from a senior official in Brussels indicated dissatisfaction with the 'vagueness' of my outline evaluation plan and suggested that it should be revised straight away 'to secure as much *systematic* feedback as possible from the second year of the programme'. The letter clearly put the onus on the LEA to make more appropriate arrangements for the evaluation. This was only two months after I had been appointed.

It was not clear precisely what was meant by 'systematic' here, though it may have meant testing of pupil performance, as this was being conducted in other countries where there were pilot projects. I had excluded testing from the evaluation for the following reasons: the difficulty, given the late start, of establishing a baseline; lack of appropriate tests; my lack of appropriate linguistic background. Also I was not in a position to undertake more systematic feedback in view of the distance from the programme and the part-time nature of the evaluation. On the positive side, of course, I argued that such a focalized evaluation would be inappropriate, particularly in a pilot project (and one that was contentious) when there was a need to learn as much as possible about all aspects of the innovation and its context of implementation. It therefore fell to the LEA to meet this need for 'systematic feedback'. Internal evaluation, also an EC requirement, became more imperative and may have led to some of the conflicts which arose.

Other conflicts related to personalities and, in some instances, skills. Where managerial demands were intensified by personality conflicts within the development team and between individuals in it and the LEA officials, the programme and the evaluation was at its most vulnerable and political. As the evaluator I was caught in the middle of these pressures, participants each putting forward their perspective of events more and more strongly in the hope of establishing their view as '*the*' view of the problem.

The notion of impartial reporting in this context was severely put to the test; that of 'impartial broker' in the exchange of information even more so. Negotiation of any data for the evaluation was prolonged as participants worked through their anger, anxieties and fears. Negotiation of disputed data as relevant for the public record was even more difficult and time consuming. One day a week was grossly inadequate. Many times I felt like giving up, initially as it became more and more difficult to cope procedurally with the internal stresses and grievances within the project and latterly as it became increasingly difficult to report the evaluation in the face of persistent attempts to contain it. But I felt bound to see the task through.

The first evaluation report (Simons, 1978–79) produced during this time was a narrative history of events leading up to the inception of the programme and early experience of it. Drawing on interviews with key personnel, observations of meetings and relevant documentation, it was structured around issues which either the evaluator or participants thought significant for informing policy. These included the organization of the project within the LEA and school curriculum, aims and expectations and lines of accountability and responsibility. No fact was reported that did not have at least two sources, no issue was signposted that was not identified as significant by more than three people and individuals had frequent opportunities to check the accuracy of the reportage.

This first evaluation report was considered accurate, relevant and fair by all key contributing personnel. It was also valid in the sense described by House (1980, p. 90) where facts and truths are accepted by everyone and inferences correctly derived from the data and impartial in the sense that it aspired to represent all interests in the evaluation and did not attribute blame. The validity of the evaluation report was subsequently strengthened by the identification and documentation of many of the same issues as significant in both the evaluation written by my successor (Tansley, 1981) and the EC's comparative evaluation (Boos-Nunning *et al*, 1983). When dissemination became a contentious issue, however, there was some indication that the LEA may have changed its mind and at that stage considered the report to be invalid. Particular audiences, of course, can perceive the report as invalid, even if the other criteria for validity are met, if it does not suit their particular purpose or use (House, 1980, pp. 90–1).

The Process of Clearance of the First Evaluation Report

By the eleventh month I began the process of clearance of the first report in preparation for a phased dissemination plan: first, to those most closely involved and clearly identifiable; (these were the development team and the two LEA officials, one a senior administrator, the other the specialist adviser); secondly, to those involved in the project but less identifiable (heads and classroom teachers); thirdly, to sponsors and other local schools and teachers not directly involved; and lastly, to other 'interested parties' beyond the immediate programme (the parents of the participating children, the local community, organizations concerned with migrant education, and the evaluation/research community).

The actual process of clearance involved several stages but essentially was based on the principle that those people most closely reported upon and most identifiable should have the opportunity to check their comments first individually and to amend or add to their statements on the criteria of fairness, accuracy and relevance. They should, secondly, have the opportunity to comment on the representation of those comments in the context of the whole report. These procedures took several months to work through, the LEA indicating in the fourteenth month, through a telephone call from a junior official (the third LEA official now involved) acting as intermediary between the LEA senior administrator and the development team, that they wished to prepare a statement for inclusion.

One month later they had changed their mind. Notification of this reversed decision was also relayed to me through the junior official who indicated, when I sought reasons for the decision, that what the LEA wanted to say was outside the scope of the report, that they thought the 'domestic detail' should be excised for wider circulation and that they assumed in any case that the LEA had copyright. This was not in fact the case. Apparently, what had precipitated the change was concern expressed by some teachers about the 'domestic detail' in the report at a project meeting the week before at which I was not present and at which the LEA had decided that the report would remain confidential to them. One of the development team commented after this meeting that the LEA had assumed that because *they had paid for the evaluation* they had copyright over the report.

A letter from a senior administrator which thanked me for the report was dated two days after the above cited meeting and one month after the report was sent. In the letter he effectively made two points. The first was that he, acting presumably on behalf of the LEA, had no specific comments to make at that stage, and 'since they could not be incorporated in the body of the report' he would prefer to delay them until the report could be discussed by the development team and heads at a meeting timetabled two months on (ie, three months after the report had been sent).

My suggested means for incorporating participants' responses to the complete report (to include responses where feasible as a footnote and, where not, on a separate page at the end of the report) was a function of the previous procedures and available resources. Each individual had already had two opportunities to clear individual comments and several changes in the text had been made. There was simply no secretarial help available to retype the report, at least not at the Institute level. Procedurally it could not be typed at County Hall as this would contravene the principle of independence and threaten the impartiality of the evaluation. Clearly, my intention here was to include any further comments, though it is possible that the LEA saw the format of the response as a chance to deny that opportunity was offered to comment further. Alternatively, they may have decided, in view of the assumptions of copyright presumed above, that they need not comment at all.

The second point related to dissemination. In view of the considerable amount of 'domestic detail' which the senior administrator argued would be of little interest to those outside the programme and therefore 'would not be appropriate for wider circulation', he sought my confirmation that it was not my intention to circulate the report more widely myself.

It was not clear to me in seeking confirmation of this point, whether the administration intended to circulate the report themselves, suitably excised perhaps as the junior official had intimated. The administrator's letter had indicated that they realized that the EC must be furnished with a copy of the evaluation report. If they were seeking assurance that I would not circulate the report, then who was left to meet this obligation to the EC? There was at least a possibility here that the LEA assumed it was their responsibility and, moreover, that they may have assumed editing rights over the report as well.

First Meeting to Negotiate the Evaluation Report (held at County Hall)

The meeting at which the evaluation report was to be discussed duly took place two months later, then the seventeenth month of the twenty-month period of evaluation. Present were the three LEA officials, heads of project schools, the development team and I. The meeting started at 10.00am and was timed to end at 12.00 noon. The evaluation report was last on the agenda before 'any other business'. At 11.30am approximately, the senior administrator who chaired the meeting asked me to introduce the report. Since they had all had the report for some time, presumably read it but had not responded to my request for critique, I said that I assumed they had found the report satisfactory and that we could now go ahead with circulation to other groups (ie, the fourth stage of the dissemination plan).

The senior administrator interrupted and asked what audiences I had in mind. I replied parents, local community groups, race-related organizations and the evaluation/research community. The senior administrator then said that he was not aware that other circulation was intended, that in fact they had settled the issue of confidentiality at the last meeting (in my absence they had decided that the report would be confined to the local groups because of the 'domestic detail'). I indicated that that would not be possible. The purpose of evaluation was to inform. Parents and the public had a 'right to know' what was happening to their children and public funds.

The senior administrator then asked who had the report and I outlined again the four-stage dissemination plan, emphasizing that I had given the major groups adequate time to respond and that the report was currently in its third stage of circulation. The adviser claimed that there had been too little time to comment as the report had arrived at half-term (due to a delay in the post). Taking that into account, plus the fact that the LEA had requested further time, I had extended the deadline for a fortnight and waited even further before circulating to the groups in the third stage. They had now had three months to comment and I had received no response.

Clearly the LEA officials, though not the teachers, were surprised that I raised further circulation. I, in turn, showed surprise that they had not recognized that the report would need to be circulated more widely — that was one reason, I explained, why the procedures had been so carefully followed. And I again sought their support for this next stage of dissemination to groups outside the project.

The senior administrator then said 'Well we are not going to discuss distribution now' and asked me if I would send him a list of the people to whom the report had already been sent and the groups to whom I intended to send it, and then we would discuss it further. I agreed to do this and asked if the others present would like to say something on this issue. But they had frozen. The administrator had decided not to discuss it further. Then, in strict administrative fashion, he moved straight to the report. 'Now, any comments on page 1?'

Very few comments were in fact made on the text in the little time left for discussion of it. Aware of the time factor and aware also that the tone engendered by the discussion of dissemination at the meeting may have prevented people, particularly the development team and heads, from speaking freely, I suggested that they take a further two weeks to respond if they chose. My final remarks assume that further circulation will take place. 'May I just assume then that if I do not hear or receive any further comments by two weeks from today you are happy for me to go ahead with further circulation of the report?' All agreed except the senior official who chaired the meeting.

Dispute over Dissemination

Immediately after the meeting the senior official asked me into his office and suggested that the report be restricted to the groups to whom it had already been circulated. In support of this recommendation he argued as follows. The LEA was not aware of the evaluator's intention to circulate the report more widely (though it had been indicated in the initial statement and reaffirmed in the letter accompanying the report). The LEA believed that control lay with them, not me. In any case not enough time had been allowed for them to respond to the report. They needed to know three months in advance, for instance, that a response would be sought. The usual convention of anonymity would be difficult to employ in this report and that was a further problem. They were concerned that wider circulation might raise disputes between individuals and/or raise political troubles with teachers who were operating on the understanding that the report would have restricted circulation.

My reply emphasized the following points. The evaluation was external and independent with a responsibility to inform those who had a 'right to know' about the issues and outcomes of a publicly-funded programme. Over the past few months key personnel had had ample opportunity to clarify, add to or amend their statements and had agreed that the report was a fair account of what had transpired. I had specific agreements about confidentiality and clearance with the teachers and officials which had been worked through particularly thoroughly taking into account the difficulty of anonymizing people.

The intention to disseminate to groups beyond the immediate programme was in the initial statement they had received. Finally, I said that the local political difficulties to which he had referred had nothing to do with the dissemination of the report.

Not wishing to be coopted or collusive in 'understanding' the local difficulties, but neither wishing to pursue further dissemination without participant support, I suggested a future meeting was necessary to resolve the issue. I also said I thought it appropriate to discuss the issue with my consultant, whom I would bring to the next meeting if that was acceptable to the LEA. No date could be found in the administrator's diary until approximately one month later, by then the eighteenth month of my twenty-month assignment.

In between these meetings I sent a letter detailing the precise dates on which the report had been sent, to which groups and the principles upon which this phased dissemination plan had been constructed. The letter also specified the groups to whom circulation was intended in the fourth dissemination phase, though it was emphasized that the details would be negotiated with the LEA. I said that resource help with circulation of reports might be needed from the LEA and that resource constraints might limit circulation to particular groups. The letter also expressed my intention to make two additions to the report — a postscript that would update events taking into account many of the issues raised in the report and an introduction alerting the reader to the problematic nature of innovation in education. I hoped to be able to say in the introduction that dissemination had the support of the main participants in the study. The letter concluded by seeking the LEA's help, in effect, in furthering understanding of the innovation process.

Second Meeting to Negotiate Dissemination of the Evaluation Report (held at County Hall)

Present were the senior and junior administrative officials, myself and my consultant. By the time this meeting was held the positions of both the LEA and I had hardened, and the meeting ended in impasse. The LEA administrator had been briefed by his chief (now the fourth LEA official to become involved) and argued a narrowly legalistic interpretation of the agreement while I, supported by my consultant, maintained the right to disseminate the report. I will try to summarize the main lines of contention.

The LEA presumed that the report would be available only to

local professional participants and sponsors whereas I assumed the right to report to 'interested parties', an evaluation goal specified in the initial statement of intent. Much of the dispute turned upon competing interpretations of the concept of 'interested parties', with the evaluators contending that even a parsimonious interpretation could not justifiably exclude those parents who had volunteered their children for the pilot project. But the LEA officials remained adamant that the report was not to be made available to parents.

But who had the right to decide this issue? The LEA assumed that the evaluator had provided a paid service on behalf of the Institute solely for the LEA paymasters. The evaluation took the view that 'you can sponsor an evaluation but not buy it' (see chapter 2, p. 48). A difference of understanding then emerged over the meaning of independence. The LEA held that independence meant independence of view, not of action, whereas the evaluation stressed it meant both. From 'independence' the dispute moved to 'confidentiality'. Suddenly the LEA officials revealed (belatedly and without evidence) that they had given an undertaking to the teachers at the outset of the project that their privacy would be respected and dissemination of any resultant reports would be restricted to protect and safeguard teachers' professionalism. This was odd. I had engaged in extensive confidentiality and clearance agreements with teachers on the understanding that the report would be more widely circulated. This was the first I had heard of the agreement between the LEA and the teachers. Had I known of it I would not have accepted the evaluation commission since it effectively undermined the very concept of an independent external evaluation. In any case it did not seem reasonable to invoke such an agreement now, given that the report had been cleared independently through extensive negotiations. I was seeking further dissemination to fulfil a basic and declared function of evaluation — to inform — and was offering to negotiate to whom specifically the report should be sent. But the LEA officials assumed this meant publication which they resisted absolutely. On no account would they countenance publication.

This very strong stance against publication may have to be seen in the light of some aspects of the local history of the project. For instance, early in the history of the project, it had at one point received a bad local press. It is possible that the LEA was trying to avoid a recurrence. Also, early in the time span of the project there had been difficulties between the development team and the LEA and, quite separate from the project, between the LEA and some teachers which had involved negotiations with teachers' unions.

Perhaps the LEA anticipated unfavourable union response if the report was published. Lastly, an aspect only revealed much later in the final negotiating meeting at which an agreement was reached, that the local councillors were not in touch with the programme and its difficulties.

Time was passing, patience wearing thin. The fact that the LEA had now had four months to comment while the report was held up received no acknowledgement from the LEA, nor did my offer to update events and locate the report within a sympathetic treatment of the problems of innovation. The central issue, in summary, was one of control over dissemination and the fact of the matter was that the prolongation of the dispute favoured those who were against dissemination. At no stage in the discussion was the fairness and accuracy of the report in dispute. The LEA negotiator (the first senior official to be involved) agreed that the account was a fair record of what happened. Failing to reach any resolution the suggestion was made that the Institute as main contractors be informed and invited to state where they stood on the issue. The senior official indicated that he had reason to believe that the Institute would support the LEA's view. I, on the other hand, assumed that the Institute would support the independence of the evaluation. They had, after all, taken out copyright to secure it (I had not raised this point at the meeting to avoid generating a further disagreement).

Immediately after the meeting I wrote extensive notes on the positions that each of the four people in the meeting had taken. These were effectively the same as those reported in the minutes of the meeting prepared by the junior official (though these were much less extensive) with one exception — the conclusion. On this, the minutes suggest a possible compromise, that the LEA, rather than resist absolutely any further dissemination, would agree to consider an anonymized version of the report which, '*if it received the consent of the LEA*', (my emphasis) would then be published by the evaluator: in this case the original report would not be published or further disseminated. In the meeting itself two conditions were cited: that written agreement for publication of such a form of the report be obtained from *all participants* and that the anonymized version receive *consent* from the Chief Education Officer (CEO).

This proposal, in fact, had been flatly rejected at the meeting by me on the grounds that it would be impossible for all personnel so closely involved in a programme to ever agree that the report was effectively anonymized. Neither was I confident, given the power relationships (employers and employees) that project and school personnel would be free to respond autonomously. Such an agreement *'if it received the consent of the LEA'* would also effectively mean that control over dissemination lay with the LEA. They could simply refuse to give consent.

What was agreed at the meeting was that a negotiated settlement would be a preferable resolution to the issue than unilateral action by either side, my consultant pointing out here that both sides had a lot to lose by non-dissemination: the LEA by being seen to suppress a report, the evaluation by being seen to be co-opted.

It is perhaps important to point out here that the senior LEA official (negotiator) in this meeting would not commit himself to any decisions, deferring to the CEO who was not present. He adopted an extremely formal line management position emphasizing both his accountability to his superior and to the schools. In other words, he was only carrying out his duty. The effect of this was to hold up negotiations and delay resolution.

The day after the meeting I wrote a memo to my consultant commenting upon the tone of the negotiations and raising a number of points that might prove useful in subsequent negotiations. I pointed out that it was the LEA, not me, who had pushed a hard line on the issue of publication. I commented that the LEA seemed to have an odd view of the professionalism of their teachers. Did teachers not have the right to decide what professional issues they wanted to discuss? I found it difficult to believe, I wrote, that the LEA could have expected me to subsume my report under their conditions of confidentiality; if I had, it would have meant that I was co-opted and that I could not have written the second independent report which was in fact almost entirely about teachers' views. I emphasized that my contract was not with the EC or with the LEA but with the Institute and, in less formal terms, with participating project personnel in terms of agreed purposes and procedures. The memo concluded by expressing concern about taking too entrenched a position in negotiations with the LEA — 'reacting strongly to publication in proportion to the degree to which they are resisting it' — and too strong a view on wider dissemination with the Institute as they carried the secretarial load 'and might be inclined to side with the LEA to keep down what might seem to them to be inordinate costs in broader circulation'.

Involvement of the Institute and the CEO

Following up the suggestion at the end of the second formal meeting, the Institute was then involved. There followed over the next six months (and well beyond the period of evaluation) a series of letters between the CEO (now the fourth and most senior official to take up the negotiations), the senior administrator for the Institute and my consultant trying to resolve the dispute. Letters previously signed by the senior administrator on behalf of the CEO were now signed by the CEO himself.

I was still involved in evaluating the work of schools attempting to complete the second report under increasing pressure from the LEA to meet the delivery deadline. The formal period of the evaluation was over and a second report expected. This proved very difficult to do given the time that was taken up in negotiation and the uncertainty that prevailed over the fate of the first report. One advantage of bringing in a consultant in such circumstances is that the evaluator is not totally prevented from carrying on with the primary task. Clearly by now any time I devoted to dissemination of the first report and completion of the second had to be spare time over and above commitment to a full-time university teaching position.

The LEA emphasized to the Institute promises they had made to the teachers and sought the Institute's support for restricted circulation. Before the Institute responded they asked me for copies of all correspondence to the LEA on access to or release of any report. At the same time as sending this, and anticipating perhaps at this point that the Institute would side with the LEA, I wrote a long memo to myself and the consultant, noting the issues at stake. The tone of the memo clearly indicates frustration at the seemingly unending negotiations in sight. The memo began:

> I'm beginning to believe that we have been altogether too soft in this matter. After all, I do not, as independent evaluator, have to consult them at all. Most evaluators don't. So they have no rights, absolutely no rights over the dissemination. I have given them personal rights over their own data — rights to edit on an individual level; and rights to comment on a group level and individual level once the complete report was circulated to the main actors involved ...

The memo then detailed again precisely the steps I had taken in this process of clearance, indicating that it must have been clear from the letters accompanying the report and negotiations that further circulation was intended (something the LEA claimed that they did not know) and that they had now had nine months to respond and I had not circulated the report further.

Anticipating issues which may come up in future negotiations, the memo continued with the following points. The fact that written procedures were not sent to all at the beginning could not justify the LEA's claim to ignorance as they had had many opportunities to work through the procedures. The Institute knew the evaluation might be problematic which is why they took out copyright to secure the independence of the evaluation, though we (the consultant and I) ought to check precisely what 'copyright' means. Before circulating the report to anyone for comment, I had informed the Institute that it might be problematic, and that I would need institutional backing; the Institute had agreed to support the evaluation as long as it was not perceived to be taking sides. I did not think that the Institute should be too involved. The dispute was between the evaluation and the LEA. I felt I was being asked repeatedly and unfairly to justify my actions when it was clear that I had carried out a competent evaluation, one that had been negotiated with all key actors and been declared by them to be a fair, accurate and relevant account. The memo concluded:

> It seems that maybe they just do not like the report and are using their hierarchical position and bureaucratic criteria or way of acting to stop further circulation.

When the Institute made its response (to the CEO, copy to me) my worst fears were realized. The Institute, in effect, agreed with the LEA (after pointing out that none of the three parties had clarified the independence of the publication of the report at the outset)[2] stating that the rights of the participants should be safeguarded (this included the right to control the use to which accounts were put), and that if wider circulation was proposed, the approval of every individual consulted would be needed and opportunity provided to reply.

This was precisely the process I had been through (though not giving such total control to any one) and the thought that the process might need to be repeated created a feeling of despair, reinforced by the fact that there were now two organizations contesting freedom of reporting, including the one which had underlined the independence of the evaluation at the outset and on whose behalf the independent evaluation was being conducted.

I drafted a two page letter to the Institute in reply, pointing out that the letter did not actually help resolve the issue of dissemination, that the procedures for clearance had been rigorously adhered to, that the rights of participants had been safeguarded but that no one person, of course, had the right to control the use of a negotiated account which is what it seemed was being sought then; that the LEA's position of granting blanket confidentiality to their teachers only revealed in the second formal meeting over the dispute and seeking to subsume the evaluation within it, was incompatible with independent reporting and inappropriate in the event. The letter, in effect, repeated yet again, for the Institute this time, the precise, lengthy and rigorous procedures that had been followed to safeguard participants' rights and reminded the Institute that an independent evaluation had a responsibility to report to the public.

In the event the letter was not sent, the consultant taking up the issues in a more strongly worded letter and, significantly, in view of the eventual resolution of the dispute, pointing out the Institute's obligation concerning copyright. After a resumé of the crucial issues involved, the letter concluded as follows:

> The fact remains, however, as you point out in your letter to me, that the Institute has the copyright of the report, and therefore the power to suppress publication. It is, of course, the most ludicrous of ironies that this power, an arrangement that by tradition guarantees freedom of reporting, should in this instance be invoked by an academic institution to obstruct the dissemination of a report which has gone to great lengths to present an accurate, relevant and fair account of an educational programme. The extreme view of the participants' rights articulated and endorsed to the LEA in your letter would, if implemented, virtually eliminate the possibility of public and professional reporting by the research community. That view would appear to confer upon every participant the right to veto the publication of an entire research or evaluation study. Such a view of participants' rights is held by no academic institution except, it would seem, the Institute. I find it hard to believe that your view is shared by the Institute's Research Committee or practised by its research staff.
>
> We have offered to publish the report in anonymized form. This offer has not found favour with either the local administration or the Institute, but we are not yet ready to discard the idea. In any event our intention is to publish the report as widely as possible unless the Institute intervenes, on

the basis of its copyright, to frustrate this intention. We must, of course, bow to the Institute's decision but I must advise you now, that in the event of the Institute prohibiting publication, I shall seek to promote public discussion of such an act.

One further point. As you know, Miss Simons is currently working on the second of the two evaluation reports she undertook to produce. In this connection the CEO has written to Miss Simons (letter dated last week, nineteenth month) asking her to 'ensure that any official communication with the EC about the (project in the LEA) should take place through my Department'. Again, I would like to know whether the Institute considers this request to be consonant with its understanding of 'independent evaluation' and compatible with your view of the Institute's 'central role' in this particular evaluation process.

This letter was sent to four personnel in the Institute (two research staff, the senior administrator/negotiator and the Director), the CEO and myself.

Dispute Over First Report Continuing; Solicitation of Second Report

While this dispute was in progress over the first report the CEO sought access to the second report which he indicated was needed by the EC by the end of the twenty-second month in preparation for an international conference the LEA was hosting the following year. The letter indicated that the LEA had to submit its own report *and* mine to the EC by the first of that month, and sought some indication of the contents of the second report. I replied accordingly, noting that the second report concentrated upon the experiences of the participant teachers, their judgments of pupil benefit and their evaluation of the pilot scheme, but indicating that the time-scale the CEO proposed for the second report was unrealistic. It was more likely that a final version of the first report including an introduction, a postscript updating events and an account of the principles and procedures of the evaluation would be available by that time.

I deferred comment on the request to send the report to the EC through the LEA. This was an issue affecting the independence of the evaluation that remained to be resolved by the consultant together with the outstanding issue of dissemination. It was referred to the consultant now handling the negotiations to allow me to devote what little time there was available for completion of the two reports.

In his reply the CEO indicated that the EC were anxious for some assessment of the effects of the project even though the evaluation and the project were not yet complete. This was not surprising in view of the early intimation from the EC that they would like more 'systematic feedback' and may have been quite significant in the events which followed. A second evaluation report focussing more on the project, less on the LEA's role and responsibility might well have appealed more, particularly with an international conference to be hosted by the LEA in the near future.

Only two weeks later than anticipated (ie, in the third week of the twenty-second month) and in time for the translation date for the international conference, I wrote again to the LEA enclosing the last, and final, version of the first evaluation report (now drafted three times to take account of participants' comments, both individually and at the meeting where the report was discussed, and including the postscript updating events, the introduction locating the programme within a context of understanding about the innovative process and the principles and procedures of the evaluation). The letter indicated that on the consultant's advice, and bearing in mind the urgency with which the EC requested the reports for translation for the international conference, that the report had been sent to the EC. This was not inconsistent with the decision already agreed in the dispute over dissemination (see pp 161–2) that the LEA and Institute accepted that all the people to whom the report had already been sent were de facto legitimate audiences. The final version therefore fell within established practice.

This letter enclosing the final version of the report crossed with another written by the senior administrator anxious to receive the first report in its final form for 'onward transmission to the EC', and the second report by the end of the month (ie, the twenty-second month).

Mounting Pressure for Second Evaluation Report

During the next six weeks (twenty-second and twenty-third months) there were several telephone calls from the junior official (now a different one from the one present at the meeting where the impasse over disseminaton was reached) seeking definitive dates from the evaluator for delivery of the second report. One of these calls was followed up by a letter from the CEO documenting the dates at which I had said I hoped to have the second report finished (this was taken as definitive that I would) and indicating that it would be helpful to have at least two copies initially, one for use at LEA level, and one 'for despatch to the EC'. Their papers for the same meeting, it may be added, were not yet complete either (information sought and given by a junior official in a telephone call).

My reply to the CEO a week later (in the fourth week of the twenty-third month) indicated that the junior official's interpretation of the likely delivery dates for the second report (by the third week of the twenty-third month) was somewhat optimistic and that it was, in fact, hampered by the prolonged altercation over the fate of the first report. While this had been resolved three days previously (see next sub-section) the nature of the agreement allowing participants one more opportunity to improve the account required continuing attention of the evaluator to the first report thus detracting from the very limited time available in any case for the completion of the second report. No doubt responding to the pressure I felt I was under, I also pointed out strongly that the LEA could not both expect me to deliver reports on time and engage me in prolonged negotiations about their use and sought their confirmation that, as a result of the agreement, there would be no more repetition of the time and energy consuming process that followed the production of the first report. The letter concluded by revising the time-scale, 'as a result of all these unanticipated delays and communications' to match the deadline the EC had indicated for translation for the international conference (the middle of the twenty-fourth month of the evaluation period) confident that their understanding of the circumstances which had led to the delay would make them sympathetic to the problem.

Justifiable though I thought my protest and request for no more prolonged negotiation over the use of the reports was, it may nevertheless have been this letter, or more likely, the need to revise the time-scale for delivery of the second report which the LEA urgently required, that led to the CEO taking a most pressing imperative tone and action in the days which followed. But I move too quickly.

While this correspondence was taking place between myself and the CEO over delivery dates, my consultant, the Institute and the LEA (through the senior official) were attempting to resolve the dispute over dissemination of the first report.

Resolution of Dispute Over Dissemination:
Third Formal Meeting to Discuss Dissemination of the
Evaluation Report

Finally the Institute convened a meeting between the LEA, themselves and the evaluators to try and resolve the impasse. A date was reached in the twenty-third month (ie, three months after the formal evaluation period had ended, twelve months after negotiations for clearance first started, nine months after the second draft had been sent to participants and discussed and one month after the third and final draft of the first report had been sent to participants and the EC). Many of the issues concerning confidentiality agreements, the right to know and to disseminate, publication and publicity, independence and externality of the evaluation were again discussed at this meeting and a resolution finally reached. The decisions were as follows:

- that copies of the evaluation report would be made available, distributed by the Institute, to a list of people and groups, including LEAs with similar concerns, representative organizations (related to the substantive area of the project), research libraries, and academics with a substantive or methodological interest in the study. The list was to be agreed between the evaluator, the Institute and the LEA;

- that a copy of the report be lodged in the participating schools and *steps taken by the LEA* to make the report accessible to the parents of the pupils involved in the project;

- that the evaluator was free to draw upon the experience of the study in contributions to the literature and development of her professional field whilst maintaining the anonymity of the material;

- that the evaluator write again to the participating heads and teachers informing them of this dissemination plan and asking if they wished to add any further comments on the same principles as before.

The resolution was a compromise on both sides.

These decisions were reached at the very end of a two-hour meeting. Significant factors which led to a resolution included the recognition:

- that an internal evaluation existed as well as an external one, thus offering counter-balance;

- that in order to establish copyright, copies of the report had to be placed in copyright libraries, a requirement compelling some degree of dissemination and public access;

- that parents were perhaps a less problematic audience than the elected officers of the LEA, who had not so far been informed of the dispute;

- that an international meeting was shortly to be held in the LEA to discuss the work of the project, and that this would guarantee a more extensive circulation of the evaluation findings than the LEA had so far contemplated.

The dispute was, then, resolved but the resolution itself generated more work for me. As part of the resolution I was asked to write again to the participants informing them of the intention to circulate the report more widely and seeking further comments in the light of this — a procedure I considered superfluous (it had already been done) and time-consuming. This was done the next day and further time allowed for participants to respond by the end of term in the twenty-fourth month, and for me to update and adjust the report accordingly. This meant that participants had now had five opportunities to comment on the fairness, accuracy and relevance of the report.

Only one development team person responded welcoming the news on agreed circulation and offering three pages of comments not substantially changing the issues but for clarification and to prevent misunderstanding by outsiders. These were included in the final account offered for circulation. The first evaluation report was then finally cleared for agreed wider circulation thirteen months after the first negotiations began. But it was not circulated then. For another reason.

As part of the agreement, too, I had to prepare and negotiate the circulation list for the final stage of dissemination. Since disagreements arose over this as well — and it all had to be done by post between three parties — the Institute, the LEA and myself — it took twelve months to finalize. In the end circulation of the evaluation reports to groups beyond the programme did not take place until two years after the initial negotiations for clearance of data began, and fourteen months after the evaluator's contract had officially ended.

Further LEA Intervention

While processes were set in train to meet these two further demands of seeking additional comments from participants and agreeing the circulation list, I was under increasing pressure from the LEA to complete the second report for the international conference (see p. 160). Though aware of the time pressure I wished to proceed on the same clearance principles as before, and so did the teachers whose views and experience formed the central part of this report. In discussion with the teachers and taking the deadline into account, the teachers agreed to respond within two or three days if they knew the day on which the report would be arriving and some idea of its contents; and one of the teachers offered to collect the report for distribution to the teachers before Christmas. In this way both the EC deadline and the consultation procedures would be met as before.

The LEA intervened to impede this arrangement (not allowing the teacher to collect the report). On their suggestion, the report was then posted, the teachers not receiving it until the beginning of the school year. The LEA also intervened with the procedures of clearance I had established with the teachers by deciding that comments on sections of the report sent to the teachers by me should be collected by the LEA for transmission to me. They also decided that teachers would have a second opportunity to comment upon the report when they had the complete version.

Demands for Delivery of the Second Evaluation Report

Again I had to call upon my consultant to take issue (and he did not mince words) with the CEO, whose staff were by this time making quite unreasonable demands for delivery of the second report whilst at the same time impeding completion of it. I received a stream of demanding telephone calls at my office, at the Institute, at my home. I often had to speak with a junior official, then confirm or clarify with the senior official, who then communicated with the CEO who wrote to seek confirmation.

In one letter written in the twenty-fourth month, the CEO confirmed that he had asked project staff to forward comments direct to the LEA office rather than to me, the previous procedure. The nature of the intervention was a curious one and an example perhaps on both sides of the lack of acceptance or commitment to the procedures each was following. The LEA was pressing for the *utmost* (their emphasis) speed in the completion of the second report, 'it is vital that any further delay be kept absolutely to a minimum', yet were intervening to set their own deadlines later than mine. In the process they were overriding the procedures I had adopted to safeguard participants' rights and creating the inevitable further delay that they were pressing me to avoid.

At the same time (in the twenty-fourth month) the LEA were requesting copies of the *whole report* to be sent to the development team leader and the LEA so that comments 'could be coordinated' and 'forwarded with the minimum delay', and 'in order to expedite its dispatch to the EC for translation'. What the request did not respect was that individuals had a right to clear their individual comments first.

It is possible that what was at issue here was the two-stage process of clearance, particularly the fact that the LEA, this time round, were only involved in the second stage. Unlike the development team, heads and classroom teachers, they were not direct contributors to the report. The procedures the evaluation was following were, moreover, endorsed by the development team and schools. The LEA administration may have felt excluded.

It seems reasonable to infer that this direct intervention of the administration in procedures that were in fact safeguarding the rights of their staff, was an attempt to wrest control of the second report or at least establish oversight of what their employees said in it.

The development team, heads and classroom teachers caught in the authority structure had no option but to comply with the request of their employers, although one team member sent comments in a sealed envelope marked confidential and addressed to the evaluator. By the time it reached me it had been opened. Another team member reported at the same time that a report addressed to this person confidentially at project headquarters had been forwarded on to the home address, opened.

One month later (in the twenty-fifth month of the evaluation) the consultant wrote again to the CEO protesting at this bureaucratic intervention in my consultation procedures with the staff of the programme. No comments had been received on the second report by this time. The consultant also informed the CEO of his advice to me to forward the second report for typing and dispatch to the EC indicating that there would be an opportunity for participant critique before wider dissemination, as before, in fact.

This I did, thereby ending the delay caused, in my view, by the LEA's intervention in the evaluation clearance procedures and fulfilling the evaluation agreement for delivery of a second evaluation report. The report was sent simultaneously to the EC, the development team and the LEA administration. It was received five weeks in fact after the EC indicated it was needed for translation for the international conference (the Christmas holidays had intervened) and five months after the official evaluation period had ended. The story does not, however, end here.

Aftermath

In the negotiations that had continued over the second report the LEA had repeatedly requested that it was needed for the international conference, despite incurring a delay by their intervention. Finally, one month after the deadline for translation for the conference, the LEA forwarded the teachers' comments on the second report explaining the delay on the grounds that they were waiting to see if participants could view them in the context of the whole report. It was now however 'clearly important for the matter to proceed with all speed'.

The letter with three pages of notes from participating teachers had been typed by the LEA and concluded by saying that the LEA looked forward to receiving the full report in the near future so that it might be included in the papers for the international conference.

I responded immediately, reaffirming procedures that individuals would have the opportunity to see the whole report once the process of individual clearance had been completed, ie, the same procedure as before. The letter also pointed out, however, that seeking further comments at this stage would have resource implictions not to mention a further delay and questioned whether the matter was now less urgent than before. It was difficult to reconcile the previous demands for speed in completion with further suggested delays.

The letters between the CEO and myself now take a different turn and the request for completion of the second evaluation report fades.

Exclusion of the Evaluator from the International Conference

The day after receiving the letter with the teachers' comments noted above I received another letter from the CEO suggesting that now that another organization had taken over the evaluation it would not be necessary to attend the preparation meeting for the international conference as previously arranged or to attend the conference itself. This message was in direct contrast to a letter dated eighteen months earlier seeking reassurance that, though the official period of the evaluation would have ended, I would be available to present the evaluation at the conference. Subsequent planning had involved me at every stage, and space specifically allotted on the programme for me to speak to the external evaluation report.

This letter of the CEO's was written three days after the consultant's protest letter at the bureaucratic interference in the completion of the second evaluation report. The two letters may not be unconnected. In reply, I indicated that I did not wish to be released from the commitment to present the external evaluation at the international conference as previously arranged.

The very next day, the CEO replied to both my letters (the first on the report [see p. 165], the second on the conference) separately. It was now the fourth week in the twenty-fifth month. The evaluation period had officially ended seven months earlier. To the first, he simply said that the contents were noted and the LEA would not meet any additional costs whatsoever. In response to the second he indicated that his purpose in suggesting that I might want to be released from commitment to the international conference was to avoid placing me in some embarrassment, following the difficulties connected with the preparation of the evaluation report. The letter went on to say that it was probably better for all concerned if my commitment to the LEA was terminated and since the responsibility for issuing invitations to the international conference lay with the LEA (not the EC or the development team), he did not intend to continue the connection.

The letter commented further on the structure of communications. I had indicated that when the second report had been retyped

I would forward it to the LEA, the development team, and the EC simultaneously as before. The CEO clearly did not approve of this procedure, stating that my intentions in this matter were clearly set and although the correct channel of communications would be for the report to be sent to him for 'onward transmission' to members of staff in the project, he had no doubt that I would, in any case, continue to act upon my own initiative.

It was, it seemed to me, rather too late for the CEO to be pointing out the official procedure of communication more than two years after my work with the project had begun and despite an acceptance throughout of the procedures I had followed (though these, of course, had been seen through by the senior official). Had this 'official channel of communication' been pointed out to me at the beginning, just like the confidentiality agreement the LEA belatedly claimed they had made with their teachers, I would not have accepted the evaluation commission. It is difficult to see how such a framework for communication could facilitate the conduct of an independent, impartial evaluation. This second letter of the CEO's was a clear indication that neither side accepted the other's procedures, and that goodwill had, in effect, irretrievably broken down.

I replied to the two CEO's letters separately, to the first simply reaffirming progress with completion of the second report and stating that participants' comments, if any, on the whole report could be added at the end for wider circulation as before. The second reply pointed out that presenting the external evaluation at the international conference would not embarrass me in any way (relationships with all the personnel in the project, with the exception of the senior officials at this stage, were entirely amicable); that the difficulties were entirely procedural, and reaffirming my willingness to complete and present the evaluation at the international conference. The three-page letter also outlined once again the procedures of the evaluation. It was clearly too late to affect the current project but bearing in mind future projects and the responsibility of the evaluator as educator (Cronbach *et al*, 1980) they seemed worth repeating.

The CEO replied a week later (ie, early in the twenty-sixth month of the evaluation period) acknowledging the receipt of my two letters and reaffirming that the contents of his stood. His letter crossed with another from me forwarding the final draft of the second evaluation report to the LEA, the EC and the development team requesting further comments, if any, to be sent direct to me to be taken into account at the international conference and in the report for wider circulation.

No comments were received, only an acknowledgement from the CEO two weeks later (ie, the third week of the twenty-sixth month) that the report had been received, that he had not yet had time to study it and that in view of the fact that it had missed the deadline for the EC to translate the documents for the international conference, the report would not be considered at the conference, a clear reversion of the previous intention.

No thought was apparently given to the fact that the reports might not need to be translated as most of the participants attending the international conference were familiar with English.

Fulfilment of the Dissemination Agreement

While negotiations over the dissemination of the report(s) were now over, negotiations continued over the list that had to be agreed for circulation. Once it had been agreed it was up to the Institute to finalize copy and distribution. Negotiations here were three-way, between myself, the Institute and the senior official in the LEA. The CEO had by now ceased to take a front role though he no doubt continued to be consulted by the senior official.

The Institute indicated willingness to proceed with speed saying, in the twenty-ninth month since the evaluation had started, six months after the agreement to circulate the evaluation report more widely was made and nine months after the evaluation period had officially ended, that 'something will be lost with every month which passes since the evaluation period ended'. But in the event the list was not finalized until two months later (ie, in the thirty-first month of the evaluation period).

One year after the meeting resolving the dissemination of the first report (ie, in the thirty-fifth month) I wrote to the Institute enquiring if the arrangements for circulation had been met in accordance with the agreement of the year before. The administrator responded indicating some difficulty with the copyright libraries expecting more copies but indicating that the letters had gone out and orders were coming in. Their part of the agreement had been fulfilled. Mine had already been fulfilled in circulating programme participants for further comments. There remained the LEA.

Eighteen months after the meeting resolving the agreement I wrote to the LEA asking if they had met their part of the bargain by making the report accessible to parents. Their reply indicated that no application had been received from a parent to see the evaluation report. In making this response they had referred to the minutes of the meeting written by the Institute administrator which stated that 'parents should be able to have access to the report in their children's schools on application to the head'.

In fact, the inference of the resolution was that a copy of the report be lodged in the participating schools *and steps taken* by the LEA to make the report available to the parents of pupils in the programme, giving the LEA an active role to play in seeing the agreement through just as the Institute and I had an active role. The minutes did not convey this *active* intention and I, preoccupied at the time by having to renegotiate to fulfil my part of the resolution agreement, did not take it up at the time. One might, in any case, reasonably assume that giving people access meant that they should have knowledge of its existence. It is difficult to escape the conclusion here that the LEA did not inform the parents of the fact that they *could have access* to the report lodged in their schools.

And that is the end of the case, closed, three years six months after it began, and two years after my official evaluation period ended. In such circumstances, and I must say with the greatest reluctance, I was left with no choice but to publish this account, name the institutions involved, and place the record in the sphere of public judgment.

Notes

1 The statement outlined the 'responsive' approach I would take to evaluation contrasting this with more formal preordinate designs. It would focus on issues identified in the development of the project, and perspectives of participants at all levels with a view to informing all the 'interested parties' of the process and outcome. Qualitative methods in the main would be used to facilitate this flow of information. The statement also emphasized the boundaries of the evaluation, what it could and could not do in the timescale; and that two reports were required as part of the commission.

2 The Institute seems to have forgotten in this response that they took out copyright to underwrite the independence of the evaluation, though they may not have been aware at the time that copyright effectively ensured public accessibility of the evaluation, if not direct publication.

7 What is Reasonable?
Reflections on the Case

Bureaucratic organizations tend to distort or deny information they cannot select. (McLaughlin, 1975, p. 42)

The evaluator will probably have moved to another job once
his contract has finished and this will not usually have
covered dissemination time. He will want to get away from a
subject that has probably drained him. Dissemination is a
laborious occupation involving.... and continuing to meet
those who have been evaluated. None of this is academically
rewarding. It is unlikely to be funded. Yet dissemination is
the point of evaluation. (Shipman, 1981, p. 123)

At the end of chapter 1 I said that it was not clear whether evaluators
distinguished between respect for legitimate authority and docility to
the exercise of power. In subsequent chapters I explored that central
issue further with respect to democratic evaluation, offering an
answer to the charge, mounted principally by House, that the
approach is 'weak on social justice' and does not do enough to secure
the 'distribution of choice'. I think we should keep that issue in mind
as we review this particular case. For me it was a test case of how the
democratic persuasion responds to the exercise of power by legitimate authority.

This is a two-dimensional question. We have to consider the
response to the exercise of power within the case, in terms of
employer/employee relationships that link the Chief Education
Officer to classroom teachers. That is one dimension. The other
dimension concerns the relationship between the evaluator and those
authorities — administrators at the local district level, at the Institute,
and at the European level, who at various points and in different ways

made it difficult for me to make known to others the story of the project. It may be useful here to quote House's statement on power:

> Power occurs where there is a conflict of interests. If sanctions are employed, then power becomes coercion (threat of deprivation) and force (no choice) and is not based on authority. One has imposed against the other's will. (House, 1980, p. 181)

The case described in chapter 6 exemplifies both coercion and force. When the tactics of delay and interference with negotiated agreements and procedures for the conduct of the study did not produce the effect the administration desired, they resorted to coercion and force. It could be argued that the evaluators responded in kind, but that argument would be difficult to sustain in a context where the 'obvious' solution, release of the report to the local and national press, was not adopted. The evaluation was perceived by the administration, despite espousals to the contrary, not as one which would inform policy but one which would legitimate development decisions. When it did not, in addition to the tactics noted above, the LEA adopted the strategies of denying the account after previously accepting its validity, refusing to comment, placing unreasonable demands on the evaluator, seeking to suppress dissemination of the evaluation, to limit its accessibility and, eventually, to thwart public discussion of it. The kind of public decision process that House, Cronbach and MacDonald all aspire to in evaluating public programmes was thus seriously undermined. The question is whether my efforts to secure through negotiation the survival of the evaluation as a source of public knowledge constituted a defensible response to the exercise of power, or an indefensible concession to pressure.

> What if the evaluation feeds in impartial reports reflecting all interests and some interests are continually ignored? What if decisions are usually taken on the basis of power rather than consensual deliberation? To that degree, the radical critics of liberalism are correct. Power really decides the issues, and evaluation is only cosmetic. (*Ibid*, p. 187)

It was clear in this case that power became an issue when interests conflicted. The formal balance of power was unequal to start with both within the LEA and between the evaluator and the LEA. The evaluator has no formal power in the structure of the system. She can only proceed on the assumption that rationality and reasonableness will persuade. And she can only defensibly offer a service from a position of impartiality and independence. In this case the evaluation was forced into a prolonged dispute over dissemination of evaluation reports because these assumptions of rationality and reasonableness, while accepted in rhetoric, were challenged in practice by the most senior of the local actors who resorted to power to decide the issues.

Test cases are rarely as clear as this one. Let me remind you that the dispute was about the dissemination of a report and not about the validity of its content. Before the dispute arose all parties involved had agreed that the report was accurate, relevant and fair. The dispute was clearly about 'the right to know', and about my right to make known. And let me make it clear, if it is not already clear, that I took no pleasure from this dispute. I have argued that for me the democratic approach is an educational form of inquiry, offering the possibility of relationships that are developmental for all concerned. I am no 'commodity broker' in the market-place of information exchange. That kind of discourse, in which MacDonald sometimes discusses the theory (see MacDonald and Sanger, 1982) has no appeal for me. 'Reasonableness', the other side of the 'democratic' coin, does, so my question is, with respect to the case, 'What is reasonable?'.

Let me put that question more precisely. What is reasonable, at this time, in this place, in these circumstances, with regard to all relevant considerations? 'Why the hell didn't you just publish it and be damned?' demanded one exasperated member of the audience when I presented a paper on this experience (Simons, 1981b). There are some very simple answers to that, all of them plausible. Lack of money, lack of backing, lack of confidence, fatigue, hints of legal action, job precariousness (mine), fear of unanticipated consequences. Most of the theory of evaluation is propounded by tenured academics. Most of the practice is carried out by people on soft money contracts with at best a precarious toehold on the bottom rung of a career that has no precise structure.

Although by the end of this evaluation I had a tenured post, for most of the time I had only a part-time, then a temporary full-time position. I offer this data, not because I believe it explains my course of action, but because I am inviting the reader to judge the case, and therefore s/he is entitled to take such data into account as she sees fit. But I quoted the exasperation, not to immediately answer it, but as a way of introducing a range of possible responses.

Let me now cite another and very different response. A senior administrator from another LEA with whom I discussed the case said, 'I can't agree. My sympathies are with the LEA. I might well want to restrict the dissemination of a report that described early mistakes and grievances'. It is this reaction, and some of the reasoning that lay behind it, that I want to explore further, before revisiting some of the details of the case.

The UK is a very secretive society, with very few levers available to make it less so. There is no equivalent of the American Constitution, no Freedom of Information Act yet, though the issue is much debated, as indeed is a Bill of Rights. Investigative journalism is severely constrained by a combination of legal restrictions and a highly developed lobby system at Westminster by means of which political journalists are kept informed of what ministers are willing for them to publish in return for silence about what ministers do not want the public to know.

Of course not all journalists are lobby journalists, not all of them obey all the time the rules of confidential patronage, but there is a high degree of collusion between such journalists and the seat of political power. The public 'right to know' is not served as well as it might be by the press. It may be worth adding that, by a curious anomaly, educational journalism is arguably better developed in this country than it is elsewhere, certainly on a national level. But education is, itself, rather a secretive service in a country where the civil service in general has evolved an unobtrusive style and has, on the whole, managed to resist political appointments to its upper ranks. In terms of transatlantic comparison, there is some agreement that British administrators operate more informally, often secretively, whilst the USA is procedurally more open (see Kogan, 1978; Smith, 1980). There is another consideration to be borne in mind with respect to the British tradition:

> ... in our country teachers, headmasters, inspectors and administrators all have similar professional qualifications, so the hierarchy of staff is based on experience and is consultative. Expertise cannot be claimed on extrinsic criteria and used as a basis for authority. This characteristic of the structure, allied to mythological aspects of the culture, creates an inherent need for secrecy that is all-pervasive. (MacDonald and Walker, 1975, p. 8)

I have made much, in my arguments so far in this book, about the threat to schools and teachers posed by close-up and detailed study. Yet in a sense teachers at least have some experience of their performance being subject to scrutiny, either individually, while they are trainees and probationers, or collectively, by national inspectors. But when the focus of case study is widened to include administrators we must keep in mind how much more threatening, and how novel that experience is for people who are accustomed to being free from external observation and to rendering accountability through self-report to an elected committee. And when we take into account the fact that, at least in Britain, their fitness for the responsibility they bear is in principle an empirical issue — a question of the skills and judiciousness they bring to the discharge of that responsibility, then surely we can understand how vulnerable they feel to the kind of public judgment that is entailed in the right to know.

In the remaining chapters of this book I shall be dealing with evaluation in a context of school accountability rather than a context of programmes of curriculum intervention involving professional actors other than teachers. This shift of focus from programmes to schools has tended to divert attention from the lack of accountability data at other levels of the educational system, a deficiency which democratic evaluation is intended to counter, and which the theory has highlighted. Categorical funding continues to grow as governments increasingly prioritize economic goals, and administrators are increasingly called upon to act as curriculum developers and implementers. The pattern of funding, responsibility and accountability which I have documented in a particular case is one that has in the eighties become the dominant pattern of curriculum intervention.

The change is very significant for evaluation. Whereas in the sixties and early to mid-seventies administrators would commission evaluations of projects and programmes for which they had no direct responsibility, now they are commissioning evaluations of enterprises for the success of which they are directly accountable. The result is, not surprisingly, that they typically insist upon bureaucratic evaluations backed by contracts which give them ownership of the data. This is true of both nationally and locally commissioned evaluations associated with categorical funding programmes. As for the evaluation of European educational programmes, the decision of the Commission to dispense with evaluators for the second phase of the 'Transition from education to working life' programme drew this comment from its meta-evaluator:

> Dispensing with evaluators does not dispose of the need to establish and sustain effective means for the disinterested accumulation of sophisticated, experience-based understanding of planned change. All it is likely to achieve is the total

insulation of Community adventures from the possibility of public scrutiny. (MacDonald, 1983b, p. 10)

The notion of the pilot as a learning experience is still so poorly understood that it needs to be emphasized. For nearly everyone, new curricula, under whatever label they travel, carry promises: promises for change, for resources, for success. Hope, optimism, and commitment continue to generate unrealistic expectations in participants and inappropriate criteria in spectators. For participants the rewards are uncertain, the risks great. Careers and reputations are at stake in enterprises where success is elusive and difficult to demonstrate. Achievement is hard earned. If more account were taken of the realities of practice curriculum aspirations might promise less and have more chance of meeting expectations.

My evaluation reports in this particular case were consciously concerned with the need to promote understanding of the problems of change, to inform planning and policy at the international and national as well as at the local level. That improvement is needed can be in no doubt. Take this particular case, one of four pilots launched under the 'Migrant education' label by the European Commission. The LEA is given three years to demonstrate the merits of mother tongue teaching, a concept of enormous complexity. The LEA has neither administrative nor curricular experience of such an innovation. It knows so little of its linguistic communities that it initially assumes, wrongly, that Hindi is the main language of its Asian community and that standard Italian is the mother tongue of its Italian community. Neither the time-scale nor the resources provided for the pilot allow for a research phase upon which a sensible approach might be based. Indeed the LEA is under pressure from Brussels to provide evidence of student accomplishment. The Commission itself needs success stories to maintain political support for community initiatives in education. Such initiatives require the voluntary support of all member states, and some have been consistently critical of a European role in education. The Commission needs good news from the projects it funds and is sensitive to critical publicity. This probably explains why the LEA, at the height of the dispute about dissemination of the report, was able to claim support from Brussels for its interpretation of the right to control dissemination, and why it was able to exclude me from the international conference which it hosted.

But what about the right to know? Was it important in this particular case? It is not difficult to make a case that it was very important. At the international colloquium in 1980 the Chief Education Officer questioned, on the basis of the pilot experience, whether mother tongue teaching was desirable or practical or could be afforded, announced that the County could not afford to go ahead once the EC money stopped (*Times Educational Supplement*, 1980). Tosi (1986) has described how this 'conclusion' of the CEO, much publicized in the press, was used by the Department of Education and Science to buttress its known opposition to bilingual schooling. He also notes the restricted availability of external evaluation reports. My own evaluation reports, though lodged in copyright libraries as well as in the Institute, and advertised to the agreed list of individuals and agencies, are still less than freely available. The NFER report was confidential to the LEA, and the comparative study of the four pilots has to date only been published in German.

The case for the right to know in such circumstances is clearly a strong one, both locally and nationally. The central issues raised by the pilot are of great educational and political significance. Judgments were made on the basis of this pilot, and policy justified with reference to such judgments. But the basis of these judgments was not, and is still not, widely known. The restricted availability of evaluation reports made it difficult for people to challenge apparently authoritative and supposedly well-founded conclusions. Given the prior disposition of the central Ministry to oppose bilingual education for migrant and immigrant communities, and the subsequent pronouncement of the Chief Education Officer, it is hardly surprising that concerns about the lack of availability of external evaluation should be expressed. I understand that at the colloquium two separate attempts were made from the floor to ask questions about the missing evaluation but that these were not pursued from the platform. I also understand that delegates to the colloquium were recommended to read my evaluation reports on the pilot by the NFER representative who took my place.

Before reaching conclusions on what course of action is reasonable in such circumstances I would like to reconsider and elaborate upon my own responsibilities and behaviour in the conduct of this evaluation. Disputes of this kind can often be traced to inadequacies in the actual performance of roles, so it is appropriate that I reflect upon this with as much objectivity as I can muster.

Performance Factors

Not learning it seems from Castle Manor I undoubtedly let the negotiations become too protracted, allowing five opportunities in the case of the first report for participants to comment. Each opportunity raises the possibility that participants will find more to say, or change their minds and the report may have to be rewritten to accommodate such changes. My reasons for allowing these further opportunities were two-fold: to democratize the shaping of the evaluation report and to demonstrate that the evaluator was acting 'reasonably' in the context. While reasonableness may have been demonstrated, the cost was high in terms of time and delay in completion. Three opportunities may have sufficed to demonstrate the same point.

   Not unrelated to the above action was my feeling that I allowed participants too much scope to talk to me. This was a difficult issue for in order to learn about the setting up and effects of the programme, I had to empathize with participants' concerns which were often more with the internal difficulties and personalities in the programme than analysis of the programme in action. Participants took this to mean I was in sympathy with their position and saw it as a licence to reveal their anxieties or anger towards other participants that they would not express to each other. This was particularly true of members of the pilot development team, short-term contract people who felt undersupported, misunderstood at times, and isolated. The social and interpersonal processes entailed in naturalistic case study, allied to conditions afforded by confidentiality, inevitably provide opportunities for participants to express their frustrations and to look to the evaluator as a source of legitimation and sympathy. These outpourings were time-consuming to deal with, but, of course, highly relevant to the evaluation. The disinterested but empathetic outsider in this context took the flack. I find it difficult to conceive that I could have done otherwise where the social and professional relationships were so fractured — one had to work through the individuals in order to gain data for the evaluation — but perhaps I empathized too strongly with each of their concerns and possibly exacerbated the problem of establishing data for the evaluation.

   It could also be said that I invited the political difficulties in this case by adopting a style of evaluation which was antithetical to the prevailing management style. Clearly so. But the only defensible starting assumption for evaluative activity of a democratic persuasion is one of egalitarian discourse, which seemed to be endorsed at the beginning of the study. It was only in the course of the study that the far-reaching effects of the line-management style of the local administration became apparent. Access in the beginning was open and the autonomy of all professionals involved apparently respected. Even if the bureaucratic management style had been clear at the outset, would I have acted differently? In retrospect I think not, though I would have tried to negotiate for greater access to the CEO at the outset and throughout the evaluation. It was not clear to me that the CEO totally shared the decisions of his subordinates. Access to him from the beginning, I felt, might have established a basis for more reasonable negotiations.

When discussing the difficulties raised by this case colleagues have sometimes asked, why not work within the structure that is given? Surely this is more realistic and likely to lead to greater acceptance of the evaluation. No doubt. But working within the structure in this case would have meant allowing some participants access to knowledge while denying it to others. The LEA officials were trying to ensure that all communications went through them. There was doubt as to the extent to which information would be shared. Acceding to the LEA's request for control of information flow might have only served the interests of the most powerful group involved. It would not have been impartial, it would have lacked credibility. It would not, in short, have been worth doing.

In not complying with the structure I was agreeing with Mac-Donald and Norris's (1981) position that if we accept that the social and political function of evaluation in a democratic society is to provide a disinterested information service, then the principles which guide and legitimate our actions should be derived not from the existing structure of social relations (where society is) but from where society would like to be (the rhetoric of liberal democracy). To have operated within the social structure would have meant helping to reproduce it.

> If we *are* in the business of helping all people to choose between alternative societies, that is, to enter into the democratic political process, then it is essential to help effect a more equitable access to the policy-making, policy implementation and policy evaluation processes of our societies. (*Ibid*, p. 16)

Not acceding to the LEA's request to send the evaluation reports to the CEO first, especially in the case of the second report, was not an in-principle challenge to the power structure of local authority management but simply a function of the agreed procedures for clearance of reports. It was not a question of whose side the evaluator was on (Becker, 1967) though it may perhaps have appeared that way to the local administration. The assumption on which the evaluation was operating was one of equality of access to information, once individuals had cleared their comments in the context of the report. No group including these individuals had the right to see the whole report first. It just so happened that, in regard to the second report, the administration was not directly reported upon so had no right of access to the data until the second stage of dissemination. This was contrary to the position in relation to the first report where some information had to be checked with the administration in the first stage. Overall, it was subordinates rather that superordinates who were more prominently featured in the reports. The process of clearance of data therefore had to begin with those lower in the hierarchy. The process of distributing the report, however, was subject to the principle of equality of access, which is why I insisted on sending the complete negotiated report simultaneously to the EC, the CEO, the development team and schools. And this was the crux of the problem. This principle of horizontal communication was at odds with the LEA's custom of vertical flow of information. This difference in operational style and assumptions about information flow undoubtedly led to the conflict over dissemination.

Finally there are the actions I did not take in presenting a written account of the procedures at the beginning of the evaluation and my persistent correspondence with the CEO at the end of the study.

While the precise procedures could not have been written at the beginning — some observation of the field situation was necessary to see precisely what procedures would maximize the democratic process, the principles could have been spelled out in advance. I should not have accepted the LEA's intimation that they were not necessary. While I do not think that written principles would have avoided the difficulties which arose in the study — other conditions are necessary for principles to be respected (see House, 1980, p. 170) — they, nevertheless, might have provided some clarification. Unclear contracts are helpful for neither side.

My actions in pursuing the written correspondence with the CEO over control of dissemination and establishment of procedures undoubtedly prolonged the negotiations and, towards the end, given my reluctance to give in to the demands of the LEA, precipitated the decision to ban the evaluation from the international conference. It could be said that my actions, or the actions of my consultant in protesting at the interference of the administration in the procedures of the evaluation, curtailed any possibility of gaining immediately wider access for the evaluation and thereby fulfilling the aspiration to inform. Possibly so, and another time I would not perhaps take such a strong stand nor allow the consultant to react so strongly.

The point of continuing to explain the procedures to the CEO, even though the cause was lost, was an educative one. It was too late to affect that evaluation but maybe not another. The CEO had not been involved at the beginning of the evaluation, but he took a more prominent role as the evaluation proceeded and the dispute took its form. In alerting him to the logic of the evaluation procedures which might operate in future evaluations, I was still operating, even at this late stage, on the assumption that rationality and reasonableness might persuade, though it is possible to question my motives here, I guess, and claim that I only wanted to have the last word.

One indication of the success of this 'educative' mission would be if that same LEA commissioned another evaluation either of the same type or by the same evaluator. In this regard it may be worth noting that the LEA subsequently granted access to its schools for case studies utilizing similar principles (Elliott *et al*, 1981) and that I have had co-operation from the LEA on a subsequent evaluation/research inquiry (see chapter 9, p. 229).

There are three points related to the structure of the evaluation that also had an effect on the actions of the evaluator in this case: the part-time nature of the task; the large number of participant groups; and the formal structure of relationships within the LEA. The part-time nature of the evaluation meant that I had to opt for correspondence where face-to-face negotiations would have prevented misunderstandings arising or being prolonged. Being located at a distance from the LEA did not help. Secondly, having so many groups to negotiate with inevitably incurred more time than was allocated for the evaluation. The fact that the five groups — LEA, EC, college, development team and schools — were at different levels in the system with different lines of command and accountability to each other only intensified the negotiation process and made it all the more necessary to pursue exactly the same principles with each group. I could only have taken less time with any one group to the detriment of the principles of the evaluation process.

The formal style of the LEA with its hierarchical line of command undoubtedly created difficulties in the programme and in the negotiation of data for the evaluation and dissemination. It is possible that I should have been more aware at the beginning of the precise chain of command and its effects, although in other authorities in which I had worked professional advisers and administrators, as well as schools, have had a great deal of real autonomy to pursue initiatives and make their own judgments. The effects of the hierarchical line of command were not explicit at the beginning. When they did become clear, I possibly contributed to the assertiveness of the LEA by refusing to comply. This action undoubtedly prolonged negotiations.

The management style of the LEA had another effect. The CEO at first delegated the task of management to a senior official, who was, throughout, the key negotiating person. Many of the negotiations were face-to-face. When the dispute arose, the CEO became involved but only from a distance. His views were relayed and decisions deferred to him so that each negotiation could never be completed. The role of the CEO here had two effects — it prolonged the length of time needed for the negotiations and it laid the evaluation open to inadequate representation through secondhand reportage. The effect was to give the LEA the power to delay completion of the evaluation. Had I been able to discuss the evaluation with the CEO from the beginning, or even throughout, some of the difficulties that arose over the evaluation and for his staff might have been avoided. I sought his direct involvement at the point of the dispute but this was denied. He remained throughout a distant figure, although letters increasingly came to be written and signed by him.

There were several actions on the part of the participants that also had an effect on the way the evaluation evolved. I have already referred to the distant role of the CEO, attempts by the local administration to delay completion of the evaluation and thwart its accessibility, and the tendency on the part of the development team and LEA officials to vent their anxieties and fears about the programme. All these actions lengthened the time it took to gain access to, and negotiate data for, the evaluation, and dissemination of the evaluation.

The lack of financial support for the evaluation and the LEA's unwillingness to seek extra financial support for dissemination clearly limited the scope of the evaluation and exacerbated the difficulties which arose over clearance and circulation. The only resource support the evaluation could draw upon was the Institute administration which had offered to provide some back-up from within its normal resources. No extra funds were allocated. For this reason the reports that were finally made accessible could only be made so at cost. In my view the price determined by the Institute was excessive and effectively limited the report's accessibility. The lack of resource support for an adequate evaluation and dissemination did not prevent the LEA, however, from demanding more than the evaluation and an evaluator working alone could possibly deliver.

The evaluation report, plans for dissemination and the democratic procedures of the evaluation received support from the development team and schools but when the administration opposed the report so strongly and intervened in the process of clearance of the second report, there was little the team could do but comply. They were all on short-term contracts. Further funds for development were unlikely to be forthcoming, so they were very dependent on the favour of the administration for references and future jobs. The participants were in an impossible bind. It was no part of the evaluation's task to prevail upon the teachers to pursue the procedures they clearly endorsed in defiance of their employers, and so the administration effectively secured control and undermined my attempt to sustain a communal process of rational discourse within the case.

The local administration's action reflected the anxieties and priorities of those who have a vested interest in the success of the innovation and the maintenance of their system and sphere of influence (Weiss, 1975a). It is possible that I did not have enough insight into the way this particular administration operated — a limitation Weiss (*Ibid*) suggests is common among evaluators. But it is difficult to conceive how I could have acted differently given the structure of relationships, the lack of resources and an organization threatened by adverse publicity, internal staff differences and political pressures of their own. More insight and understanding carries with it a high risk of co-option and may pose a threat to independent reporting. Weiss's point however, is well-taken. In general we may need to understand better the way bureaucracies function but our action must remain consistent with the aspiration to democratize evaluative inquiry and evaluation reports.

One Person Case Study

The changing circumstances brought about by a policy focus in evaluation underline a political weakness peculiar to case study. It is now generally agreed by experienced practitioners of the approach that case study is best conducted by one person, although Denny (1977) is one of the few to have written about it. Both the complexity of processing and the need for coherence of style and content require that it be a one-person task. Certainly in the UK it is the prevalent practice to assign one person to a case rather than attempt a composite study even when a team is available (see, for example, the designs of the SAFARI Study (MacDonald and Walker, 1974), the UNCAL Study (MacDonald *et al*, 1975) and the Cambridge Accountability Project (Elliott *et al*, 1981)). Parsimonious funding policies reinforce this pattern by typically providing for only one full-time evaluator.

The case, on the other hand, usually involves a number of individuals organizationally linked through hierarchical relationships. Some of these individuals may want the story told, some may not. The hierarchical relationships mean that opposition to an evaluation that may begin with one group or individual can quickly escalate into a unified organizational opposition that places the evaluator working alone in an impossible position having to complete the evaluation, defend it and sometimes argue for its dissemination as well. In practice it becomes very difficult for one person to defend the evaluation and protect its independence in the face of sustained and organized opposition. The case study worker is outnumbered and can be overpowered. This is so even when the case study is issue-oriented, focussing on persons only indirectly to reflect the origins and shaping of the policy in action.

The differential of power relationships is usually exacerbated by a differential in resources. Evaluations in the UK are typically under-resourced. Most evaluations now have secretarial support built into the funding (this part-time evaluation was an exception) but contingency funding is rare and few have built-in funds for dissemination (for an exception to this see the 'Careers guidance observed' evaluation based at the Centre for Applied Research in Education and funded by the DES (Kushner and Logan, 1984)). Any extra resource backing provided by the academic institution — the base from which evaluators usually work — more often than not fails to match the back-up resources available to the organization studied. This places the evaluator at an even greater disadvantage in contesting opposition by a powerful group within an organization. In this context also, one advantage of working in academic institutions — the freedom of individuals to pursue their own lines of inquiry — can become a disadvantage. The process of marshalling support for individual action is not a familiar process in academic institutions, and this stands in contrast to the way in which hierarchical organizations can be mobilized by their most powerful members to generate support and compliance for a particular policy or line of action.

The case I have described is one where, as the dispute developed, the LEA gradually moved from a single representative, providing a manageable person-to-person negotiation, to a collective front involving the evaluator in multiple interactions with LEA personnel who had no power to make decisions, and from verbal to written interactions, a time-consuming and protracted process. Where such disputes occur, a small evaluation works from a very weak resource base compared to an organization able to marshall human resources from its normal administrative flexibility. It is difficult to see how an evaluator can match this capability at the point of need. I tried, but at some cost to my own time and that of the institution in which I then worked.

One or two resolutions to this issue — the individual against the institution as it were, are suggested at the end of this chapter, but there is one final point to be made here. This issue did not arise in the Castle Manor study and might not have arisen so sharply in this case had the boundaries of the evaluation not included high-level superordinates. Reporting of executive action has different consequences from reporting of development action primarily because those in power can mobilize effective resistance to efforts which undermine their boundary control and their image management. The case for extending the boundaries of evaluation studies to include such superordinates has been argued most extensively by MacDonald and Norris (1981), but the consequences of studying superordinates have not yet been fully explored.

In the case under discussion the administrative actors (unlike the development project personnel) were not extensively studied. Their early decisions were traced and related to the progress of the development programme, but even this degree of reporting was sufficient to generate resistance to circulation of reports and recourse to control strategies when the evaluation did not capitulate.

It is perhaps worth noting here a more general point about UK rhetoric and reality. In this country there is a cultural distaste (challenged by the accountability movement) for explicit examination of relationships between levels in the system in terms of power, and a pervasive rhetoric of familial consultative relationships. It should be understood that this is only possible because power is so rarely challenged. Those who challenge it can expect 'powerful' reactions. I think this is one important message from the case.

Where Do We Go From Here?

The conclusion of this particular evaluation must give everyone concerned a feeling of dissatisfaction. We reached a complex agreement with the Institute and the LEA that at least appeared to guarantee that the parents directly involved in the pilot would have the opportunity to inform themselves about what had happened. The agreement also guaranteed that dissemination of the reports would take place, albeit by a slow process. Was this a reasonable course of action in the circumstances for an evaluator committed to the democratization of evaluative inquiry? Did the compromise help or hinder the promotion of social justice, in this particular case and more generally?

This separation of the particular and the general is an important distinction in terms of my own answer. I think I have made clear in the course of this book that I take an educational view of evaluative inquiry, that I seek to establish and sustain educative relationships through evaluation, and that I believe that the cultivation of such relationships has an important contribution to make to the social transformation of our society and thereby to social justice. My interpretation of the democratic argument in evaluation theory suggests that there are two ways in which I can make this contribution. The first is by directly employing a process of inquiry that offers equal franchise to all those within the case, and that in this sense is bound to be in most cases non-aligned with established practice. This means I only take assignments where the procedures embodying such principles have been accepted. The second is by embodying these beliefs in my relations with those whose behaviour in the course of the evaluation is not reciprocal.

This is a long-haul view of change which has regard not just to the particular case but to the future. And this means that in any particular case my actions will be governed by a search for balance between immediate and cumulative achievement. My answer to those who ask why I didn't abandon the negotiations and go public by whatever means came to hand is that any immediate gain in social justice obtained by such a power-based strategy would have ill-served such a general aim. It would have meant that I resorted to the very strategy to which I was objecting. Of course had I known that the parents were to remain in ignorance of the pilot experience through the failure of the LEA to take reasonable steps to inform them, I might well have acted differently. It might be argued that, on the basis of my experience prior to the agreement, I should have known.

Perhaps I should, perhaps even I did, but isn't it also true that the only way to promote trustworthiness is to engage in trust?

Having said that in defence of my course of action, I now want to argue that such prolonged disputes about rights and obligations, though they may in the end have educational outcomes for those involved, are highly detrimental to the conduct of the evaluation and the important goal of feeding policy deliberations at the point of maximum relevance and impact. It is clear to me that the independence of evaluation needs strengthening and that the right to disseminate, with appropriate safeguards for participants and the appropriate level of resourcing needed to operationalize that right, should lie with the evaluator as Shipman (1981) suggests. This view is clearly against the tide of contemporary practice in the UK, where the context of command is much more prevalent than is the case in the USA, if Cronbach is correct in asserting its rarity there (Cronbach, 1982). In this country there is now a crisis of credibility in programme evaluation as a source of public information about the exercise of delegated authority, and a need to repair the damage inflicted on the evaluation enterprise by the power of the bureaucratic purse.

One solution is to propose that negotiated contracts be extended to include considerations of the rights of all relevant constituencies. Contract setting has been a dominant feature of sponsored evaluation in the USA for some time. Proposals for funds are subjected to detailed scrutiny in terms of aims, methodology, outcomes and costs and may be quite changed as a result: setting up conditions for fieldwork often involves mandatory negotiations with stakeholding groups including parents, teachers and administrators who are also able to exact changes. Contracts are usually written and agreements signed by the appropriate parties acknowledging acceptance of the study under the terms eventually agreed. The Right to Privacy Act (1974) added further protections for the subjects of research, compounding the growing complexity of prerequisite clearance.

In the early days of sponsored evaluation in the UK the equivalent requirements were much less exacting. The pre-funding phase was usually confined to two parties, sponsor and evaluator or sponsor and director of the project. Arranging access was subsequent to the award of the contract, and typically informal. Sponsors did not specify their needs in any detail, leaving the evaluator largely free to follow her own preference and restricting the sponsor's role to a go/no-go decision. The contracts covering the evaluation usually took the form of a conventional research proposal and an exchange of letters signifying support for the proposal from the sponsors and commitment to its implementation by the evaluator. Frequently the evaluator was only employed once the funding negotiations between the sponsor and director of the programme or institution were complete. In such circumstances opportunities for the evaluator to negotiate an agreement fair to all parties and conditions for independence could be severely restricted. One such case is described by Adelman (1979) who half-way into an evaluation working to certain principles found that an earlier contract existed which conflicted with the one drawn up by him.

In the case reported in chapter 6, the evaluation had to take second place to the financial agreement determined between the LEA and the Institute, the evaluator having no access to the LEA personnel until the financial agreement had been finalized. The only professional discussions which took place were between the evaluator and the Institute, which approved the style of evaluation to be conducted on its behalf. This had several effects. First, it meant that only the Institute had forewarning of the procedures and approach the evaluator would adopt before a commitment to the evaluation was made, though in the letter of contract from the Institute, the LEA were alerted to the evaluator's previous work and publications. Secondly, it was too late to negotiate precise procedures with the LEA. Having secured the external evaluation they needed, they did not appear interested in the details except in a very general sense of approving the style of evaluation. Thirdly, it established a strong administrative connection between the Institute and the LEA, one that conflicted in the event with the professional negotiations that were necessary in the conduct and dissemination of the evaluation. In the initial negotiations, the evaluator was more an object of discussion than an active negotiating partner to the agreement. Fourthly, it meant that funding for the evaluation was entirely in the hands of the Institute and the LEA administrators whose understanding of the financial support necessary for evaluations left something to be desired. The evaluator had no direct negotiating power with the paymasters of the evaluation.

The UK scene has now changed, of course. From the late seventies increasing attention has been paid to the formulation of evaluation contracts bringing us nearer to American practice (see, for example, MacDonald, 1980a; Parlett and Dearden, 1977; Adelman, Kemmis and Jenkins, 1976). This initiative has stemmed primarily from evaluators out of concern for fairness to evaluatees and the need to ensure accessibility of the evaluation. For the most part contracts drawn up by evaluators have been designed to secure fair procedures (fair to all parties) for conducting the study, to prevent misunderstanding and to provide a basis for review in cases of dispute. This trend to secure contractual guarantees for the evaluation process is in part a reaction to the growing assertiveness of bureaucracies in matters of programme control and accountability. This assertiveness characterizes bureaucracies which sponsor programmes and bureaucracies which have administrative responsibility for programme implementation.

For instance, in the five-year National Development Programme in Computer Assisted Learning, which funded more than thirty development and evaluation projects, the negotiation of contracts involved detailed discussions between programme and project directors concerning the aims, methods and costs of the proposals, and strict forms of subsequent accountability (see MacDonald and Jenkins, 1980). In a similar vein those now seeking investigative access to the schools of inner London are faced with a set of stringent requirements in the form of a contract drawn up by the administration, with similar accountability intent. With the escalation of categorical funding in the eighties, bureaucratic sponsors are also taking the initiative in contract setting, both in pre-specifying their requirements in the request for proposals (RFPs) to an unprecedented degree and in limiting in the contract the extent to which findings may be published, if published at all. In most cases control over publication lies with the sponsor.

Whose interests do such contracts serve, and do they help to further the cause of independent and fair reporting? Where contracts are unilaterally drawn up it would be surprising if the contract did not reflect a special interest. A specific case was the evaluation of the EC's 'Transition from school to work' programme (MacDonald *et al*, 1981). All but one of its twenty-eight evaluations were contractually subject to bureaucratic control. In this context the evaluators capitulated to the funding body.

House (1980) outlines some twelve conditions that must be obtained for an agreement to be considered fair. These include non-coercion, rationality, acceptance of terms, joint agreement, disinterestedness, equal and full information and participation. Fulfilling such conditions requires that a great deal of time is spent negotiating an agreement before an evaluation can begin, time that frequently is not available given the timing of evaluation funding. Evaluations are often sought after programmes have begun, as urgent after-thoughts. Nevertheless, the conditions remain an important aspiration and at least some evaluators are increasingly cautious about taking on evaluations without an agreement meeting at least some of the conditions outlined above. It is perhaps significant in this context that House does not talk about contracts but agreements. His notion of a 'fair agreement' emphasizes the moral, rather than the legal, dimension of the setting of contracts. It takes the debate beyond vested interests to consider the conditions under which policy agreements are morally acceptable (*Ibid*, p. 162). While democratic evaluation has gone some way to ensure that evaluation has a moral dimension through negotiation of data and reports on the criteria of fairness and relevance, House's conception of a fair agreement here extends the moral dimension to pre-conditions for the evaluation.

It might be some time before such agreements become an accepted part of evaluation in this country given the current trends at one level and the informal tradition noted earlier, but some such agreement along House's lines might well have helped avoid some of the difficulties noted in chapter 6, where lack of acceptance of, or adherence to, the contractual principles generated unilaterally can lead, as it did there, to conflict and confrontation. Such agreements will not in themselves, of course, resolve the particular issues in a case. These must be negotiated through continuous dialogue with the different parties to the evaluation. The purpose of agreements is to clarify the function of evaluation, the procedures by which the evaluation is to be conducted and reported and to generate the conditions that allow a fair evaluation to be carried out. But, as House warns, such agreements offer no guarantee;

> Things like the degree of coercion, disinterestedness, etc. of the participants are important influences on whether an agreement reached and the consequent evaluation will be a fair one ... If proper procedures are followed *and* the other conditions are met, then the agreement should be a fair one. ... The point is that procedures by themselves do not guarantee either that these conditions are satisfied or that the evaluation agreement is a fair one. (*Ibid*, p. 170)

Fair agreements may offer one way forward, although negotiating them will not always be easy, and may easily lead to disqualification. As we have seen it is not difficult for sponsors to find biddable alternatives. But there are other important ways in which evaluation may be strengthened. The first is to establish a stronger institutional base from which an evaluation operates. One of the major difficulties in my case stemmed from the fact that I was working as an ad hoc employee for an academic institution under whose auspices the evaluation was being conducted but in which I was not based. The issue here is not simply one of location, though that might well have avoided some of the more detailed negotiations with the Institute and facilitated more direct negotiation with the EC, but the fact that I had to negotiate with three groups which had an investment in the evaluation ie, those who funded it (the LEA), those under whose auspices it was being conducted (the Institute) and those who required it (the EC).

If I had had a stronger institutional base, the LEA might not have been able to claim that all communications should go through them to the EC — the institution would have had more muscle to negotiate directly. If the evaluation commission had been direct from one institution to another the evaluation would not have been caught in the conflict of interests of the Institute and LEA and the prolonged three-way negotiations that ensued. Finally, the evaluation would have had a more certain basis of support from the institution responsible for the evaluation.

The second proposal, particularly important as a back-up for lone evaluators, is to have consultant support throughout the evaluation. The consultant would have several functions:

to generally support the conduct of the evaluation;

to check on the impartiality of accounts in cases of dispute;

to safeguard the evaluator against cooption or collusion;

to insulate the evaluator from the stress that an organization can exert to establish their viewpoint or suppress an evaluation;

to ensure that the evaluation is completed and the right to report to legitimate groups beyond the institution involved is established and maintained.

This concept of the function of a consultant is based on two conclusions: first, that it is important to protect the work of the evaluator against additional demands which may compromise completion; second, that it is useful in highly political contexts where vested interests conflict and the evaluation is at risk to have a colleague take up a negotiating role. The solution is apposite to a one person evaluation, though it may well have relevance to team evaluation for the same reason. Such a proposal is additional to any consultative committee that frequently is part of evaluation arrangements. While such committees exist to advise the evaluation, they are often composed of representatives from different organizations with their own interests and may not actively support the evaluation in the way my experience suggests is necessary.

The third proposal is to build in funds for the dissemination of evaluation reports. There were two major points at issue in the case I have discussed. One was the struggle to establish dissemination as a legitimate function of the evaluation; the second was the mechanics of dissemination itself. Funds were certainly needed to secure the dissemination and the lack of funds had an indirect effect on the issue of legitimacy. Knowing that there were insufficient funds for dissemination, and that more would be needed to secure it, the LEA which provided the money for evaluation simply refused and thereby effectively contained the dissemination. The Institute also refused though, in the end, it took some responsibility for producing the evaluation at cost. It is difficult for any evaluation to sustain an argument for dissemination without the resources to see it through.

A Final Comment

There is an irony in this particular case which should not be over-looked. When Robert Kennedy, then a young senator from Massa-chusetts, successfully negotiated a 'reporting requirement' codicil to the ESEA enactment (see chapter 2, p. 32) which released a billion federal dollars for compensatory education, he had in mind that the parents of poor children would be kept informed of what was being done for them with these dollars in their local schools (McLaughlin, 1975). That initiative of Kennedy transformed evaluation into a big (and increasingly privatized) industry, but after fifteen years it seems that the idea of delivering that simple service still poses severe problems. At least in England, so far as an independent source of such information is concerned.

8   The Demand for School Knowledge: For Whom by Whom?

The Changing Context

In this chapter and the next my attention will be focussed upon what schools themselves can do and should do to improve schooling and to make their work more accessible to those who have a right to know and a need to judge. This will take me away from programme and project evaluation, the context of the work I have described up to this point, and into the world of teacher in-service education, the context of the work I will elaborate later in this chapter. This change of context, however, does not entail a discontinuity of aspirations on my part, or a suspension of interest in working out the logic and potential of a democratic theory of evaluation. I declared in the second chapter of the book that my main interest in this theory was whether it could yield a basis for *justified*, professional self-direction in schooling as an alternative to both professional insulation and external control. My emphasis on the word 'justified' is intended to evoke and endorse the need for a form of accountability, but a form that must be consonant with the conditions of school improvement.

I want to locate this thinking within the naturalistic school of case study evaluation, and the legacy of development theory that was carried into the seventies by those whose thinking about curriculum development was shaped by their experience of the national projects that characterized the centre-periphery initiatives of the sixties. Let me summarize, albeit somewhat crudely, the message of those early evaluations. We cannot change for the better what we do not understand, and our current understanding of how schools change is limited. Schools have many common properties, but they are in each case idiosyncratically configured in ways that are important for curriculum decision-making. Individual freedom of choice, both at the personal and institutional level, is much more constrained than the myths of autonomy would have us believe. Even a curriculum reform programme conceived, as was the Schools Council programme, in terms of support for teacher choice, failed to take sufficient account of the constraints, and made participant teachers feel hostile or guilty about limited success.

That was the message that the evaluators, at least those who met in Cambridge in 1972, sought to deliver to policy-makers, planners, curriculum developers, local and national administrators. In the UK it was intended to temper both the goals and the means of large-scale interventionism then being rethought in the corridors of power, and the optimism of those curriculum developers like Stenhouse and Elliott who saw in the concept of the 'teacher as researcher' (Stenhouse, 1975; Elliott, 1973) the basis of a new, localized thrust forward in curriculum development.

Was the message received and understood? In part, I think is the answer. There were enough disillusioned sponsors of curriculum development around to provide work and opportunities for the new evaluators in the years following the conference, sponsors who at least took the message that more effective implementation of policy might require a better understanding of the contexts of implementation. That was, of course, only part of the message, but the new, aggressive curriculum politics of the seventies had little patience with the rest. The DES, which had in the early sixties lost the battle for curriculum control to the teachers[1], was preparing another bid to directly influence the curriculum (see, for instance, Salter and Tapper, 1981; Atkin and Simons, 1977). The era of managerial centrism soon followed fuelled by the economic cuts and the perceived need in government to restrict public expenditure to economic growth.

At the same time, and much more promisingly, in-service teacher education began to change in the seventies, supported by the arguments of the James Report (1972) which suggested in-service begin in schools and later INSET (In-Service Education and Training) initiatives (DES, 1978). Curriculum studies in higher education was also reshaped to reflect the experience and wisdom of those teachers and teacher educators, veterans of the sixties reform movement, who moved on to promoted posts in this expanding sector. This meant more than simply that the artefacts of curriculum reform — its theories, strategies, products, self-reports and evaluation reports, became the curriculum of teacher education courses. A number of those providing such courses engaged their students increasingly in researching their own work as a key element in the course. People like Elliott and Adelman with their Classroom Action Research Network[2], Stenhouse and Rudduck with NARTAR (National Association for Race Relations Teaching and Action Research), Eraut and Becher at the University of Sussex, Lewis at the University of York and others with courses in curriculum development that had a major research component, began to generate the possibility of a teacher-led grassroots curriculum development movement that largely bypassed the formal management structure of the school system. This meant, of course, that throughout the seventies government and its executive infrastructure, and academia and its course infrastructure, were in some cases pursuing divergent, if not mutually opposed ideologies of development. It is important to keep this in mind in reading what follows.

In 1976, while I was coping with the escalating effects of teacher proactivity in Castle Manor, the Labour Prime Minister, James Callaghan, made an important speech about education in which he said the time had come for a public review of curricular responsibilities. 'The implication was that the professionals had tried to keep control of the curriculum and therefore of the aims of education to themselves, and had resisted attempts to get them to explain themselves to their paymasters and clients' (Maclure, 1978, p. 9).

Although this might sound like an assertion of the 'right to know' it was much more an assertion of the government's right to govern, and of an ailing economy's need to shape its educational institutions in conformity with its economic goals. A somewhat farcical Great Debate followed the speech, but its main effect was to reinforce politics and directions already in train. The Schools Council for Curriculum and Examinations, the tripartite but teacher-controlled body that had sponsored the national curriculum projects of the sixties, was already in terminal decline, reduced to programmes of small-scale and piecemeal funding of local initiatives. The Council was eventually to be disbanded in favour of two new, DES-serviced central bodies as a new, hard-nosed model of central intervention in curriculum emerged (see note 3, chapter 2).

The prototype was the National Development Programme in Computer Assisted Learning, set up much earlier in 1974 at a cost of a then staggering £2½m, a sum that was soon to look very small indeed as more and more categorical funding programmes emanated from Whitehall, and as the Manpower Services Commission (MSC), an off-shoot of the Department of Employment, began to buy its way into an educational system that was systematically subjected to resource contraction. Neo-vocationalism was the name of the government's game, a message somewhat bafflingly tied to a theory of skills-led economic regeneration, and replete with deficit models of unemployable youth, industry-phobic schools, and incompetent teachers. The singer, but not the song changed in 1979 when Mr. Callaghan left a million plus unemployed and high inflation for Mrs. Thatcher to deal with. She made a virtue out of what the Labour administration had seen as a necessity. Inflation was successfully controlled, but unemployment rose alarmingly, educational institutions at all levels lost resources and confidence, and both national and local intervention in the preserves of teachers became more substantial, and more narrowly focussed on matters important to government.

The notion of school self-evaluation emerged in the late seventies as the result of a convergence of these varying interests, beliefs and commitments. System managers, both national and local, needed audit data to meet accountability demands and to facilitate administrative influence over curricular aims and performance. Teacher educators, fearful that such demands might deprofessionalize schools, saw in school self-evaluation a means of both protecting schools against reductionist pressures and of providing a stimulus for reflective practitioners.

It would be difficult to do justice to the range of voices clamouring to be involved in schooling throughout the seventies and eighties, and it may well be that I have over-emphasized those strands that were of particular relevance to my own thinking, and underemphasized those, such as the involvement of parents and industrialists in curricular determination, that were also prominent. This may seem odd in one with an interest in democratization, but it is not difficult to explain. By 1976, as a result of all my experience of school case study, and encouraged by the potential revealed by the Castle Manor study, I had come to two conclusions. The first was that the school, rather than the classroom, should be seen as the major unit of change and focus of development efforts. The second was that intra-institutional evaluation, conducted along democratic lines, could provide a basis for both development and for volunteered public knowledge. In 1977 I wrote the first of several papers advocating and expounding such a view (Simons, 1977c, 1980b, 1981a and 1985). I am aware that those who have read the preceding chapters may well consider such a view, and the commitment I made from that point on to encouraging and supporting schools that were persuaded by it, a departure from a concern to make schooling accessible to public judgment. But within an evolving scenario of change in the power relationships that create or deny learning opportunities we have to choose, at any point in time, how our long-term aspirations can best be protected within what opportunities we have or can foresee. Much of the argument in the seventies was concerned to promote and make explicit power-based control of the curriculum. The form of democratization involved in opening up schools was one that was hostile to the values of democratic evaluation, hostile to the promotion of mutually educative relationships, between pupils and teachers, between teachers and parents, between schools and their managers. As Apple and Teitelbaum (1986) say: 'Yet while curriculum planning and determination are now more *formally* democratic in most areas of the curriculum, there are forces now acting on the school that may make such choices nearly meaningless' (p. 179). One counters such developments where one can.

I saw my future opportunities lying largely in working with schools, promoting such relationships within them, enhancing the capacity of individuals and institutions to understand what they could and could not achieve within the constraints and licence of their social and political location. This was a view that was to be reinforced rather than undermined by the further experience of programme evaluation which I reported in chapter 6.

Of course a commitment to work with schools on such a task does not entail a view that schools can transform a society, but rather that the individuals within them have a part to play, a space to exploit. The same is true of programme evaluators, even with access to the spectrum of power relationships that define the space that schools will have. They have a role to play like everyone else. As I have said a number of times now it's a long haul, and those who think in this way need to recruit others to the persuasion, wherever and whenever we can get access to them. We will not succeed, in my view, unless our own actions and relationships embody the values we seek to promote in others.

In September, 1977, when I was preparing to embark on the work with teachers which is reported later in this chapter, the Educational Research Board of the Social Science Research Council convened in Cambridge a small invitational seminar on accountability as a guide to research policy initiatives in this area (Becher and Maclure, 1978). Evaluators were well represented, particularly members of the naturalistic group, some of whom had been active on both sides of the Atlantic in attacking accountability based on a product model of schooling. Becher, House, Stake, MacDonald, Elliott,

Eraut and Harlen (see chapters 2 and 3) all participated, as did DES members of the Assessment of Performance Unit (APU) set up in 1974 to monitor standards of performance in schools.

A major issue at the seminar was whether there was a viable role for the kind of large-scale testing of pupil performance that seemed to be underway at both national and local level as both a direct and indirect result of the APU initiative. Both Stake and House warned of the dangers of the techno-bureaucratic schemes of accountability which were already widespread in the USA. MacDonald, who denounced large-scale testing in no uncertain terms ('biased, obsolescent, coercive and authority-based') outlined an alternative, process model of accountability consisting of graduated stages of self-investigation leading to self-report exposed increasingly to public critique (MacDonald, 1978b). For some at this seminar this was 'too little, too late'[3] but one outcome was the allocation of funds to support local initiatives that fell broadly within a process conception and pro-active teacher engagement (Becher *et al*, 1981; Elliott *et al*, 1981). As we shall see in the next chapter, such initiatives were very much against the predominant approach to school accountability at the LEA level, and to the seemingly irreversible spread of managerialism in the British school system.

Before giving an account of the 'teacher as school evaluator' experiment which I undertook in the late seventies, I will now give an outline of the process model of school self-evaluation which I articulated at this time.[4] Although in some respects (see the end of chapter 9) I have since reconsidered aspects of my advocacy, my thinking at this time has not fundamentally changed, and shows how my experience of evaluation in the naturalistic tradition was reinterpreted in terms of the needs of schools.

Process Evaluation in Schools

Evaluation should aspire to reflect the processes of teaching, learning and organization. We need to know not so much what pupils can be demonstrated to have learned (the focus of product models) but rather what transpires in the process of learning and teaching, the outcomes we could reasonably expect from such transactions and the strengths and weaknesses of educational provision. We need, in other words, to educate our judgments about the adequacy of provision for learning and the quality of experience pupils have.

One of the best ways to improve these judgments is to study the processes of teaching, learning and organization in order to be able to compare practice with intention, opportunities with aspirations. And one of the best ways to represent and promote understanding of these processes is to accumulate and make available detailed descriptions of teaching and learning and the values and effects of curriculum policies within the context of particular schools and classrooms. Such an approach could take into account actual as well as intended practice and indicate the range of ways achievements might be demonstrated.

Product models emphasize measurable learnings, teaching intentions, and how efficiently the intentions have been achieved. The concept is an economic one and fits best within a system where resources can be allocated and assessed directly in relation to outputs by measures such as achievement tests. Such an approach has an appealing logic, but its defence rests upon a dangerous oversimplification of education and evaluation.

I want to make a case for process evaluation in the context of evaluating the whole school. Process, as already indicated, can refer to the teaching/learning interface and several authors have written extensively about the need to understand these processes (see, for example, Elliott (1978), Stenhouse (1975). Others refer to the whole process of schooling (MacDonald 1978b)). Both have been suggested as alternatives to current accountability models. Both have been closely linked to self-evaluation, thereby challenging the political as well as the content assumptions of orthodox thinking.

The particular stance towards school self-evaluation advanced here is one which encourages a high degree of participation in the conduct of the evaluation and the sharing of knowledge. The major justification for school self-evaluation is enhanced professionalism and it is best introduced as a continuing part of professional practice, not as a short term response to political pressures. In the short term, development of the process model needs to be insulated from accountability demands. In the long term, such evaluation will provide an effective and constructive model of accountability. If schools initiate evaluations in response to their own needs (and these may include producing accounts for outside audiences) these efforts are likely to be more sustained, to reflect the actual experience of schools and to lead to a quality control which is in the hands of those who have the prime responsibility for educating children and running the schools. It is primarily for these reasons that I wish to emphasize that the most appropriate justification for school self-evaluation is educational and professional and to suggest that it should be established as an integral part of professional practice.

Over the past two decades evaluation has become a highly specialized activity — the end of a chain of central development and diffusion invoked to see whether such central investment has been worthwhile. It has generally been costly, technical and specialized. Results and learnings from project evaluations have not been easy to apply to the varying circumstances of individual schools and classrooms. What I am suggesting here is:

1 that the sequence be reversed — evaluation should precede curriculum development and not follow in its wake;
2 that the style of evaluation more closely reflect the ways in which schools do evaluate the quality of education they provide;
3 that the evaluation be undertaken and managed by the schools themselves;
4 that the evaluation focus on intra-institutional issues.

Schools are under increasing pressure from parents, politicians and employers to demonstrate their worth. But many of the indices being sought focus solely on pupil outcomes. These are only one measure of the worth of a school. Much more needs to be evaluated including curriculum policies, learning opportunities, the interrelationships between levels (pupil, classroom, school) and forms of provision and achievements. The specific case for such a broader evaluation is outlined below. The emphasis is on evaluation of the school as a whole, or a policy issue which concerns the whole school. Information on pupil achievement or teacher performance may form part of the evaluation if it is relevant to the issue chosen for study, but is not focussed upon directly.

The case for studying the school as a whole is based on the following assumptions:

1 that better understanding of the organization and policies of the school could improve the opportunities and experiences provided in classrooms;
2 that systematic study and review allows the school to determine, and to produce evidence of, the extent to which they are providing the quality of education they espouse;
3 that a study of school policies can help teachers identify policy effects which require attention at school, department or classroom level;
4 that many policy issues (remedial education, for example),

cut across departments and classrooms and require collective review and resolution;

5 that there are many learning experiences (fieldwork and extra-curricular activities, for instance) which do not take place in the classroom and which require the cooperation and appraisal of the whole school;

6 that participation in a school self-study gives teachers the opportunity to develop their professional decision-making skills, enlarge their perspectives, and become better informed about the roles, responsibilities and problems of their colleagues.

It is perhaps important before proceeding further to describe some of the characteristics of school process self-evaluation. What distinguishes it from other forms of evaluation? In what ways can it contribute to our understanding of education.

Studies of the process of learning and schooling will tend to be descriptive/analytic, particular, small scale. They will record events in progress, document observations and draw on the judgments and perspectives of participants in the process — teachers, pupils, heads — in coming to understand observations and events in a specific context. Close description both of practice and the social context is an important part of the study. Such descriptions provide opportunities for interpretations that elude other models of assessment or evaluation based on assumptions of comparability and elimination of variation. Such descriptions also provide opportunities for more of the complexity of educational experience to be grasped and articulated, and for implicit theory and values to be made clear. Descriptions of practice, examples of outcomes, observations and analysis of different perspectives on issues may all form part of the process.

Reports to governors and parents are changing in many schools with the giving of more detailed information, and that provides, of course, a basis for outside evaluation to begin to take place. The evaluation process described here emphasizes that evaluation should start within the school in a context of informing the school's policy-making and improving educational practice. Reports with this aspiration are likely to be more interpretative than factual, to focus on particular policy issues, to expose different value positions, to provide evidence for decision-making and to raise options or alternatives for action.

Subjective judgments are an important part of the process. This needs to be emphasized, so undervalued are such judgments in many approaches to educational research and evaluation. Professional judgments are an integral part of classroom transactions and policy decisions. The subtlety of judgment may be difficult to capture but in evaluating the processes of teaching, learning and organization, judgments of people are an important source of data it would be foolish to ignore if understanding of the complexity of these processes is sought. There are difficulties, of course, in relying solely on judgment or, rather, on any one person's judgment, but in an evaluation utilizing a range of different methods and different people as sources, cross-checks on the accuracy of information can be established and the validity of judgments assessed.

While the focus may be particular, the data base is broad and may include quantitative and qualitative indicators of progress or events, and evidence of the outcomes as well as the processes of teaching, learning and organization. Both may be needed, if relevant to the issue under review. But what is also important here, whatever kind of data is selected, is that it be considered within the context of the particular school. The point has often been made (but is nevertheless worth stressing again) that our understanding of schooling is likely to be more complete if we try and capture more of the detail of what actually transpires in classrooms and schools, and more accurate if we interpret findings in context, be they examination results, achievement scores, qualitative judgments or observations.

It is also important to stress here that process approaches to evaluation (emphasizing description and interpretation, dynamics and context) do not reject quantitative data or suggest that, in paying more attention to the process, outcomes be neglected (see, for example, Stake (1967b), Parlett and Hamilton (1972). But there are many outcomes of schooling (qualitative and quantitative), and these need to be related to the aims of teaching, the opportunities provided for learning and to the transactions which occurred in the classroom and school.

Part of the argument against existing models of accountability rest on the fact that they do not, as Stake has pointed out, provide *relevant* information on the *quality* of educational practice and provision (Stake, 1976). Descriptions of classroom practice and the ways in which policies are determined and translated within particular school contexts are likely to yield more relevant information for local decision-making, particularly if they utilize a range of information and judgments in describing and analysing the values, implicit or explicit, of policies and practice. An understanding of different attitudes and values towards the policy issue under discussion is essential if change in policy is to be an outcome of the evaluation. It need not be, of course. Evaluation is undertaken initially for the purpose of reviewing current practice and coming to understand some of the strengths and weaknesses in present provision. Change is a possible outcome but the decision may be to leave things as they are. If the decision is to change, it is hoped that the evaluation would have provided insights or leads as to how this might be done.

Much information which can form a data base for analysis already exists in the school. It includes, for example, information on examination results, the academic and pastoral structure, the option system, the qualifications and allocation of staff to subjects, the resources available and their allocation to departments. Implicit in such information are questions of values. Even a brief analysis will provide a basis for the elucidation of policies, priorities and assumptions.

Where evaluation of a policy issue is sought for the explicit purpose of review, additional data may have to be collected. Useful methods which need not take a lot of time and which utilize skills teachers already have include questioning, listening, observation, and the noting of critical incidents and dialogue between different members of the school. Data collected in these ways does, however, have to have credibility and validity for those with whom it is shared. Similarly, data will not provide information to help decision-making unless it is presented in a form that is easily assimilated, a mechanism exists for the discussion of such evaluation, and a commitment is undertaken by the whole school to considering the evaluation as a basis for decision-making. Written reports are economical and the most usual way of presenting information. But if they are to be used as a basis for discussion they need to be evocative rather than prescriptive, ie, to raise questions, options, alternatives. Reports which are closed — tendentious, argumentative or conclusive — are rarely helpful for collective decision-making purposes. Written reports can, of course, be supplemented by recordings, examples of pupils' work, photographs. But in general these take more time both to produce and assimilate.

How any particular school sets up the appropriate procedures to evaluate the policy issue chosen and to utilize the evaluation to inform decision-making can only be determined in the particular context of each school in relation to the time available, the personnel who will undertake the evaluation and the ethos of the school, but some general principles are necessary to ensure that the evaluation has a reasonable chance of being taken seriously and is instituted as part of a continuing process.

In the short term, I suggested earlier, development of the process model needs to be separated from accountability demands. For several reasons. Opening one's policies and practices to critique in a system characterized by privacy for so long can be a challenging but threatening exercise. What was once implicit now becomes explicit. What was once informal or the province of one or two staff now becomes an accepted part of the school's agenda for study. Even the most commonplace events and policy statements can raise controversy when the assumptions underlying such events and statements are discussed.

It is also the case, of course, that maintaining fictions about practice or the institution may be functional in preserving its stability, and this is a stability that many may not want to see disturbed — at least without some control over how and to what extent. For this reason I have, elsewhere, (Simons, 1977c) suggested a set of principles and procedures which give participants some control over the process and some protection from the risks of self-evaluation while they gain experience in documenting their own work.

Secondly, it seems important that school self-evaluation be protected for a time from public scrutiny to allow schools to build up the necessary evaluation skills to produce self-accounts. The ability of teachers to engage in this activity is not in doubt, but a certain amount of time is needed for schools to produce self-accounts and for teachers and outsiders to become familiar with the kind of data which is offered and the criteria by which self-accounts should be valued.

Given this situation it would be unfair at the present time to use a school self-evaluation as a school audit. Reflecting on one's practice can be disturbing in itself as those who have been through the process testify. Support is needed to sustain the exercise. Honest accounts of one's practice could be construed as evidence of weakness and possibly used as a basis for alleging incompetence. With so many highly qualified teachers on the market, it is not inconceivable that some heads and LEAs might want to use self-evaluation for this purpose.

A third reason is the use to which these accounts may be put. Pressures to go public too soon, particularly in a context of threatened closure of schools and teacher unemployment, may simply result in window-dressing or positive, glowing accounts. After all, what school is going to open itself to critique if that critique, undertaken in a genuine spirit of self-examination, has any chance of being used to arm its critics or put individuals at risk? Given the changing nature of governance and management of schools and the increasing interest by parents and employers about what goes on in schools such an outcome is a possibility. One hopes, of course, that LEAs would not put the schools in such a position should they decide to undertake school self-evaluation; that they would respect their need for time to experiment with the process and production of such accounts and not expect to use them as an accountability mechanism before an appropriate time. Given the way the system is structured at present, more information about schools means more information in the hands of those who have the power to control resources: the DES gets more information about schools; the LEAs get more information about schools; the heads get more information about their staff and pupils. Those in a hierarchical, and usually more powerful position, in short, get more information about those who are less powerful in the system. What is more, they may use their power, as already implied, to get access to evaluations undertaken by other sectors of the service for one purpose (for example, self-reflection of schools policies and practice) and use these for another purpose (for example, resource allocation, employment decisions). If schools are to be more open to public scrutiny and be called to account for how they carry out their responsibilities, it does not seem unreasonable to suggest that the other sectors of the education service do the same. Information flows one way at present — upwards.

How fair is it to encourage schools to produce self-accounts detailing their practice and school policies, the grounds on which decisions are taken and the achievements reached, if other institutions to which they report are not to do the same? In a democratic society the principles of openness and sharing of knowledge cannot be confined to particular groups.

It is perhaps important to point out here that in suggesting that schools control the availability of self-reports to outside audiences, I am not advocating that they become less open to public scrutiny. Quite the contrary. The issue is one of timing, confidence and credibility. I believe teachers and schools should be accountable and report upon the work of the school to parents and the community. But in order to demonstrate accountability they must have autonomy. The most effective way of ensuring accountability is not to restrict people's autonomy but to make them accountable for it. The argument is not one for greater secrecy on the part of schools but for quality control as the first stage in a process of gradually making information more accessible.

The dominant mode of accountability, House argues (1973b), is mechanistic, having 'productivity' as its ethic and power rather than professionalism at its core: 'Most accountability schemes — whether they be performance contracting, cost-benefit analysis, performance-based teacher education or whatever — apply a mechanical solution, a power solution, to reform complex social organizations' (p. 2).

Evaluation on process lines allows schools to demonstrate and to account for what they can reasonably be held to be accountable for, ie, creating the opportunities for children to learn and for the quality of provision. Given the wide range of factors affecting pupil learning (home influence, social factors, individual differences, interest and motivation, relationships between pupils and teachers), in the last analysis teachers cannot be held to be entirely accountable for what pupils actually learn or fail to learn. Teachers should be held accountable not for the precise learning gains of pupils but for providing the appropriate opportunities for children to learn and for demonstrating the ways in which they have learned. Similarly, the LEAs should be held accountable for national provision, policy priorities and administration. All sectors of the service, in other words, should be accountable for those parts of the service they are responsible for. Evaluation which takes a broader view of pupil achievement and pays more attention to process may lead, in the long term, to a form of accountability that reflects the quality and breadth of learning and teaching.

Teachers as School Evaluators — An Experiment

The school self-evaluation I explored in 1977–78 with a group of teachers was essentially an extension of the case study approach to curriculum evaluation that was adopted in external evaluations utilizing naturalistic methods of inquiry but in this case the process was *initiated, conducted* and *controlled by the teachers in their own schools*. It was actually a more modest and partial form of the process just described, a beginning if you like. This was partly by design and partly by default given the opportunity which came my way and the constraints which accompanied it. The study evolved in practice from a research interest to explore the relevance and utility of democratic procedures for the conduct of evaluations conducted entirely by the schools themselves. Encouraged by the facility teachers demonstrated in Castle Manor to participate in democratic evaluative research, I wanted to explore how they might manage this process without the catalyst of an external facilitator producing a case study. Originally I intended to examine the use of the democratic procedures in three intensive case studies of schools undertaking their own self-evaluations. An invitation to design and conduct an in-service course in school self-evaluation offered an alternative opportunity: to explore this process with the support of consultant course guidance; and to examine, at the same time, the utility of the democratic procedures, through the teachers' experience, in a larger number of schools.

The democratic procedures were an extension of those adopted in Castle Manor strengthened in response to the rising demand for public reporting and the growing awareness, at least to evaluators, of the political dimensions of the school self-evaluation process and modified to take account of the fact that the evaluators were internal to the school. The central concepts of *confidentiality*, *negotiation* and *impartiality* were retained and those of *collaboration* and *accountability* added to emphasize the collegiate nature of the task. The precise procedures are documented in Simons (1977c). Teachers were asked to adopt the procedures in conducting case studies of a curriculum policy in their own schools and to report periodically on their implementation. On the basis of these reports, the procedures would be examined for their appropriateness in school self-evaluation and, if the evidence so indicated, local or general amendments suggested.

The unit of analysis was to be discrete, ie, a department or subject, house, pastoral system, year group or management group. This meant that each teacher would have a small group of colleagues with whom to discuss the issues. The procedures were to be negotiated with them and any other colleagues who became part of the evaluation study. In giving teachers permission to attend the course heads had to agree to an evaluation study being conducted in their school.

The course itself lasted two terms, a total of twenty weeks. It took place at a local teachers' centre from 6.00–8.00pm one evening a week. Twelve self-selected senior teachers (heads, deputy heads, or heads of departments), a mixture of primary and secondary, attended the course which introduced them to the concepts and techniques of evaluation and the analysis and reporting of results. The course had a workshop style interspersed with input from the course leader on specific topics.

The first session concentrated on exploring teachers' expectations and motivations for undertaking the course, the concepts of evaluation teachers brought to the course, and the structure and scope of the course itself. To the second session they were asked to bring a statement of an evaluation problem in their school and they were encouraged to start their evaluation studies by the fourth week. Choice of topic, method and style of reporting for each self-evaluation study were determined by the teacher-evaluator him/herself. Most chose to interview, observe and/or conduct a questionnaire. Data from course members' ongoing evaluations were used during the course itself, and their completed evaluation studies were the basis for discussion of data analysis and skills in reporting.

My research interest in this study was to examine the extent to which democratic procedures were relevant and useful in school self-evaluations; and to extend my understanding of the appropriate conditions for schools to effectively evaluate. The first aspiration was quite unrealistic, in fact, and did not get far. Teachers did not at the outset perceive the procedures to be important in evaluation practice. Their concerns were more with threats to their own competence in the process of undertaking evaluations than with the protection of others. When the procedures were introduced (in the third week), they did not see the need for them in practice. Several pointed out that the relationships in their school were open in any case. What was the need for confidentiality and negotiation if there was no conflict of interest? Others felt that the introduction of the procedures might inhibit co-operation in the study. Most importantly of all perhaps, teachers were primarily concerned with the methodology of evaluation. They did not perceive evaluation to be a political process.

In the face of these observations it would have been pointless to impose my research interest, so I abandoned the aspiration to get course members to systematically test the democratic procedures in practice[5] and concentrated on understanding their experience. To this end, throughout the course I documented their reactions to the process, the issues they found problematic and the questions they raised. At the end we discussed their perceptions of progress and early in the third term after the course had ended I interviewed course members about subsequent action, if any, since the course. The following observations are based upon these discussions and my observations of the teachers' experience.

Techniques

Teachers involved in evaluation in their own schools do not readily respond to the notion of building upon 'natural practice' (Walker, 1974a). Given a formal responsibility for evaluation they seek a corresponding formality in the means of data collection and analysis. Rather than a disciplined extension of their existing repertoire of skills and practices, such as intelligent questioning, observation and informed judgments, they look initially to the models of survey and experimental research for instrumentation. The effect is to deskill the teacher-evaluator in a manner akin to that observed by MacDonald in Hamingson (1973) of teachers experimenting with a novel pedagogy. In these circumstances theoretical explications of the parallels between systematic process evaluation and teacher decision-making may convince intellectually, but some period of immersion in the evaluation role is required before the resemblance begins to be seen in their developing evaluation practice.

Partly this is a matter of confidence, partly a matter of prudence. Instruments such as questionnaires not only have the appeal of research respectability, they offer depersonalization of inquiry and distance from the potentially disruptive and alienating effects of close-up observation and questioning. In the early stages of an internal evaluation political survival may be problematic and seem to depend upon the adoption of relatively unthreatening approaches. Over time the deficiencies of such instruments, particularly for those who want to get at the social construction of curriculum realities, lead to their abandonment in favour of more qualitative approaches once the evaluation activity has gained an institutional niche.

At first sight the teachers' experience here sharply confounds one of the assumptions underlying the case for school self-evaluation — that teachers do have skills for this activity, and can build upon 'natural practice' (Walker, 1974a, p. 25). Though not necessarily so. In the context in which these observations were reported the teachers had only twelve weeks to work through the process. They need to be involved in the process for a longer period of time in order to test the assumption fully. More important, perhaps, what the observation points up is that formal school self-evaluation stimulated by an external source has more affinities with the effects of externally developed curriculum projects than with informal school evaluations. The common and surprising factor here, given my initial assumption, was the innovativeness of the activity.

This was an observation immediately picked up by the first CEO interviewed in my initial investigation into LEA support (see next chapter, pp. 219–20). School self-evaluation on the process lines I was proposing would be regarded, he surmised, as an innovation in most of the schools in his authority. My failure to see this initially lay with my own beliefs in the capacities of teachers to respond to formal invitations to evaluate. I underestimated the time which a transfer from the informal to the formal would take, the support that was needed to help teachers identify their strengths and utilize them in an evaluation and the problems it might promote, such as seeking to approximate research skills, which might sidetrack the process.

It is difficult to know whether it was the innovativeness of the activity or the fact that the initiative, despite the focus on the school, stemmed from an external source which generated unrealistic expectations of the research task. But these expectations had two effects, one on the participant evaluators themselves, the second on their colleagues in cooperating schools.

The initial reliance of the teacher-evaluators on formal research techniques was to some extent a function of their own diffidence but also, of the expectations of their immediate colleagues. In some instances this lack of confidence was seized upon by colleagues and together with the unrealistic expectations used to discredit the evaluation.

One course participant, from a secondary school, the head of a department in the lower school, in the end had to abandon her evaluation study through lack of cooperation from other staff. One of the reasons given by the head was that the person could not do a satisfactory evaluation as she lacked the time, experience and the methods that Elizabeth Richardson (1973) adopted in her study of Nailsea school.[6] A totally inappropriate parallel in the context of an informal school evaluation, it was invoked to effectively curtail the evaluation (of an area in the upper school) which the head, despite having given his initial agreement, decided could not be competently carried out by a member of the lower school.

These observations do not necessarily invalidate the assumption that teachers can build upon natural practice, particularly if we believe, along with Eraut (1984b), that the origins of the perspectives and views teachers offer in responding to formal interviews and questionnaires in a formal evaluation study lie in their informal evaluations which are part of the daily practice of their profession. What the observations do question is the naturalness of the transfer implicit in the assumption. It is possible too that the context in this study was not favourable for bringing these tacit criteria and judgments to the surface and utilizing them in a more formal evaluation. It had more affinities, given the stimulus of the course and the outsider initiative (even though that outsider was a member of the school staff), with an external evaluation than internal school self-evaluation generated by the school itself.

Procedures

The second major problem was the teachers' lack of recognition of the need for procedures to govern the access to and release of data. Despite exhibiting a generalized nervousness about initiating an evaluation process in their schools the teachers did not anticipate a need for carefully thought out and negotiated procedures to guide the use of data. It was not until they actually encountered difficulties in collecting data or encountered objections to the evaluation from other members of staff that the political complexity of the activity began to crystallize and compel the teacher-evaluators to think through the conditions of their contract in the school, their role and position, and that set up for the evaluation.

The precise nature of some of the difficulties course members encountered are indicated by the following incidents. The course member whose study was abandoned encountered objections from other staff at three points. First the 'illuminative' approach to evaluation she introduced was disapproved of, then her competence doubted and finally, even when an alternative questionnaire approach was approved, the questionnaire itself was rejected by some members of staff, notably the head of the upper school who had suggested the area for study and the head who had endorsed it. In an account of her attempt to conduct a school self-evaluation this course member points to her growing awareness of the political aspects of evaluation:

> Internal political struggles seemed to be drifting round this study, and here it becomes difficult for me to comment, since I try to avoid entanglements of this kind. The school has its share of ambition, empire building, manipulation, dishonesty, autocratic decision-making 'divide and rule' ... I would suspect some political moves were in action, and I was about to attempt to bring openness into an area, which the head or someone close to him wanted left alone.

Another course member, a deputy head from a primary school, discovered halfway through his study and to his dismay, that two teachers did not wish to be interviewed by him. Even more to his dismay, he discovered that the head wanted, and expected, to use the report of the evaluation to demonstrate the weakness of one particular member of staff in order to effect some changes in his staffing policy. The teacher-evaluator perceived the head's intent as one of 'using' the evaluation he had conducted in good faith with staff to explore curriculum policy, to weed out an incompetent teacher. His response was to change the focus of his study mid-stream so that it could not be used for this end.

Would clear procedures over the use of data have helped to avoid these two diversions of intention and prevent ill will arising? One would need to have access to a more detailed account of the exact circumstances to check this out. Some of the difficulties may have arisen from inadequate explanation and the diffidence or inexperience of the teacher-evaluators. As one commented, 'I think my inexperience led me to confuse an illuminative technique with not taking control (of the study)'. But these explanations do not account for all the political difficulties encountered. What the teacher-evaluators did in the event was to begin to generate their own rules (for subsequent work) taking up some of the procedures outlined in the democratic principles but by no means all.

On reflection the initial reaction of course members to the procedures is not at all surprising. The fact that teachers did not immediately perceive their utility is no different from external evaluators' initial political naivety in case study evaluation. As noted in chapter 2, in the early days of naturalistic evaluation the need for procedures was not so immediate a concern as methodological appropriateness. The detailed procedures that evaluation research has developed over the past decade[7] for the access to and release of data have partly arisen from the political complexities evaluators experienced in conducting and sharing information between different groups with different interests. Evaluators did not undertake their first evaluations with such procedures clearly articulated. We should not be surprised that teachers in their first attempt at formal evaluation did not perceive the need for them.

Language

The third major observation also has links with innovative developments, in this case with action research as formulated by Elliott and Adelman (1976). The early experience of teachers undertaking school self-evaluation confirms the findings of these authors from their work with teachers in the Ford Teaching Project that teachers lack a precise enough language through which they can share their professional concerns. The prior existence of an adequate language cannot be taken for granted, and meanings need to be clear.

There was much confusion initially over precisely what was meant by evaluation. While some teachers equated evaluation with pupil assessment — and here they often meant measurement of pupil performance ignoring other forms of assessment — others perceived evaluation more broadly to include the value-judgments they or parents made of the activities of the school in general. In no instance did they link evaluation with decision-making. It was typically thought of as a summative one-off judgment. In no instance did they consider that exploring the opportunities and resources provided for children to learn was an important part of evaluating school perform-ance. At least initially. The emphasis was predominantly on pupil achievement. Broader concepts were introduced to the course and widening the data base suggested but it was only when teachers were engaged in doing their own study that they began to see the utility and relevance of a broader data base for understanding the issues they had chosen for study.

The question of ascribing value in relation to criteria and making judgments based on evidence raised another issue of language. While not reluctant to make judgments — these were evident from teachers' observational reports and the studies themselves — teachers were diffident about specifying the criteria underlying their intuitive judgments, and, in some cases, valuing their judgments vis-à-vis the judgments of 'expert' evaluators. They were also not very skilled, in the first instance, at writing descriptions of practice that might offer some evidence for judgment, presenting, instead, past judgment of pupil performance and personality much as might be written on a report card.

One interpretation of these observations is that the teachers lacked a theoretical language to articulate criteria and the skills to describe classroom and school practice; another that they felt depro-fessionalized by the formality of the exercise and felt their judgments to be worthless; a third that they perceived the exercise to demand the adoption of the 'language of formal evaluation' with which they were not confident.

In the event it was not a question of whose language or which language to adopt but the process by which meanings come to be shared and understanding generated. Language refinement, especially to gain equivalence of meaning, is a daunting task for the teacher-evaluator who has successfully generated in his colleagues an aware-ness of shared problems and an interest in exploring them. And for some, as we have seen, generating this awareness brings its own problems. The process of self-evaluation gives schools a chance to think through and operationalize the criteria by which they would want to be evaluated, but it will take time to develop the discourse and the forms of evidence that would adequately realize their convictions.

What may help in this process of generating shared understanding is to work from a close analysis of the language and forms of evidence teachers *do use* in informal evaluations in a non-threatening context without pressure for the production of reports. We may then begin to see how teachers *can* build upon this 'natural practice' in more systematic evaluation.

Constraints

The fourth set of concerns centres on intra-institutional arrangements for conducting school self-evaluation. Two constraints cited by the initial teacher group, confirmed subsequently by many other teachers, are time and motivation. Many teachers do not feel that they have enough time to engage in this 'additional' activity of formal evaluation, and few are prepared to give it a high priority, especially where, as is often the case, there is no firm commitment on the part of the school to consider the results. Although many regard official schemes for evaluating school performance as inappropriate, the threat of external auditing is insufficient to motivate teachers into active exploration of alternative practices. It seems that some catalyst from within or outside the school is needed to provide the initial and continuing stimulus for self-evaluation.

At that time I took the view that within the school the deputy head, despite the objections that may be made to the managerial aspect of her role, was ideally placed within the school structure to initiate a process of school self-evaluation. She has a whole school responsibility, so that her interest is seen to be legitimate. She has dual access to the head and teachers. She can support the evaluation through the creation of time and structures for participation. Teachers, on the other hand, often see their major responsibility to be their classroom or, in secondary schools, their subject. Interest in whole school evaluation is often not perceived by them, colleagues or senior management as a central facet of their role.

Some years later, my observations and discussions with teachers lead me to conclude that the process is best initiated, not by any one person, although the deputy head may still be a useful ally in the creation of time and support, but a group of teachers strongly supported by the head and deputy. The process, furthermore, is best conducted by a team of teachers, a cross selection of staff, supported by a horizontal management structure. These conclusions rest on the assumptions that the school is a community with overlapping and interrelated interests and that any one teacher has a responsibility to the school over and beyond her particular subject or classroom interest.

There was some evidence from the studies of course members to indicate that teachers working alone were powerless in their study of whole school issues, even those who perceived that they had a legitimate interest in them. It was clear in the case of the study which was abandoned that the head and some members of staff did not view that course member as a 'member of the school' rejecting her as inappropriate to study the whole school issue chosen. It was clear, too, from the second incident cited that the deputy head was not necessarily the best person to initiate and support the process, though this was a primary school where the status of the deputy vis-à-vis the head and the rest of the school is perhaps less strong. The head in both cases certainly exerted the more powerful role.

The legitimacy of the person for the task is a serious constraint on individual teachers who want to extend their evaluation interests beyond the boundary of their own professional responsibilities. Course members who chose issues within their immediate subject or classroom concerns encountered few political problems. Those who chose to focus on whole school issues either encountered severe problems in the execution of the evaluation or found their task undermined. The key issue here is legitimacy of interest. The competence question is secondary. Teachers on the course indicated that sometimes the most appropriate person to be an in-school evaluator was one who had responsibility for influencing policy in that specific area (ie, the person in charge of the sixth form might be the best person to study sixth form provision; the head of the pastoral system the best person to study the pastoral system). Against this, however, others claimed that a disinterested person or team would be more appropriate.

The teacher whose study was abandoned experienced both these views. Her involvement in the study had been sought as a 'disinterested outsider'. The head of the upper school had suggested the topic and it had been welcomed by the head as well. The study was curtailed when some staff of the upper school objected. While several objections were raised, the teacher-evaluator herself analyzed that it was her role in the school (she was head of a department in a lower school) that effectively led to the demise of her study of an aspect of the upper school, more so than her own competence or the adequacy of the illuminative approach to the study both of which had been criticized by her colleagues. It simply wasn't seen as legitimate for a member of the lower school to study the upper school. The teacher-evaluator commented of the experience that 'I was too much of an outsider' and that 'the head, when trying to stop the study, used my role in the school as the reason for the study's failure'. Her words suggest that this may not have been the real reason for stopping the study, merely a useful one ('they wanted to stop the study for different reasons'), but it was effective, nevertheless, and a real constraint on the innovative process.

The team approach suggested earlier especially if the team is chosen from a cross section of staff whether by subject/topic, interest, age, experience or status, may offset such a response. It is unlikely that all members of a team would be regarded as inappropriate, incompetent or not having a legitimate interest in the task.

The outside catalyst often thought to be helpful in stimulating school self-evaluation is the in-service course. It is highly doubtful, however, that this alone is sufficient to sustain the exercise unless the in-service is arranged as a series of courses with follow-up locally in particular schools or collectively at a local teachers' centre. We have little evidence of the force of the one-off course for sustaining activity in schools though to some extent it depends upon the length, quality and organization of the course (Rudduck, 1981). Longer term involvement in research activity is similarly not necessarily sustained once teachers are back in the school (Elliott, 1976). Even if an external catalyst provides the stimulus then, an internal one is needed as well to sustain the interest and create the necessary conditions for effective self-reflection.

Support

The final observation relates to teacher support needs and is based not only on observations of teachers conducting school self-evaluations but numerous discussions with other teachers on perceived support needs. Teachers conducting school self-evaluations require support in the following ways: *in-service course support* that focusses upon evaluation rationales, concepts, advantages and disadvantages of different approaches, and provides training in the *conduct* and *reporting* of evaluations; *on-site* support in the form of acceptance by the head and colleagues of the relevance and importance of the exercise, time for the evaluation and a structure to facilitate participation and discussion of the evaluation issues, progress and results; *intermittent or continuing consultancy support* in the form of outside advice on specific aspects of the evaluation — design, testing, interviewing, processing data, or whatever is most needed by the school at different times; *off-site support* in the form of regular meetings with teachers/teams from other schools to share experience; and back-up services — reprographic, typing, duplication of case studies — to facilitate this process; *LEA support* in terms of the in-service mentioned above, extra resources to buy in release time, consultancy or material support, and realistic expectations of the time needed to build up skills and confidence in the process.

In summary what these observations point to is, first of all, that despite the oft-quoted and non-disputed adage of teachers that 'we are evaluating all the time', school self-evaluation that focusses upon curriculum policy issues, is systematically pursued and maximizes participation of staff is as innovative an activity as many of the curriculum development projects of the sixties and seventies. Secondly, the observations suggest that teachers beginning more systematic evaluations initially perceive evaluation to be a methodology or a set of techniques rather than a political process. Political consciousness only seems to emerge once individuals have conducted evaluations on cross-curricula issues in their own schools. This raises a rather serious problem in planning collaborative evaluations in schools. Accounts of the problems that can be anticipated, preferably in case study form, may help teachers to judge in the context of their own school (the 'naturalistic generalization' suggested in chapter 1) the need for such procedures to sustain the process. But more than this is needed.

At the end of the next chapter, in the light of a critique of the school self-evaluation movement, I outline some steps towards a reformulation of the concept, and consider at a more fundamental level the preconditions of effective school-based curriculum development.

Notes

1 In 1960, the then Conservative Minister of Education, David Eccles, who had criticized the school curriculum for being a 'secret garden', not given to public scrutiny, announced his intention to make the Ministry's voice heard more forcefully in curriculum matters. In 1962 he set up a Curriculum Study Group in the DES to further this intention. Opposition to this Study Group by both the LEAs and professional teachers' associations led to its demise and the setting up instead, in 1964, of the

Schools Council for Curriculum and Examinations for England and Wales, funded jointly by the DES and LEAs and with a teacher majority on its committees. For further comment on the Curriculum Study Group see LAWTON, 1980; MANZER, 1970; KOGAN, 1978.

2 The Classroom Action Research Network (CARN) was established in 1976 following the Ford Teaching Project (Elliott and Adelman, 1976) to stimulate and strengthen links between individual teacher-researchers and teacher-based research groups. Through its annual Bulletin, CARN disseminates the ideas and reports of these individuals and groups and papers from the annual conference it has held since 1978. The network includes teachers and researchers interested in teacher-based research in Europe, the USA, Canada, Australia, New Zealand and the UK. Supported originally by a grant from the Ford Foundation the network was established and coordinated from the Cambridge Institute of Education, England, initially by John Elliott. In 1987 the coordinator is Peter Holly.

3 I am grateful to JOHN ELLIOTT (personal communication) for giving me an account of this conference.

4 For a more extended account of the process model see Simons (1981) 'Process evaluation in schools' in LACEY, C. and LAWTON, D. (Eds) *Issues in Accountability and Evaluation*, London, Methuen.

5 The procedures were not entirely abandoned, however. Different course members adopted some of the principles in seeking access to and clearing of data with colleagues in their schools and, subsequent to the course, the appropriateness of the procedures was discussed and critiqued with over 500 teachers in various in-service and MA courses.

6 This is a reference to Elizabeth Richardson's work in Nailsea school. For three years she acted as a consultant to the school studying staff relationships, management structures and leadership patterns in the school. The experience is written up as a 300-page book (Richardson, 1973).

7 See, for example, the procedures developed by MacDonald and Stake (1974), MACDONALD *et al* (1975), ADELMAN (1979).

9 School Self-Evaluation — Schemes and Scepticism

> One way government becomes an influential participant in education-related decisions is by requiring that certain procedures be employed even if there is no direct suggestion about the curriculum to be used. (Atkin, 1980, p. 15)

My exploration of the concept of 'teacher as evaluator' was conducted in parallel with the early stages of the LEA evaluation reported in chapter 6. It revealed a great deal of the problem structure encountered by individuals who venture beyond the confines of their cellular location in schools. The message was much the same as that derived at the end of the previous decade from studies of innovating teachers in the context of national curriculum projects. Support was needed at different levels of the school system if such inquiry was to have any chance of being sustained. This was not just a matter of intra-institutional support structures, though these were quite evidently crucial, but of external forms of support (and legitimacy) such as in-service provision, consultancy, release time, physical resources. If school self-evaluation was at least as innovative as the curriculum projects of the sixties, as seemed to be the case, then early discussion with, and involvement of, LEA administrators and school advisers was needed to facilitate such a development.

In mid-1979 I began to explore the feasibility of LEA support for curriculum development based on institutional self-evaluation, by conducting interviews with chief education officers and advisers. Neither this, nor a later more extensive effort to monitor LEA initiatives in this area, were funded projects. By this time I had registered for a part-time PhD with the provisional title 'The democratization of evaluation processes' (Simons, 1984b) and these inquiries were conducted within the framework of this pursuit.

My concerns, reflecting the anxieties as well as the difficulties experienced by the experimenting teachers, were not restricted to the need for positive support. In a context of accountability and financial efficiency, could teachers be assured that evaluation carried out for one purpose — curriculum improvement — would not be used for another — course audit? In a context of falling rolls, school closures and teacher redundancy, would the honest exposure of failings be seized upon as a reason for intervention, external control and punitive measures? Would the LEA accept the notion that some of the critique, and some of the data generated by self-evaluation, might be withheld from them in the interests of sustaining the process of open reflection within the school?

In the event, my explorations of the possibility of LEA support for the process model of school self-evaluation were abandoned after a small number of interviews, when it became quite clear that such a possibility had been overtaken by events. Chief education officers, harassed by budgetary problems and a myriad of local and national pressures, were too preoccupied with crisis management to engage such issues seriously in action, reflective though they were in conversation. Plans for school evaluation were already in hand, and these plans, though they embodied the rhetoric of self-evaluation, were conceived primarily within a managerial framework. Later in this chapter I shall take a close look at LEA initiatives. First it may be useful to place these within a broader canvass of the self-evaluation movement.

The School Self-Evaluation Movement

In the last ten years we have witnessed a rapid growth in school self-evaluation models and practices, not dissimilar to the spate of evaluation models that followed the growth of curriculum development in the late sixties/early seventies. We might do well here to recall Stake's (1967a) warning: 'Let the buyer beware'. The scale of the movement, as it very quickly became, can be noted by the range of activity that developed in the years 1977–87. Many academic conferences and in-service courses were held on the topic, universities and colleges introduced units on school self-evaluation in diploma and degree courses, the DES-funded regional courses and the Schools Council supported several research and development projects on the subject. Within these years the Open University developed and published a course on curriculum evaluation and assessment in educational institutions, one part of which was devoted to institutional self-evaluation (Open University, 1982). Books and articles on the subject burgeoned (see, for example, Shipman, 1979; Elliott, 1979b; Simons, 1981a; Eraut, 1984b) as did an evaluation journal devoted almost entirely to the topic: *The Journal of Evaluation in Education*.

The speed of production of school self-evaluation guidelines was another sign of the rapid growth of the movement. Prominent in the development of these were LEAs. The initiative taken by the ILEA[1] in publishing *Keeping the School Under Review* (1977) was quickly followed by others and by the end of 1980 approximately three-quarters of the LEAs in England and Wales had initiated discussions on school self-evaluation and one-fifth had issued guidelines for schools. One year later this had increased to approximately five-sixths having initiated discussions and one-third having issued guidelines (Elliott, G, 1982).

The movement has not been confined to the UK. It has its counterpart in other countries. In Australia, for instance, school self-evaluation has been growing in popularity, supported by project initiatives (Hughes, 1979; Hughes *et al*, 1981), in-service and academic initiatives (see, for instance, Davis, 1981) and, in Victoria, by the state government *School Improvement Plan* (SIP) (1983) which offers some financial support for individual school self-evaluation initiatives. An OECD initiative, the *International School Improvement Project* (ISIP), extends the scope of the activity further, and a summary of current practice (Hopkins, 1983) indicates that school self-evaluation is a major trend in several other OECD countries as well.

While conceived by some as a counter weight (at least in the UK) to technocratic trends in administrative theory and practice, the movement in school self-evaluation is neither as coherent nor as 'subversive' as such a conception would suggest. Under the many labels[2] which are in currency are a variety of activities all broadly pursuing the same aim of encouraging schools to evaluate themselves but with different underlying assumptions, purposes, audiences and emphases. What is least clear and most controversial in this range of activity is who has control of the process, who has access to any product that emerges, and whose interests are served. School self-evaluation is obviously for the school to conduct but depending upon such factors as whether the source of the initiative is external or internal, there may be significant differences in both espoused and implicit theories of control of the educational process.

For the most part interest has centred on schools rather than other institutions, although there are parallels in some sectors of higher education (see, for instance, Adelman and Alexander, 1982), and on the school as a whole. It is a movement ostensibly concerned with institutional self-evaluation, not pupil, teacher or classroom self-evaluation, though aspects of classroom practice or pupil assessment may well form part of the whole school evaluation.

The origins and motivations of this movement are many and complex as I intimated in chapter 8. It is a conflation of interests, trends and opportunities. Initiatives in the UK have stemmed from at least five sources: LEAs, funded projects, individual academics, the DES and schools themselves. LEA schemes for local school self-evaluation have provided perhaps the readiest index of activity comprising, as they do for the most part, published check-lists of questions for school review with, in many cases, mandatory status. The funded projects, most of them supported by the Schools Council Programme I and II developments,[3] vary in scope, but include those which emphasize analyses of the organization (McMahon *et al*, 1984), those supporting process evaluation at an institutional level within schools (*Education Bulletin I/82*) and those focussing upon classroom process and its relationship with the organization of the school (Elliott, J, 1982). While academics such as Bolam, McMahon and Elliott have led such projects, they and others (see, for instance, Eraut, 1984b; Nuttall, 1982b) have also played another role in the school self-evaluation movement, clarifying concepts, aims and assumptions, and supporting development through conferences and in-service courses on the topic. Yet others have provided a critique (see, for example, Shipman, 1983). The DES, though not dealing directly with school self-evaluation have, nevertheless, provided impetus for the process through the issuing of circulars (14/77, 6/81 and 8/83, for example) asking LEAs to report on the curriculum in their schools.

Last, but not I hope least, are schools themselves who have initiated self-evaluation in response to their own curriculum needs (see, for example, Mitchell, 1984) or as a reaction to imposed forms of accountability. The extent of this activity is difficult to ascertain. It is particular to an individual school, often not documented and, for both these reasons, not widely known. But one survey undertaken by Mary James for the Open University begins to document the direction and shape of individual school initiatives (James, 1982b).

While at least three different contexts provided an inspiration for school self-evaluation activity — the curriculum reform movement, in-service education and accountability — undoubtedly the most powerful influence according to several commentators (Holt, 1981; Nuttall, 1982a; Elliott, 1983) was the centrally-inspired accountability movement which began in the early seventies and by the late seventies had gathered considerable momentum.

1977, the year in which I rather hopefully set out a model of school self-evaluation directed primarily towards self-development rather than immediate accountability was a key year marking the build-up of bids for greater public control of the curriculum. That was the year which saw the publication of the ILEA school self-evaluation booklet, the year the DES issued Circular 14/77 asking LEAs to review their curricular arrangements; the year the Taylor Report into the governance and management of schools recommended that parents and governors should play more of a role in curriculum matters; the year the Schools Council changed its constitution to give teachers less of a majority on its key committees and increased lay representation; and the year the DES published a Green Paper on education in schools expressing a variety of concerns about curriculum provision. These were all signs that the tripartite balance of control in education, for so long an assumed virtue of the British education system, was beginning to crumble. It was in particular a sign that LEAs and individual schools would both have to find acceptable responses to the demand for school knowledge.

The signs of a change in the balance of power were borne out. Although the Great Debate initiated by Callaghan's 1976 speech fizzled out, the actions which followed it (see DES documents 1980 and 1981) confirmed what many suspected was the intent of the 1977 activities, an increase in centrism and managerialism (MacDonald, 1979; Becher and Maclure, 1978; Holt, 1981; Lacey and Lawton, 1981; Salter and Tapper, 1981).

In the short term the DES backtracked a little on the core curriculum thrust intimated in the Green Paper and given shape in *A Framework for the School Curriculum* (1980), but there were stronger moves afoot. In 1980 central government produced a new Education Act requiring schools to publish their examination results and in 1981 the DES issued a new Circular (6/81) calling for curricular review by LEAs. This was followed two years later by a further Circular (8/83) declaring the central government's intention to continuously monitor curricular activities. It was clear with this announcement, if it wasn't before, that central government was demanding more accountability of LEAs, which could, logically, only be rendered by greater accountability of schools to LEAs.

It wasn't only initiatives by central government, however, that produced an accountability climate for LEAs. At the local level itself there were contributory factors stemming back to local government reorganization in 1974 when, within the corporate management structure many authorities adopted as a result, education lost its independence as the big local spending department, CEOs were forced to provide more local justification of educational spending and advisers ceased to have such a prominent support role in relation to schools. Add to this the increasing concern of parents, employers and councillors over standards in schools, and the pressures of financial stringency which led, in some cases, to cutbacks in the advisory services, and we have many local reasons as well why schools should be asked to account.

The two main developments that can be seen to arise in this accountability context are the school self-evaluation schemes introduced by LEAs and the broad curriculum review initiatives promoted by the DES (through their circulars 14/77, 6/81 and 8/83). The DES initiatives reflect a determination to call LEAs to account for their constitutional responsibility for curriculum. The initiatives of academics and schools themselves, on the other hand, tend to reflect opposition to the means of accountability proposed and designed by central and local government: central government through its APU[4] monitoring of national standards on the basis of tests of pupil learning in core subjects; and local government through schemes advocating and embodying an objectives approach to curriculum planning (Elliott, G, 1981a).

Reaction against these forms of accountability stemmed not only from intellectual and political dissatisfaction with a production model of schooling (MacDonald, 1978b; Simons, 1981a) but also from knowledge of the evidence of the reductionist effects of mechanistic forms of accounting emanating from the USA (see, for example, House, 1973a and 1973b; Stake, 1973; Read, 1973).

Increased interest in teacher education and in-service education provided the context for a quite different orientation towards school self-evaluation. It is in this context that the concepts of the teacher-as-researcher (Stenhouse, 1975) and the self-monitoring teacher (Elliott, 1976) were further developed along with concepts of teacher self-evaluation and, somewhat later, school-centred in-service training (Bridges and Eynon, 1983). What unites this range of activities and enables them to be loosely grouped is a commitment to enhancing the professionalism of teachers (*Ibid*). Activities prompted by this commitment typically involve self-reflexive inquiry by teachers, usually of classroom practice (see, for example, an account of the Ford Teaching Project, Elliott and Adelman, 1976.) In-service courses, whether within or outside the school, have similarly focussed upon the individual teacher.

More recently, as Bridges and Eynon (1983) have pointed out, the emphasis in in-service education has shifted to school-centred activity, a term they prefer to school-based or school-focussed to make the point that in-service provision is generally designed to enhance the competence, authority and professional control of teachers and implies an advanced level of professional responsibility and consciousness. However they note that by 1979 what was missing in school-centred initiatives was a sharing of experience of the processes of school-centred in-service work, an observation that links such in-service activities with the emergence of institutional self-evaluation initiatives that have a process orientation.

These then are the contexts in which the growth of school self-evaluation has flourished. It is not insignificant, as many have pointed out, that the growth of the movement and the shape it took within these contexts occurred in a period of economic stringency. In hard times less money is available to support curriculum developments that are not government priorities. And financial cuts, forced upon the education service by both central and local government, increase concern for the efficient deployment of a dwindling resource base. The promotion of school self-evaluation and school-centred in-service in a period of severe economic constraint, can be viewed as a form of provision 'on the cheap', particularly when, as is often the case, it is justified as a form of professional development for teachers.

It is interesting to note that administrative agencies such as the LEAs and the DES made little use of professional development rhetoric in the era of innovatory curricula and resource expansion. The fact that the professional development appeal has coincided, or been linked, with lack of resources has led some commentators (see, for example, Holt, 1981; Elliott, 1983) to suspect that the use of this rhetoric is a mask for gaining acceptance of schemes that have managerial rather than developmental professional interests at heart.

The concept of 'institutional' self-evaluation, however, compels us to note that much of the professional development activity proceeding from teacher-educators reflects, and therefore arguably reinforces, the division of teacher labour within schools. The emphasis on the individual teacher, worthy and necessary though it is, and difficult to avoid in any case within the opportunity structure of course provision for teachers, fails to fulfil the logical rationale that is entailed in the more collegial concept of school evaluation. It is difficult to see how institutional self-evaluation, involving the collection and consideration of curricular policy and practice across the whole school, can be understood other than in terms of collaborative teacher action, both in the process of evaluation and in the subsequent consideration of evaluation-based action. If this argument is accepted, then the democratic theory of evaluation, which essentially concerns itself with the social and political dimensions of a process model of inquiry, provides a possibility for institutional development. Within the present organization of schools, a democratic approach to school self-evaluation would, of course, be potentially transformative of intra-institutional relationships, just as the best of the teacher action-research movement is potentially transformative of teacher-student relationships. Such a development at school level is in any case required to facilitate and reinforce the work of the reflective practitioner in the classroom.

The notion of school self-evaluation as a basis of self-direction, as I argued earlier, grew out of the naturalistic evaluator's critique of centre-periphery innovation strategies. The implication of this critique was that more devolved structures of curriculum decision-making would facilitate the need for problem-solving processes more responsive to idiosyncratic contexts and practitioner definitions of deficiency. In this sense the rationale has much in common with the action-research movement, which is also responsive to context and felt needs.

Both aspirations are consonant with MacDonald and Walker's (1975) goal of promoting a 'self-monitoring educational community' and both have found, in the naturalistic adaptations of methodological traditions, a useful source of ideas for conducting teacher-initiated inquiry (see Walker and Adelman, 1975; Walker, 1985). But a question of undoubted importance is the relationship between such aspirations and the widespread guidelines for school self-evaluation that have issued from LEAs and now constitute the 'official' framework within which many schools have been asked or required to respond.

The First Wave of LEA School Self-Evaluation Schemes[5]

Most of the formal LEA self-evaluation guidelines published in the late seventies take the form of an extensive checklist of questions for schools to ask to 'keep themselves under review'. While many of the questions are addressed to the head teacher, some are for class teachers, and there are different sections for primary and secondary schools. Some require a written response, some do not; some are voluntary, others mandatory. Most have been devised by administrators and advisers, only in some cases in consultation with teachers. None of the thirty-one schemes examined in detail by Elliott, G, (1982) had been devised by teachers alone.

The questions in these guidelines cover a range of topics, from lessons and knowledge of children (under the teacher's role) to objectives and organization and staffing (under the head's role) to basic school arrangements and communication with parents and outside agencies (see ILEA, 1977; and Oxfordshire, 1979, for example). Some (for example Salford, 1982) focus on subject areas and take an even broader focus including sections on educational aims and philosophy, and curriculum and leadership in schools. Most lists are long and cover anything from 200 to, in one case, 2000 questions or statements.

From the booklets themselves one notes first and foremost the professed aim of development, sometimes referred to as school development, staff development, or development of professional skills (Oxfordshire, 1979, p. 3; ILEA, 1977, p. 1). Closer inspection reveals the documents have another message — to report back or account to the LEA. The focus and substantive nature of the questions tends to confirm the theme of accountability. Many are implicitly prescriptive and focus primarily on organizational and management responsibilities (see, for instance, Solihull, 1979; Lincolnshire, 1981), an observation that is confirmed by Elliott (1983) and Clift (1982). Despite the frequent references to the checklists as starting points for discussion (Oxfordshire, 1979; Lancashire, 1980) or as a resource for adaptation by the school to its own purposes (ILEA, 1977), or explicit denial that the questions are leading (Suffolk, 1981), the documents clearly represent the LEA's framework of values.

In addition to professional development and accountability to the LEA a third purpose that can be detected in several schemes is a link to central government interest in the notion of total curriculum review. In several of the forewords and questions there are references to central documents: the *Green Paper* (1977a) (see, for example, Lincolnshire, 1981); DES *Circular 14/77*, HMI *Curriculum 11-16* (1977) (see, for example, Suffolk, 1981; Kingston-upon-Thames, 1980); and the HMI *Primary Survey* (1978) (see, for example, Lancashire, 1980). Other authorities refer explicitly to *The School Curriculum* (DES 1981) which states that schools should 'analyze and set out their aims in writing, and make it part of their work regularly to assess how far the education they provide matches their aims'. Later schemes refer explicitly to Circular 6/81 which suggests that schools prepare to meet the government's monitoring intent by evaluating themselves first. In this way school self-evaluation is seen as instrumental to an external need for review.

To call such approaches school self-evaluation is to make a mockery of an essentially educational concept. The checklist approach is guaranteed to keep schools busy. Not on evaluation, unfortunately, but rather on the construction of reassuring responses to questions that on the whole reflect the LEA's sense of its accountability to local councillors or central government. This can take up a great deal of time, time that might be more profitably devoted to curriculum development, or to actually finding out what schools do. Seen as guidelines, the checklists are, in most cases, remarkably thorough and comprehensive, though few questions are addressed to the processes of teaching and learning. The view of curriculum is a narrow one, consisting largely of syllabus content. The view taken of the school is a mechanistic and individualized one, with different sets of questions corresponding to division of responsibilities.

The notion of the school as a professional community is notable for its absence from these LEA documents. They contain no sense of, or advocacy for, the collective discussion of school policy, or concern about the school's deliberative processes. 'Checklists are essentially an instrument for increasing technical efficiency and control rather than the capacity to make reflective professional decisions' (Elliott, 1983, p. 242).

The checklist is in effect, if not in intent, a preordinate device for standardizing curriculum planning and school management. The emphasis on objectives setting (Elliott, G, 1981a) tends to reinforce the view that central or local monitoring is the intent of these schemes. It undoubtedly is easier to introduce a monitoring scheme across schools if they can be persuaded to adopt the same approach to curriculum planning, even better if they adopt the same priorities and objectives. It would not be too far from the mark either to suggest that this emphasis reflects a resurgence in the management by objectives approach, long favoured by the Treasury in Whitehall and pressed upon the big-spending departments such as education. This approach failed to gain popularity in the sixties and even in the mid-seventies when attempts were made to introduce it as part of the new managerial style following the reorganization of local government (Atkin and Simons, 1977). Some LEA guidelines (Salford, for example) note the origin of early forms of objectives setting in this context.

This means-ends engineering model of curriculum was, of course, the one that was rejected in the UK by curriculum strategists as unresponsive to diversity of situations, legitimate teacher discretion, and to the psychology of creative professional work. It is, as its origins in engineering suggest, a model of specification and control. The tendency of such approaches, by separating conception from implementation, is to downgrade the status of teachers, to deprofessionalize schooling in the same way as the application of the approach in the manufacturing industry has deskilled labour forces more generally. It is in this sense in direct opposition to the values of a process model of school evaluation for curriculum development.

Let the general objections rest there. I want now to consider some of the more positive developments. For, despite what may have been conveyed from the foregoing critique, LEA approaches to school self-evaluation are not monolithic. Checklist schemes may have predominated in the late seventies but in the eighties there are other moves afoot.

1982 Onwards

In order to ascertain whether there had been any development in the scope and scale of LEA school self-evaluation, in June 1982 I made my own brief inquiry, sending an open letter to all LEAs in England and Wales asking if they had formulated self-evaluation or self-assessment programmes, whether these were mandatory or voluntary, and if they would send a copy.

Although the response rate of 82 per cent of this survey in 1982 was less than the 98 per cent and 100 per cent of the Elliott surveys conducted in 1980 and 1981 respectively, it was sufficient to indicate that the LEA initiatives in school self-evaluation had not abated. What was of more interest, however, was the reflectiveness of some of the 1982 replies. My assumption was that sooner or later some of the LEAs would realize the deficiencies of many of the school self-evaluation schemes published from 1977–81 and would begin to develop alternatives. There was some evidence that this was so.

Rather than develop their own guidelines, several LEAs chose to be involved in the external initiative of the GRIDS (Guidelines for Review and Internal Development) project (McMahon *et al*, 1984) funded by the Schools Council. The GRIDS project was commissioned to provide advice for schools on how to conduct a school review and to effect actions for improvement, a framework that was missing in the predominant checklist approach (GRIDS Project, SCDC, 1985).

Phase I of the Project in 1982/83 tested Guideline materials that consisted of five stages (Getting Started, Initial Review, Specific Reviews, Action for Development, Overview and Restart) in thirty-one primary and secondary schools in five LEAs. Results were fed back to the Project Team and LEAs and the Guidelines revised. Dissemination conferences were held in each of the five LEAs in 1984, and two handbooks were published. Phase II, to review the handbooks, produce supplementary material and disseminate further was funded by the School Curriculum Development Committee[6] in September 1984. A further eight LEAs have joined the original five in a working partnership with the project and another stage of review is gathering pace.

The aspiration of the project is to stimulate institutional development through the five-stage process noted above. Each stage is broken down into separate steps and tasks which assume consensus from one step to the next. The initial review, a survey of staff opinion to identify priority areas (not very different from the areas covered by many of the self-evaluation checklists) is followed by one or more specific reviews, also broken down into steps and tasks.

The underlying principles of consultation with, and involvement of, staff suggest that control of the review and development lies with the school and that it is a process for internal school improvement. But the project also emphasizes the usefulness of consultancy help at different stages of the process and a supportive management role for the LEA. This can take at least three forms: the appointment of a supervisor to assume overall responsibility for the project within the LEA, including ensuring that GRIDS is seen 'in the context of the overall LEA policy'; an LEA coordinator to provide day-to-day support for the project schools; and an advisory or steering group to monitor what is happening in the schools, provide feedback and advice for the LEA supervisor and coordinator and to keep other groups in the LEA informed about events (McMahon *et al*, 1984, pp. 70–1).

Other LEAs took a different path and began to generate their own departures from the checklist/guidelines approach indicating an awareness of the complexity of the self-evaluation process. One Education Officer for Curriculum and In-Service Training commented:

> Here in ... therefore, we have shifted our ground quite considerably from what now might be regarded as a somewhat naive notion that all that is required is the production of a set of questions which, when truthfully answered, will result in improved practice, to the rather more sophisticated and infinitely more difficult concept of involving teachers at every level in the school in a continual process of appraisal of their own and their colleagues' work and the *systems and values which operate in the institution.*

An adviser in another LEA wrote:

> Evaluation goes hand in hand with reconstruction — there are no self-evident fixed criteria for separating good from bad, only a programme for penetrating the complexity of a rapidly changing world, for keeping pace with it, renewing it and establishing how we can share this demanding task.

And a working party on secondary school self-evaluation in the first authority referred to above concluded:

> There should be no question of self-evaluation becoming obligatory for schools.
>
> If self-evaluation is undertaken then the school should determine the areas to be examined and have the right to restrict circulation of the findings. A self-evaluation exercise should not in itself lead to the writing of a report for the CEO.
>
> A school should not embark upon self-evaluation unless and until the ground has been well prepared and especially there is a readiness to accept and above all act on the findings.
>
> As part of the 'ground preparing' exercise, of crucial importance especially in the context of falling rolls, is the need to allay the fears and suspicions of even the best of teachers that self-evaluation is to be used as an instrument to measure their performance as part, perhaps, of some staff appraisal scheme.

It is clear from a summary of the significant features in these later school self-evaluation schemes which all have professional development as their major aspiration, that the voluntary, long-term nature of the evaluation process is recognized. The importance of the whole school focus is also recognized to some extent by the identification of issues for study which affect the whole school, by the need to engage a team of staff in the process and by the need to demonstrate the validity of the exercise in terms of its benefits to pupils. Some have gone further and argued that the process of evaluation must take place within a structure that will engage the value systems of teachers and provide appropriate procedures for the generation and control of information.

There are other signs too, that changes are taking place in some LEAs. The Chief Education Officer of Oxfordshire, for instance, has indicated his dissatisfaction with the Oxfordshire self-evaluation booklet. Pointing to the inadequacy of its individual orientation he has moved towards a system that involves teachers collectively in working on single issues within their schools. Oxfordshire has also begun to recognize the political and professional point that if there is anything of value in the self-evaluation exercise it is important to introduce it at LEA officer level as well and a self-evaluation scheme has been produced for this purpose.[7] The ILEA has reviewed its initial document (though more in terms of extending its scope than critically changing the format and content). One of its senior employees has voiced concern about the administrative problems of dealing with the 'load of paper' that is being generated from the mandatory reporting schemes without clear ideas about how to process and manage it.[8]

Whether such critiques of school self-evaluation will be sufficiently strong to counter activity that has a narrow accountability intent, remains to be seen.

Reflections on the School Self-Evaluation Movement

On a frequency count we must conclude that school self-evaluation, an idea that was initially formulated to embody the value of decentralizing the responsibility and the opportunity for curriculum development, has taken a form which reflects more powerful interests in the management of schooling. It is not difficult to see why in broad political terms. Governments faced with a failing economy and a five-year lease on power have to be seen to act decisively to stem decline. Schooling has for government a vital role in cultivating skills and attitudes appropriate to plans for economic regeneration. Governments put pressure on their civil servants to do something about it. In Britain, where the power of the state in matters of curriculum has been historically implicit, masked by protocols of action that emphasize shared responsibility and a spirit of collaboration, such pressures in the post-war era reached irresistible levels in the seventies. Senior civil servants found themselves increasingly under the direction of determined ministers. What followed was the 'decentralization of blame' (MacDonald, 1983a), and the passing of pressure down the line from the LEA administrators, and from them to the schools.

This is, of course, a rather crude and partial view of the processes that produced such artefacts as checklists for school self-evaluation, but I introduce it to qualify an impression some of my comments may have given that *administrators* at the national and local level have been single-mindedly engaged in a bid for curriculum control on the continental model. As MacDonald has observed, 'Some bureaucratic actions that look like assaults on the entrance to the secret garden are better understood as desperate attempts to find the nearest exit' (MacDonald, 1983a). Does this qualification really matter if the effect of such actions is to promote external control? Indeed it does. It helps to explain why the ILEA, for instance, now has a 'lot of paper' it doesn't know what to do with. It explains why some LEAs, in the aftermath of a hasty resort to checklists to relieve the pressure, are now having second thoughts about their utility for any other purpose, and why others are increasingly attracted by voluntary schemes responsive to professional concerns. In this sense, though perhaps I am being over-optimistic, it is possible to see the present unhelpful orthodoxy of LEA initiatives as a temporary setback to the kind of school self-evaluation which I, and others, have been trying to promote.[9]

To say this is not to deny that in recent years the latent and largely obscured exercise of central power has become manifest and in many ways explicit. This is undeniable. But it is also worth keeping in mind that many of those who are required to represent and execute centralist policies, including technocratic models of administration, are neither by temperament nor conviction persuaded of their merits. It is just as big a mistake to caricature administrators as power-driven as it is to idealize academics as disinterested, or teachers as educators. We must take each as we find them and, as I suggested (see earlier chapter 2, p. 53), seek with them to understand the compromises that structure their actions.

Turning now to procedural models of school self-evaluation, which were developed in the 1980s in response to the perceived inadequacy of the checklist approach, and the limitations of in-service provision for individual teachers, the GRIDS project is the one that has undoubtedly been the most influential. An alternative, the IMTEC (International Movement Towards Educational Change) sponsored GIL (Guide to Institutional Learning) questionnaire, trialled in this country by the NFER between 1982 and 1984, and published in 1986 as the School Development Guide (SDG), (Dalin *et al*, 1986) has yet to pass the marketability test, but is similar in many basic respects to the GRIDS model. Both are procedural models of how schools can initiate and manage self-review for development purposes and both have their roots in organizational development theory (see Runkel and Schmuck, 1984). I shall confine my remarks to GRIDS, because more is known about it and there is some experience of its use to take into account.

The experience of the teachers I involved in school evaluation indicated the difficulty they faced in trying to focus on whole school issues without a supportive organizational structure to give the exercise legitimacy. This experience was consistent with, and con-firmed, the experience of case study evaluators like myself who had found the need to develop procedures to deal with the politically and personally sensitive problems of creating shared experience within bureaucratically organized institutions. For people of my persuasion, creating the institutional conditions for worthwhile evaluation called for procedures that would equalize relationships to the evaluation, thus constituting an alternative to 'normal' relationships to meet the conditions of the particular task.

Looked at from this point of view the GRIDS project (as well as the IMTEC alternative) appears to lack this rationale. GRIDS, it is true, is a concept of collective inquiry on a collaborative basis calling for the whole staff to be involved, but the model of the school it invokes and reinforces is one of leadership and management from the top, with teachers consulted at each stage of the cyclical process. Although this entails a departure from totally autocratic styles of decision-making in schools, it does not challenge in any significant way the organizational hierarchy or the prerogatives associated with the distribution of power in institutions.

It is difficult to read the GRIDS report, which includes exemplary accounts from user pilot schools, without a growing sense of incredulity. To those of us who know schools to be institutions characterized by plurality of interests, values, beliefs and commitments, made manageable only by organizational and protocol traditions designed to minimize open conflict, the problem of collective self-review is basically a problem of how to manage the conflict that is inevitably revealed. It is in the processes of teaching and learning, and the organizational arrangements that create or deny educational opportunities, that this plurality is embedded. One looks in vain for this reality in the GRIDS report. On the contrary, schools are presented, and reported, as consensual institutions in which collaboration, self-examination, and the rectification of deficiency is a relatively straightforward matter of improving feedback mechanisms in a manner that is not too taxing for the staff. True, there are cautionary words about the need to provide staff with the option of anonymity in filling in the initial review of priorities questionnaire, which has been pre-structured by the research team. True, it is suggested that interviews conducted by review teams within the school should offer confidentiality to the interviewee. But, since the document recommends very strongly that such reviews be coordinated by senior staff with relevant responsibility for the topic under review, this latter provision must be less than reassuring to assistant teachers.

I do not want to be too harsh. GRIDS has proved to have considerable appeal to schools looking for a way to implement self-evaluation. Clearly some at least have found it practicable and useful as a way to make improvements in school management. But we should note that it is school managers who are attracted to it and who proclaim its virtues, and it is reasonable I think to hold back from equating managerial benefit with curriculum improvement. Peter Holly, who was closely involved in the GRIDS development as a Schools Council Programme Officer, suggests that it fails to engage teachers in evaluating the fundamental processes of teaching and learning: 'it succeeds only in tinkering at the organizational edges' (Holly, 1984, p. 14). He goes on to confirm my own reservations with this comment:

> The GRIDS method offers schools an on-going, natural style of working which can be assimilated (institutionalized) with comparative ease. The irony, perhaps, is that the easier it is to institutionalize, the harder it is to invoke real change. GRIDS,

despite looking 'democratic' to some, can prove a constraining, conservative force in the change process. (*Ibid*, p. 15)

Holly concludes by questioning whether real change is falling
through the GRIDS (*Ibid*). Only further evidence could answer this
question conclusively but an examination of the model of development the project advocates, reveals that it is most unlikely to lead to
institutional change.

Shipman (1983) makes a related point in a more general comment
about the school self-evaluation movement. 'The conception and
implementation of self-evaluation still tends to ignore the political
give and take, the personal and professional interests, the assumptions
behind school management that frustrated curriculum project directors' (p. 249).

Having argued that both administrative and research-based
approaches to school self-evaluation are imbued with the logic and
limitations of line-management, let me finally make some comments
on developments in the professionalization of teachers stemming
from Stenhouse's (1975) concept of 'teacher as researcher'. You may
recall that I earlier raised the question of whether the 'message' of the
evaluators in the early seventies, a message about the constraints on
individual and institutional choice, was heeded by curriculum developers such as Stenhouse and Elliott. The answer I offered was
'partly'. It was clear from case studies of innovating schools in the late
sixties that individual teachers seeking to reconstruct relationships to
knowledge in their own classrooms found themselves not infrequent-
ly embroiled in institutional confrontations they neither sought nor
anticipated (MacDonald, 1978a). In its dissemination phase the
Humanities Project sought more support for innovating teachers,
both from its own resources and through more informed facilitation
on the part of school heads and local administrations. It also set up
area group meetings of innovating teachers (as did other national
projects at this time) trying to establish peer group strength across
institutions. Such groups, related to and supported by, the central
project team, provided an alternative frame of reference for the
experimenting teacher, embodying alternative values to those embodied in the institutions in which they were employed. But it afforded
only a temporary scaffolding of course, since provision for an
after-care service when the Project ended could only be minimal.

Subsequent developments of the teacher as researcher, which
came to be better known as action-research in the classroom, tended

to concentrate on a reconstruction of that framework of external support, through further project work, course-based consultancy, and increasingly through peer group networks and associations. This had both strengths and weaknesses. Individual teachers were enabled to exploit the interpretive discretion afforded them by the closed door of the classroom and to minimize the erosion of creative energy that is entailed in venturing beyond it. And they were sustained by meetings with like minds and the support of academic institutions. But the notion of a grassroots teacher-based movement had at some point to confront the problem of institutionalization, and this consciousness came sooner than later, a fact that is itself a testimonial to the success of the movement. No doubt this consciousness was also accelerated by the involvement of some leaders of the action-research movement, such as Elliott and Adelman, in project evaluation, case study, and increasingly in the institutional self-evaluation movement. If we look, then, at recent developments in this field, what we find is a developing realization of the need to address the context of classroom-based change, and to contemplate the problem of internalizing externally initiated change, a problem not dissimilar in its structure to that of all centre-periphery models.

The self-monitoring teachers in the Ford Teaching Project, for example, demonstrated what it was possible for self-reflective teachers to achieve in improving their classroom performance but also the difficulties of sustaining that activity once they were back in their own school settings (Elliott, 1976).[10] Elliott commented at the time that 'schools have not on the whole institutionalized support for reflective teaching' (p. 7). In his later writings (Elliott, 1980b, for example) he seems to have recognized much more the importance of the institutional structure for sustaining teacher research:

> If such teachers are to increase their freedom of action at all, they need not only to understand what it is they are doing in their classrooms, but how their actions are influenced and shaped by institutional, social, and political structures. (p. 321)

In the context of school self-evaluation Elliott (1979a and 1979b) has tended to follow the same path, first by strongly endorsing that school self-evaluation must be rooted in classroom analysis (1979b) and later (1983) in emphasizing the importance of linking self-evaluative practice into the organization of the school:

> Deliberative self-evaluation is time-consuming and cannot be

simply added on to all the other demands on staff time. Priorities have to be reordered at the institutional level. Since this kind of self-evaluation also implies free and open discussion between staff, relationships need to become more collegial, and less hierarchical, information flowing laterally and 'downwards' rather than simply 'upwards'. The management style needs to become more open and participatory... (Elliott, 1983, p. 241)

Such a conception still falls short, however, of the notion of the reflective school where the aim is to focus on the school directly and to evaluate collectively how it may be changed. The action research initiative and many of the self-evaluation initiatives focus primarily upon the individual 'reflective practitioner' or group of reflective practitioners in a context of professional development. Critics may say that it is impossible to separate evaluation of the school from the professional development of individual teachers within schools and, logically, that may be so. If 'the quality of education is dependent upon the quality of teachers', as Nuttall (1981) suggests, 'any review of the first is bound to have ramifications for the second' (p. 22). There is, nevertheless, sufficient difference in the two orientations to treat them as separate for the purpose of exploring the potential for school self-evaluation where the unit is the school.

My focus, for instance, as James (1982a) has recognized, is not on individual teachers or a collection of individual teachers adding up to a collective professional school but on the development of schools themselves. Of course, it is important that schools facilitate creative professional diversity in classrooms, but to define schools merely in terms of whether they facilitate or inhibit this form of teacher freedom is surely to seriously underestimate what is involved and embodied in the organizational curriculum experience of pupils.

Nuttall (1982b) has recently cautioned that the trend toward school self-evaluation and 'modern approaches to professional development such as school-focused in-service education for teachers' (p. 2) may neglect the crucial personal dimension of professional growth for teachers and, while he does not eschew the idea of growth for the institution, makes a plea for the individual's personal professional needs not to be lost in the process. This is a point of crucial importance that is in danger of getting lost in equations between personal and institutional development. Both are needed and the problem is to determine how they may be jointly pursued and related within institutional settings.

Adelman and Alexander (1982) have also come to the conclusion that the focus on curriculum issues and collective deliberations is central to the process of institutional self-evaluation:

> Course evaluation has to be more than a collection of individual self-evaluations: it has to explore what these separate activities add up to, the relationships between them, their coherence, their consistency, their cumulative impact on and meaning for the student. Course evaluation thus is necessarily collective: an attribute usually accepted for course planning. (p. 184)

They too stress the limitations of individual self-appraisal not only because an individual's capacity to be critical of his own work may be limited but more fundamentally from their assumptions about what a course or curriculum is:

> It is not a collection of isolated teaching acts, but an inter-dependent network of activities placed in what is claimed to be a meaningful juxtaposition in pursuit of an explicit set of general goals set by the institution. (*Ibid*)

The problem in summary of much of the school self-evaluation movement to date, as the action-research movement before it, has been its promotion from without rather than from within the institution. External initiatives, especially those with potential for change, will always face the problem of how to link those initiatives into the organizational structure of the school, and many of the current external school self-evaluation initiatives to date have failed, as Shipman (1983) infers, to grasp this point. The problem for school self-evaluation as a process of institutional development, however, is quite different. It is not simply or even a case of trying to institutionalize a process generated by an external stimulus as much of the literature on institutionalization implies (see, for example, Fullan, 1982; Miles, 1983). School self-evaluation for long-term institutional development needs to be based upon an analysis of the aims, goals and values of the institution itself.

Against the Rules — Towards an Agenda for School Self-Evaluation[11]

At the time of writing a long-running dispute between teachers, their employers and the Secretary of State may be nearing resolution.

Ostensibly about pay, the terms of the dispute also reflect the cumulative resentment of the teachers at the government's onslaught on the effectiveness and efficiency of schools, and the continuing determination of the government to renegotiate the teacher's contract of employment. This determination is a result of the government's vulnerability, in circumstances of dispute, to the withdrawal of the teachers' voluntary labour, a ploy which the teachers have used to cripple the functioning of schools without incurring the costs of strike action.

I too am concerned about the teacher's contract as that has come to be understood and interpreted in the conduct of schooling. My interest in the issue is not that of the government, which clearly seeks more power over teachers' labour, but rather in negotiating a broader definition of professional responsibility as a basis of organizational reform. In the context of the Castle Manor study I observed that the promotion of self-study, both on an individual and collective basis, was made difficult by forms of institutional organization that made no provision for such activity. This observation was confirmed by the later experience I have reported of teachers attempting school-wide evaluative inquiry. It is a 'work-bench' view of teaching. Only those at the top of the organizational hierarchy enjoy a definition of their responsibilities that is broad enough to allow them flexibility in choosing how best to carry them out at a particular point in time. No-one who has engaged in the case study of schools can be unaware of the extent to which this fact skews and limits their opportunities to represent institutional life in its own terms.

There can be little doubt either that the forms of school self-evaluation that I have critically surveyed in this chapter are tailored, in different ways, to accept and work within an organizational tradition that is in many ways inimical to the extension of the teacher role that underlies the innovations. This is why, I think, such innovations strike me as either disappointingly modest, counter-productive, or unrealistic. They are at best about school improvement, not school development.

When we talk about programme or project evaluation, few would quarrel with the proposition that the task of evaluation is to inquire into the values and effects of the programme or project, so that these values may be put to the test of professional and public support in the light of some evidence of their impact in action. It seems reasonable then, in the absence of some special argument to the contrary, that we should think of school self-evaluation as an inquiry into the values and effects of schooling in a particular case. This in turn would suggest that the agenda of self-evaluation would include questions such as the following. To whose needs and interests does this school respond? What values are embodied in its curriculum and organizational arrangements and in its relationships to the world outside? Whose answers to these questions are to count? If such questions sound vaguely familiar to you, at this stage in the book, it may be because they are not dissimilar to the questions raised by the SAFARI project with respect to the interests, values and functions of a research community in a liberal democracy. If it was useful and appropriate to raise such questions for the professional research community, should we expect less of a professional teaching community. Is it just the evaluation/research sector that needs to 'raise its sights' in order to understand better its compromises with the conditions of employment? Is the task posed by Skilbeck (1985) a task that can safely be left to politicians, administrators and academics? 'Is it not time for us to examine the curriculum problems that derive from our reluctance or inability to talk frankly about the nature of the culture which the curriculum assumes, selects from, transcribes, transposes, or transforms?' (p. 27).

Some of those involved in the action-research movement that has promoted critical self-examination of teaching in the classroom see this possibility in the extension of that model to the institutional stage of collective self-critique. This is not, however, as straightforward as it may seem. Noting the tension between teacher action-researchers in the classroom and the structure of power in the institutional context, Hutchinson and Whitehouse (1986) have this to say about the problem of transition from cellular to collective critique:

> If action research is to succeed in achieving educational improvement practitioners will need to be able to regard practice and its contexts as cultural constructions rather than as social givens. In this struggle the clash between interpretative morality and technical rationality is at its most poignant. (p. 93)

I agree with this observation, and believe that if the individual teacher-researcher is not to find herself merely contained by the mobilization of managerial interests, in much the same way as the teacher-developers were contained in the Mother Tongue project I reported in chapter 6, then school self-evaluation needs to be based on an agenda of organizational change. This is a very different proposition from any entailed in current schemes, and it needs to be seen as a long-term aim. MacDonald, in his staged model of school self-report, thought ten years not too long a period for schools embarking on accountability to reach a point where they might fruitfully engage in an economic self-critique in interaction with their publics (MacDonald, 1978b). I think myself this too short a period, and am not even sure that such an ambition would ever be fully reached. I am confident, however, that without an ambition that is worth falling short of, school self-evaluation is likely to become a routinized and superficial activity that will obstruct, rather than facilitate, school development. In coming to this view I have had to rethink the implications of such an agenda for the conduct of school self-evaluation. As you will see, this has compelled me to challenge a number of assumptions which guided my initial work in this context. The major assumption was, of course, that the procedures we had evolved for the case-study of schools by outsiders could function as a model for the process of insider evaluation.

I had previously argued (Simons, 1977c and 1983) that the procedural guidelines developed in the context of external case study evaluation (see, for instance, MacDonald and Stake, 1974; Mac-Donald and Walker, 1975) applied with at least equal force to the even more sensitive context of internal evaluation, and would be sufficient to defuse the intrinsically threatening nature of the exercise.

I now see the need to go much further since it is clear that internal evaluation, if it is to serve professional development rather than managerial control, must challenge directly some of the fundamental rules of the institution. Schools are like clubs, and members must either obey the rules or change them. Unlike the external evaluator, who may be given a temporary licence to personally infringe the rules in order to complete a one-off exercise, the internal evaluator much change the organization before the service can effectively be introduced. Just as Stenhouse (1975) argued there can be no curriculum development without teacher development so I wish to argue there can be no curriculum development without institutional development.

To speak of schools, or any other institutions, as clubs is hardly breaking new conceptual ground, but it does help to underline an important dimension of the kind of fact-finding, information handling process that institutional inquiry must introduce. Members of the club know what the rules are although they are never written down. They consist of such maxims as 'mind your own business', 'stick to your patch', and 'don't get ideas above your station'.

These values, of *privacy*, *territory* and *hierarchy*, underpin the organizational structure of schools and act as constraints upon the apparently informal nature of most staff relationships. An evaluation exercise threatens to break such rules and one that is initiated by members themselves may be seen as a serious breach of long-established and widely accepted conventions. When we consider that evaluation is in any case an unwelcome activity and that such a breach means that internal evaluators begin with a deficit rather than a mere absence of the trust they require to carry out the study, then there is a prima facie case for taking steps to secure the predictability and the shared goals of the evaluation. This calls for a change in the rules.

The central difference between the external evaluation and the internal which provokes the need to review the procedures is, of course, the location and identity of the evaluators. Unlike the external evaluator who is not a club member bound by its rules and who is only a temporary intruder on a one-off mission, the internal evaluator is a permanent resident. The information she proposes to gather will upset the existing distribution of institutional knowledge, and will remain within the school as a political resource of unpredictable consequence. Any mistakes made, any hostilities generated will have to be healed or lived with within the community.

It is tempting for would-be in-house evaluators, sensitive to such pitfalls, to play down the significance of the innovation in engaging the co-operation of their colleagues, and to rely on their personal credibility. 'Trust me' they say. Such an approach is transparently a recipe for disaster, as the evidence of two of the teacher studies in chapter 8 illustrate, but equally pathogenic, I would now argue is a straight adoption of democratic procedures that were developed in an external context. In order to substantiate this proposition it is necessary to analyze this practice in terms of its consonance with the maintenance of the institutional values of *privacy*, *territory* and *hierarchy*.

The democratic procedures as we have seen were first explored in an external framework by MacDonald, Walker and associates in the SAFARI project. These principles and procedures for access, data collection and reporting (MacDonald and Stake, 1974; MacDonald and Walker, 1975) were subsequently elaborated by other evaluators in the naturalistic tradition (Adelman, 1979; Kemmis with Robottom, 1981) so that there is now a widely-shared value system with some variation of procedures to fit particular cases.

Although it might seem that by definition the case study of an institution must transgress its internal boundaries, a close look at the democratic model reveals it as a variant characterized in its process by a high degree of respect for these boundaries. In his original conception of the model MacDonald was centrally concerned with reconciling the public right to know with the individual right to privacy and protection (MacDonald *et al*, 1975). His solution was a broker role for the evaluator.

In practice this meant treating the case as a cellular structure of privatized information, negotiating access and release of information with each individual guardian. It meant gathering much more knowledge of the case than was ever released, it meant much less ascription, particularly of judgment data, than was possible from the case records. Certainly it increased the flow and the nature of intrainstitutional knowledge but accorded to individual informants at different levels of the institutional power structure the right as members of that institution to determine the volume and content of that flow. Whilst the convention of confidentiality ensured that the evaluator would gain effective access to a privatized knowledge system the convention of informant control over release ensured that she would know much more than she could ever tell.

The critical point is that a straight application of such conventions to the internal evaluator would result in an immense empowerment of the evaluator/s qua member of the institution if the conventions are accepted, or an inoperable approach if the implications of acquiescence are apprehended, a point I did not appreciate when I modified the procedures for school self-evaluation (Simons, 1977c). Only non-members can be brokers. It is quite clear, therefore, that internal evaluators cannot proceed on such a basis and that an alternative basis must be constructed. This alternative basis, I would argue, rests upon the possibility of dismantling the value structure of privacy, territory, and hierarchy, and substituting the values of openness, shared critical responsibility, and rational autonomy. In the context of current accountability pressures on schools it is worth adding that such a radical change in organizational values calls for a corresponding degree of insulation. On this point MacDonald (1978b) has written of 'self-critical communities within high walls — groups who risk enough in collective self-reflection to be spared the added risk of continuous exposure to outside observation'.

That there is a need for formal procedures in school self-evaluation is not at issue. The few published accounts of school evaluations endorse this view (see, for example, Delves and Watts, 1979; Mitchell, 1984). It is the basis on which these should be constructed that I am arguing needs reformulation. The case for formal procedures has been most convincingly argued by Nias (1981) in her essay on trust where she claims that two necessary conditions for trust are *predictability* and *perceived agreement over ends*. Behaviours can only become predictable and agreement over ends affirmed as one gains knowledge of them. For this, formal procedures are necessary:

> Trust, I have argued, depends upon the predictability of personal and institutional behaviour and of technical competence, and upon an awareness of shared goals. Yet in the educational system of a pluralist society there is bound to be conflict over the aims of education, and thus over the conduct of the schools (especially secondary comprehensive ones). To claim that this conflict can be resolved by mutual trust rather than by 'formal procedures' is to be guilty of circularity. It is also to ignore the part played in the establishment of trust by forms of organization . . .
>
> In other words, formal procedures and the interpersonal knowledge which they promote are not the anti-thesis of 'trust' but the necessary conditions for it. Moreover, they act upon each other. Formal procedures facilitate the growth of trust and help to ensure its survival. (Nias, 1981, p. 222)

By formal procedures Nias means forms of organization built into the functioning of the school (for example, heads of faculty meetings) or which routinize or give institutional recognition to existing informal arrangements (for example, giving an informal staff group the name and status of a working party) (*Ibid*, p. 212). I would want to go further and suggest that where appropriate forms of organization don't exist, new ones be set up on democratic lines to facilitate both the process of school self-evaluation and the sharing of knowledge.

The crux of the problem, evident in Nias's statement, is the reconciliation between 'shared goals' and 'conflict over aims'. Whilst one can agree with her, and I do, that formal procedures are an essential means of mediating disparate ideologies across a professional community, such procedures are not value-neutral. With respect to institutional self-evaluation the procedures should, indeed must, embody a consensual expression of the conditions of school development. In terms of my argument, therefore, procedures for self-evaluation must embody the values of openness, shared critical responsibility: and rational autonomy. Unless schools are prepared to face the fundamental reversal of institutional traditions that is clearly entailed by such a posture, and to commit themselves to a new concept of what John Elliott (1981a) calls 'intra-professional accountability', it is unlikely that school self-evaluation can lead to constructive institutional development.

Strategies for development have to be related to breaking the rules which serve old values and establishing new ones. Privacy in one's teaching, assessing and curriculum planning have to give way to public documentation and analysis of theory and practice; departmental interests have to be considered in relation to broader curriculum concerns and educational critique; working relationships have to be deduced from autonomy-based accountability rather than power-based responsibility. These values — the exposure of individual work to collective critique within a framework of professional equality — need to be underpinned by institutional processes which encourage their expression.

Is it possible that the schools we now have could evolve into self-developing communities of this kind by a deliberate, conscious process of cultural transformation? Perhaps not, perhaps in the end schools which set out on such a path will encounter obstacles to full realization that can only be overcome by renegotiating with their employers and their communities the terms of governance that presently structure their powers and obligations. The role of the headteacher, for instance, may have to change and a system of rotating chairpersons be instituted accountable to a school academic board or different groups within the school be granted autonomy for different areas of school life and a corresponding responsibility to self-evaluate in a system of mutual accountability to peers and/or governors. It is difficult to tell at this time what precisely may be needed but any experimentation that does take place must do so in the 'full consciousness' of the fundamental changes that may lie ahead.

This 'full consciousness' is what is missing from current school self-evaluation accountability proposals, even those which aspire to promote professional development (Elliott, 1979a; Sockett, 1980, Becher, Eraut and Knight, 1981). Such proposals fail to acknowledge that the cultural assumptions of their advocacies do not match the values that are deeply embedded in the formal organization of schools. Yet we have enough evidence from the lessons of the curriculum reform movement of the sixties and seventies to know that we cannot simply leave institutions intact, make new demands of them, and expect to succeed.

School self-evaluation is conceptually a major innovation. I have argued that it directly confronts three major organizational values of schools — privacy, territory and hierarchy. It follows that it can only serve institutional development if it is predicated upon a commitment to fundamental institutional change. Such a commitment must constitute, for me, the 'shared goals' to which Nias alludes. Anything less will be revealed, sooner or later, as a cosmetic rhetoric disguising an unchanging reality. In this light, the particular procedures adopted by external evaluators have little relevance. They were designed to meet the needs of external audiences whilst minimizing the consequences for schools. Internal evaluators must devise procedures on the basis of a different logic — the ineluctable agenda of organizational change.

It could be argued that the time has come to put back into schools the responsibilities and capabilities that were taken away from them with the creation of systematic and system-wide curriculum innovation. Despite their varying rhetorics the creation of specialists outside the schools inevitably weakened the status and self-image of the teacher. The task now is to reintegrate responsibilities for research, development and evaluation within a redefinition of the brief we give to our schools. This is more than just an issue of leadership styles or school ethos. It is a matter of re-examining at a fundamental level the institutional correlates of a restrictive view of the teacher's task.

Notes

1 The initiative wasn't entirely the ILEA's. Several other authorities had initiated discussions on school self-evaluation by this time, fifteen to quote one survey (ELLIOTT, G., 1981a) and at least five (CHESHIRE, SALFORD, TAMESIDE, WIGAN and BROMLEY) had issued sets of guidelines (*Ibid*, pp. 50–4). But it seems to have been the ILEA document that has been most discussed and adapted since.

2 These include school self-evaluation, school-level evaluation, in-school evaluation, school-based evaluation, school-focussed evaluation, school-centred evaluation, within institutions' evaluation, internal evaluation, insider evaluation, school self-assessment, school self-review, school self-study, self-report, self-monitoring.

3 Programme I (Purpose and Planning in Schools) and Programme II (The Competence and Effectiveness of Individual Teachers) were two of the five programmes the Schools Council instituted in 1979 in a change of emphasis from large-scale subject project funding to small-scale local curriculum development initiatives.

4 For an account of the APU's activities see DAWSON, J. (1984) 'The work of the Assessment of Performance Unit' in SKILBECK, M. (Ed) (1984) *Evaluating the Curriculum in the Eighties*, London, Hodder and

Stoughton, and for an evaluation of it see GIPPS, C. and GOLDSTEIN, H. (1983) *Monitoring Children: An Evaluation of the Assessment of Performance Unit*, London, Heinemann Educational Books.

5 This short critique is based upon two surveys of LEA involvement in school self-evaluation conducted by Gordon Elliott of Hull University in 1980–81, and a brief survey of my own conducted in 1982. I am indebted to Gordon Elliott for providing this baseline information. For a more extended critique of the conception and aspirations of LEA school self-evaluation guidelines see SIMONS (1984b). For an examination of several of these schemes in practice see NUTTALL, D.L., CLIFT, P., TURNER, G., and McCORMICK, R. (1987) *Studies in School Self-Evaluation*, Lewes, Falmer Press.

6 See chapter 2 (note 3).

7 These comments were made by the CEO of Oxfordshire in a conference at York in 1982 on *Evaluation in Education* and a seminar at the University of London Institute of Education in July 1983 on *The LEA's Response to Change*.

8 This observation was offered by the then Head of the ILEA Research and Statistics Branch in a seminar presentation at the British Council seminar on *Curriculum Evaluation*, January 1983.

9 The situation is changing rapidly, of course, and it may be that we are entering a new phase of institutional self-evaluation that is more closely linked to curriculum development. By the end of 1986, it was already apparent that, in response to further categorical funding by the MSC for TVEI-related inservice training and changes in inservice funding by the DES, several LEAs and schools were generating inservice programmes that, at least in part, utilize process forms of school self-evaluation.

10 It is significant perhaps that both Elliott (1976) in relation to the Ford Teaching Project and Holly (1984) in relation to the GRIDS project exempt primary schools somewhat from this problem. In primary schools it seems more feasible to engage all teachers in a self-evaluation exercise and to establish a collaborative ethic to sustain the process. It may also be worth noting in passing that the one LEA that I know of that has acknowledged its debt to my process model (SIMONS, 1981a) in formulating its policy for self-evaluation has done so with respect to its primary school sector (see *Self-Evaluation in the Primary School: A Pilot Study*, Royal County of Berkshire, Education Department, Shire Hall, Shinfield Park, Reading, 1984).

11 The basic argument in this section for a change in the organizational basis of schools is also published in SIMONS, H. (1985) 'Against the rules: procedural problems in school self-evaluation', *Curriculum Perspectives*, 5, 2, pp. 1–6.

10 Getting to Know Schools — The Next Step

> ... we have passed decisively out of the age of innocence in education ... (Davies, 1983, p. 135)

Unless there has been some unforeseeable transformation of circumstances in the time between my writing these words and you reading them, it will be safe to say that the background to this concluding discussion is one characterized by professional demoralization at all levels of the school system. Since I have, at various points throughout the book, located evaluation issues within a context of political and administrative trends relevant to the assessment of evaluation needs and opportunities, I see no need to recapitulate in any detail the changing countenance of curriculum macro-politics throughout the seventeen years I have spent in this country. It may, however, be worthwhile bring the picture up-to-date.

Since 1979, when Margaret Thatcher took office, the trends towards central control of schooling have accelerated and become explicitly subject to decision-making by 'conviction' politicians determined to stamp their authority on the partnership tradition. Exploiting the demand for accountability that had been carefully nurtured by the DES and the popularity of a deficit view of curriculum provision and of teacher performance, the government set about the schools with zeal and speed, and soon had the partners responding to a combination of stick and carrot initiatives. By 1985 a model of line management stretching from the Cabinet to the classroom was discernible, a demoralized teaching force was on strike, and the President of the Society of Education Officers referred caustically to the Secretary of State for Education as the 'managing director' (Hall, 1985). Others would no doubt argue that the

Secretary of State for Employment is more deserving of the title, because since the early eighties the main source of funds for curriculum development has been provided by the Manpower Services Commission's Technical and Vocational Education Initiative (MSC, 1982) (see McCulloch, 1986, for an interesting account of the MSC's intervention in the curriculum and the TVEI).

It is against this background that the effort to introduce some of the principles of democratic evaluation must be seen. Personally I do not believe the politics employed by the present government to coerce local districts and schools (not to mention higher education) to do its bidding can be sustained for much longer. In 1986 there were signals that education was becoming an electoral liability for the government, that even its own supporters were beginning to see wreckage where the government claimed reconstruction. It is a government almost without friends among professionals at all levels of the education system, and the virtual unanimity of protest against the crudity of its technocratic prescriptions, as well as the educational costs of its financial stringency, is having an impact on a public that for a time was willing to believe that aggressive government might somehow deliver employment for their children by compelling schools to deliver employability. Once that myth is well and truly nailed, and reason restored to the consideration of how schools might do better by their clients, I would expect to see some return to the checks and balances that obtained up to the mid-seventies. Until that happens it is difficult to be optimistic about the prospects of advancing the cause of reasonableness with respect to judging and developing schools.

Difficult to be optimistic, but important to be determined and committed. Governments come and go, and affect our immediate priorities rather than our long-term goals. The fact that the teaching profession is at present demoralized, for instance, has considerably influenced my thinking about the time-scale within which we can productively contemplate the opening up of school work to public critique. The accountability movement of the past fifteen years or so has talked a great deal about democratizing schooling in such terms, but in terms of action has proved to be about subjecting schools to administrative control and judgment. This has left us with a task of rehabilitation if the extension of school knowledge to school communities is not to further the process of deprofessionalization of teachers which the present government's policies would inevitably entail. Early in this book I declared an interest in justified self-direction by professional teachers, and in the last chapter I argued the need for organizational change as a prerequisite for the realization of such a goal. I also set an agenda of the kind of questions its publics are entitled to ask of a profession, and therefore an agenda that schools should prepare themselves to answer. In taking such a line I am aware that this leaves me open to the kind of criticism levelled by Gibson (1986) at action research, a criticism which can be applied more generally to what appear to be protectionist views of teacher interests. 'The insistence of "no outsiders" smacks of a desire for monopoly control which fits ill with any view of democracy' (p. 164). This is an important point but it is also important to bear in mind that the purpose of the exercise is better schools, and to seek ways of democratizing knowledge that are compatible with the conditions and kind of relationships that are essential for curriculum development. A beleaguered teaching profession is in no condition to cope constructively with the organized and eager sectors of the public who are knocking on its door and even less to reach out to those greater numbers who still do not believe that they could have a say in what schools do for and against their children. It will take time, and patience and planning to achieve at the local level any form of democratization that has a chance of empowering the traditionally powerless, both within the classroom and within the community. Nothing is to be gained by rushing the school gates, but everything is to be gained by setting ambitious goals and realistic time scales for a worthwhile process of school self-evaluation.

Let me turn now to other contexts in which the practice of evaluation has been problematic. Political and administrative interest in what schools ought to do has temporarily diverted attention from the fact that providing information about what other professionals in the school system do has proved to be even more problematic. The secret garden of the curriculum has an extensive and largely unmapped hinterland of policy-making, administration and advice that could do with more public airing. This takes us back into the arena of programme and policy evaluation.

Evaluators have had twenty years in which to explore and define a useful role in the service of education. I have concentrated on those who have not taken that utility for granted, or conceded its definition to others. In particular I have explored, in theory and in practice, an approach to evaluation which calls itself 'democratic' because it is concerned with finding more effective ways of promoting an informed public. The approach was conceived in the early seventies as a possible counter-balance to monopolistic trends in government with regard to the generation and use of new knowledge about schooling.

Since such trends also meant that evaluation opportunities would depend upon the perceived utility of the role to government agencies, achieving such a counter-balance within the context of bureaucratic funding was never going to be easy. In terms of our perception at the time we would be dealing with administrative power that, in England, was largely exercised through invisible processes of influence, protected by confidentiality and deference. We would be dealing with a school system that took for granted its insulation as a whole from public scrutiny, and that was religiously territorial in its parts.

On the other hand there were aspects of the culture that, in some respects, might be responsive to the democratic persuasion. In the first place, at the higher levels of system administration, to which evaluation would be formally accountable, we would be dealing with people who might be peculiarly dependent on evaluation to manage programmes of intervention. They, after all, had no personal knowledge of public schooling, since most of them, and their children, were privately educated. In the second place they had a known distaste, sometimes amounting to contempt, for technical research in the experimental, correlational or survey modes. The typical administrator aspired to wise advice rather than technical authority. In the third place the system as a whole supported a rhetoric of egalitarian inter-professionalism in which reasonable people with interlocking responsibilities defined and resolved problems of action through consultative deliberation. A rhetoric of community, reciprocity, partnership.

Democratic evaluation was conceived as a way of appealing to these internal values by invoking them as criteria in the internal conduct of programmes embodying power-based relationships. It was also seen as a way of persuading professionals within the school system to begin, with safeguards but with growing confidence, to create a public sphere of informed deliberation.

When the small, international group of evaluators got together in Cambridge in 1972 with representatives of public and private agencies in the curriculum field to assess past failings and set an agenda for future work, it seemed reasonable to nourish hopes that various forms of naturalistic inquiry, conducted with due regard to the complexity of change, the interests of all those involved, and the need of policy-makers to act with knowledge of the complexity and sensitivity to those interests, offered a way forward. What we underestimated, or failed to anticipate, was the sweep and radicalism of political interventionism in curriculum affairs that was to come. To be specific, whilst we did anticipate an increase in bureaucratic centrism, we did not anticipate Thatcherism, and with it the apparent abandonment of the political principle that the curriculum should not become a creature of the state, the consensual principle underlying the distribution of curriculum control. We could not foresee that the Department of Education and Science was to become subservient to the Department of Employment in the funding and control of curriculum development from Whitehall, to the extent that in 1986 a non-elected appointee, the Secretary of State for Employment, would announce a £900m programme over ten years extending TVEI to all secondary schools in England and Wales (White Paper, 1986). Nor could we foresee that categorical funding on this scale would transform LEAs into area managers of national curriculum prescriptions, in the front line of accountability for their success and failure. Such was the transformation that a Chief Education Officer summarized the astonishment of many when he said, in 1985, that the 'unthinkable' had become the 'unbelievable' (Hall, 1985).

Related to these changes, and of particular significance to those of us who believe the independence of evaluation to be a necessary condition of its credibility as a public service, was the severe financial pruning of the higher education sector, that in the eighties was to become so acute that the capacity of academics to attract research funds is now a key consideration at both the national and the institutional level in determining whether their departments survive and in what form. This change has to be seen against the backcloth of the increasing adoption by government agencies of the 'customer/ contractor' principle of research funding recommended by Lord Rothschild in 1971. Academics desperately in need of funding to bolster their institutional safety are in a weak position when it comes to negotiating the kind of 'fair agreements' which I discussed in chapter 7, or to query the problem definitions on offer. And alternative sources of funding are scarce, since the charitable foundations have suffered from the general economic decline, and it is clear that the European Community bureaucracy sees external scrutiny as a threat to the preservation of its domain of influence.

A particular weakness, in terms of the democratic persuasion, can be seen in a combination of these varying trends. Take the Technical and Vocational Education Initiative (TVEI), for example. The Manpower Services Commission which funds TVEI set up a substantial programme of evaluation to monitor the implementation of this programme in its pilot phase, both at national and local level. The national contracts stipulate the MSC's right to 'approve' publication and the local smaller contracts to academic institutions in the local districts participating in the pilot have to be 'appraised' by the MSC. But the more serious problem, arguably, is that most of these local evaluators are dependent upon the patronage of the LEAs they are evaluating for the survival of their bread and butter work in providing courses for teachers from these authorities. We should not be surprised if Lord Young, in announcing the extension of TVEI to all secondary schools as a result of the 'success' of the pilot scheme, entertained few fears of contradiction from a substantial investment in evaluation. None has so far been forthcoming.

This kind of combination of factors constitutes a powerful deterrent to the mounting of policy critique. But, in case anyone reading this is tempted to dismiss the analysis as an idiosyncratic reading of contemporary circumstances based on an unrepresentative value position, I would recommend them to read the account by Richard Whitfield and his colleagues (Baron *et al*, 1981) of a prematurely terminated evaluation in Birmingham, involving European sponsorship of a local development initiative. This illuminatingly honest account, a tour de force in an otherwise unimpressive literature of self-report by the research community, offers a comprehensive analysis of the interplay of intellectual, political and ethical factors in evaluation decisions. Apart from anything else it makes useful reading for those who doubt the claim of evaluators that the requirement to confront directly the exercise of power in circumstances of conflict constitutes a challenge that is different in kind to that faced by other forms of research. Two or three extracts from the article will serve to illustrate some of its themes. You may wish to bear in mind as you read them that it was the same Richard Whitfield who, at the annual conference of the British Educational Research Association in 1975, advanced the criticism of a more democratic form of collaborative inquiry:

> An initial period of field work (six weeks) was sufficient to discover the project's difficulties were deep and structural, and carried inevitable implications for the tasks of evaluation. The divisions of purpose and definition within the project meant that quasi experimental models of evaluation could only have been applied if one set of purposes and definitions were taken as privileged. Adapting Cronbach's formulation, the team decided to define evaluation as the collection, organization and dissemination of information in order to aid the decision making of those involved *at all levels of the project*, both during its lifetime and subsequently. This

attempt to be (to some extent) 'democratic' in our work was carried through, perhaps inevitably, by ethnographic methods. (p. 90)

We refuted claims to privileged definition and acknowledged the existence of varying and competing claims to definition within the project. (p. 91)

The logic of taking all participants seriously and denying privilege to any one group leads to differences in actual research practice and possibly to a spin-off effect. For the researcher to act somewhat democratically towards participants in an otherwise autocratic situation can be a living challenge to that autocratic situation by way of example and ethic. (p. 108)

... the importance of our emphasis on the research relationship was quickly confirmed by the reactions of participants to our attempt to move towards more equal power relationships between researcher and researched. At the grassroots level we were met, after initial suspicion, with an immense friendliness and a serious concern to understand our positions. The cost, however, of not imposing the definitions of the top of the agency hierarchy onto the other participants was great. We came under a series of ever shifting attacks which centred on the need for the evaluation team to take the powerful participants more seriously and the others less seriously. (pp. 108–9)

To gain contracts was not enough; they also had to be seen through to a successful conclusion ... in our case it produced a tension between finishing the contract to the public satisfaction of the contracting decision-makers and the fundamental impulses of integrity and honesty in intellectual and professional work. (p. 96)

This approach to evaluation met with opposition from a particular grouping within the project which ultimately led to the withdrawal of funds. (p. 91)

Looking back now it is clear that a code of ethics and politics to govern the conditions in which evaluations could credibly be conducted and which made it difficult for sponsors to find academic researchers docile to bureaucratic privilege might have furthered the cause of independent reporting and ensured the public were informed about the effects of policy. Attempts to establish such a code in 1975 received support neither at BERA that year or at the second Cambridge conference (Adelman *et al*, 1976). It was too soon in the first context, too restrictive in the second to gather support. In the UK, in the mid-seventies, there were too few researchers who had had the experience of programme evaluation, too few who had faced the problem of having to define a political stance in order to *conduct* the inquiry. One might say of the present time that it is too late, that academics are themselves too vulnerable and sponsoring agencies too powerful.

It may be worth asking at this point, in view of the detailed attention I gave it in an early chapter of the book, whatever happened to the case study movement that looked so promising in the early seventies. One might include within that question research developments in the sociology and history of schooling that, whilst not operating for the most part in evaluation roles, shared the naturalistic evaluators' interest in case study of schools. Was there no impact from these groups on the thinking of those who, at different levels of the school system, initiated or responded to the problem of the school curriculum and the quest for school knowledge?

This is, of course, an extremely difficult question to answer, since it concerns the diffusion of ideas, and the relationship between the research and practitioner communities. But I need hardly stress that it is an important question for me, since this relationship has been at the heart of the developments and experiences with which I have been associated. I have, particularly in chapter 3, already addressed it to some extent, but this seems a good point at which to add some comments which may be pertinent.

I have already made the point that evaluation theories are political theories and theories of educational change. The new wave evaluators who met in Cambridge in 1972 had as much to say about how curriculum development should be approached by sponsors and planners as they had to say about how it should be evaluated. The administrators who conceived that conference, Becher from the Nuffield Foundation and Banks from the DES, and others who attended from the Paris-based Centre for Educational Research and Innovation (CERI, a branch of OECD) were well-placed to create opportunities for the message of Cambridge to be disseminated. So were HMI representatives who were also present. But the fact is that it was still too small and marginal a group to make a significant dent in established convictions against an unfavourable background of change in the politics of curriculum development. Initially it did not look that way. In 1973, for instance, CERI organized a conference in Liege of senior educational administrators from OECD countries to discuss the issue of evaluating the programme interventions then burgeoning across Europe. Two of the three keynote speakers were Stake and MacDonald, with their somewhat startling (to that audience) message backed up by Becher and myself. And sometime later, with Banks now in the International Division of the DES and Tim McMullen, another Cambridge attender, advising the European Commission on programme evaluation, Stake and MacDonald were again prominently involved in the EC's first large venture in curriculum development, the 'Transition from education to working life' programme. As I have already noted, the EC experiment in evaluation was not successful, and was replaced for the second phase of the programme with administratively controlled reportage. At least part of the problem, in my view, was the massive gap between the tenets of the naturalistic evaluators and the positivistic traditions of research embedded in continental countries (see MacDonald *et al*, 1981).

Domestically the initial popularity of the new evaluators with bureaucratic sponsors, many of whom had little time or respect for conventional research as an aid to policy-making, gave way to scepticism and irritation as the mismatch between the acknowledgement of complexity in educational action and the increasing simplism of political imperatives became clear. Attempts to bridge the gap through the executive summary of complex data merely revealed the problem of reconciliation and to some extent raised new problems of epistemological and political compromise. Naturalistic evaluators like myself saw future influence increasingly located at local levels of the system, though some continued to direct their major effort at high level policy-makers in order to maintain and hopefully increase the space available at lower levels.

The initial movement of research funds towards evaluation, and particularly towards the new evaluators, caused ripples of alarm elsewhere in the research community. Malcolm Parlett was sought by the National Foundation for Educational Research for a few years in an attempt to broaden its funding appeal. In fact, with the setting up of the APU the NFER economy was regenerated through the renaissance of test development, its traditional area of expertise. Parlett moved to the USA to set up a centre of illuminative evaluation in higher education. Throughout this period of the mid-seventies, some of the members of the 'invisible college' became very visible for a while all around the country, talking to LEAs and conferences of advisers and school heads about the threat of technocratic trends and trying to explicate alternatives to both psychometric and managerial models of accountability. This is one reason why the group was so well-represented at the SSRC's seminar on accountability, which I mentioned in chapter 8.

By the late seventies it seems reasonable to say that, in terms of researcher orientations, preferences of students doing research degrees in education, and courses for teachers involving an element of investigation, case studies of schooling were well on the way to becoming a familiar feature of the educational landscape. Firm evidence came at a BERA-sponsored conference in 1981, where a major issue of concern for the research degree tutors who gathered there was how to supervize and how to set standards for the new wave of non-conformist field-based inquiry that their students wanted to do (MacDonald, 1981). By this time the problem of standards in qualitative inquiry had been addressed in a burst of papers by Lawrence Stenhouse, a late convert to the case study tradition that had dominated the work of CARE throughout the seventies, and to the aspirations for a more democratic process of research articulated by the SAFARI project. As his colleague Jean Rudduck observes (1985) 'Stenhouse characteristically ... immediately tried to take centre stage!', and there can be no doubt that he lent influential weight to the extrapolation of ideas that had been largely conceived and developed within an evaluation framework. Stenhouse's preference for a historical methodology of case study, first canvassed within evaluation theory by Hastings (1969) was later articulated by a SAFARI associate, Ivor Goodson, who also argued that the CARE case study approach lacked a historical dimension. 'To deprive the subject of such knowledge would be to condemn new evaluation to the level of social control — a bizarre fate for a model often aspiring to "democratic" intuitions' (Goodson, 1977, p. 160).

Historical studies of curriculum became in the seventies another dimension of a broad case study movement, suggesting but falling short of establishing collaborative links between those like Goodson and Stenhouse whose first discipline was history, evaluators like Hamilton whose search for understanding the present increasingly drew him away from evaluation practice into historical studies, and some of the revisionists following the lead set in the USA by such as Karier and Apple. There were many differences of course in focus and intent. Many of the case studies of schooling carried out in that period were conceived within single disciplinary frameworks, and in that sense were not seen by some of us in the naturalistic movement as helpful to the cause of providing a service of direct utility to educational decisions or to the goals of promoting non-specialist involvement in the research activity.

I cannot speak with any confidence about the movement in the USA in the equivalent period. Stake, certainly, remains an influential figure, and the support given to his advocacies by widely respected theorists such as Cronbach, Campbell, House, Guba and Glass, not to mention the widely used guides to evaluation practice produced by Patton, indicate a substantial diffusion of naturalistic theory. One recent trend, however, gives me some cause for concern. It was evident at the 1986 convention of the American Educational Research Association (see for instance, Guba, 1986; Lincoln, 1986) that recent academic interest in elaborating a methodological and analytical discipline of naturalistic inquiry may be leading us in the direction of a form of scientific respectability that could exclude from 'legitimate' practice all but an intellectual elite. That would indeed be a painful irony, at least for those of us who saw in democratic theory the possibility of proselytizing a much needed intellectual modesty on the part of the research community.

In retrospect, it could be said that the absence of 'common cause' politics within the research community did little to help counter technocratic trends. Whitty (1985) makes a similar point. Characteristically, academic groups with similar concerns made more of their differences than of their commonalities. The social scientists who made up the ethnographic and 'new sociology' communities trod their own, discipline-based pathways, aware of the overlaps with the evaluation group but, as I suggested earlier, misconstruing some of the continuities and failing to see some of the distinctions. Take the following statement, for instance, from the introduction to a collection of sociological case studies published in 1983: '... it (the collection) might give curriculum theorists and curriculum planners a fuller and more realistic sense of the problems they are likely to encounter when they seek to implement their ambitiously prescriptive models of curriculum change' (Hammersley and Hargreaves, 1983, p. 12). The sense of deja vu is strong. Had the sociologists been effectively linked into the new evaluators they would not, I think, in 1983 have articulated an aspiration that, in terms of the naturalistic evaluation movement, belonged to the optimism of the early seventies.

If this sounds critical, it is intended to be critical of my own UK evaluation community, which, preoccupied perhaps with the business of doing evaluation, paid too little attention to the possibilities of constructing a broad research unity around the agenda of curriculum inquiry. Some efforts were made, particularly by Walker and Adelman among British evaluators, and certainly Stake who, as I explained in chapter 3, has consistently worked towards the broadest possible membership of what he has called a 'communal' concept of educational enquiry (Stake, quoted in Cronbach, 1982). The problem with breakaway movements is, as Stake realized, that they are too small to have an impact, even more so if they fracture. Historically, I am sure that the three groups I have specified will be seen as much more similar than they have so far seen themselves. John Nisbet, in his presidential address to the BERA in 1974, made a strong plea for the reintegration of evaluation within research, but it is only recently that serious efforts have been made to bring the different strands of the case study movement together (see, for instance, Burgess, 1984b, 1985a and 1985b). This remains an important agenda for the future.

The question of impact is, as we know only too well from the evaluation of innovations, an impossible question to answer in any definitive way. That there has been a considerable diffusion of ideas and practices associated with these research groups cannot be in doubt, but there is at present little tolerance of risk among the agencies controlling the funding of curriculum development and research evaluation. We may have to wait some time before making a judgment of how far and with what effect these ideas have percolated. I leave the last word on that to a historian who, asked recently about the impact of the French Revolution, reportedly answered, 'It is too soon to say'.

Concluding Comments

The work reported in this book spans a period of seventeen years, during which I have tried, sometimes with others and sometimes alone, to do something worthwhile with the form of enquiry that is known as evaluation. Accepting from an early point in that experience that evaluation was both a threatening and a political activity I have been concerned to devise ways of handling the role that are consonant with the professed morality of liberal democracies. Being an educator first, and an evaluator second, it has been important for me to formulate and practise evaluation as an educative activity in itself and as a service to the educative intents of others. I take education to be about the empowerment through self-knowledge of individuals and social groups. As an educator and as a democrat I am committed to the promotion of education for all. As a public employee in the educational sector, in a service relationship to that aspiration, I cannot but be aware that schools fall somewhat short of unequivocally qualifying as educational institutions. Basically, like other so-called 'educational' institutions, they cannot grade without degrading. Their economic and social instrumentalism makes it extremely difficult for teachers to successfully realize educative intents. That many teachers have such intents should not be in doubt. The Humanities Project, for instance, a project imbued with the emancipatory philosophy of one of England's most articulate humanists, Lawrence Stenhouse, proved to have a huge appeal to the humanist impulse in teachers. In more recent years the action-research movement has evoked a similar response. Evaluators have been prominent in the effort to demonstrate why such educative innovations fail to stay the course. At the risk of courting accusations of exaggeration, I would say that it is precisely the educative potential of curriculum proposals that schools find most difficult to develop.

There is no need, and no justification, for being defeatist about the evident constraints on educationally significant change. No case either, in my view, for settling for an ameliorative role in softening the rather harsh realities of school experience for both pupils and teachers. We must go on reconstruing the problem of enabling schools to become educational until we have an adequate theory of action and intention that is capable of mobilizing goodwill at all levels of society. By the early seventies it was clear that the grand and seemingly powerful innovation machine of the sixties had been a marginal and precarious enterprise (MacDonald and Walker, 1976) operating in the UK on a simplistic belief in teacher autonomy, and in the USA on an equally simplistic belief in the 'teacher-proof' package.

We know better now, and many initiatives in the seventies have reflected this knowledge. Although I may have emphasized in this concluding chapter a rather gloomy picture of the macro-politics of curriculum in recent years, it is important to qualify this by recognition of a grass-roots pattern of attempts to provide more continuous, close-up and responsive support for change-oriented individuals and institutions. I am here talking mainly about the efforts of teacher-educators, often in tandem with local administrators, advisers, teacher centre leaders and researchers, to offer more context-sensitive support for what is recognized by them to be an extremely difficult process of development. At this level a more organic concept of the change process is emerging and gradually taking shape, one which acknowledges that the values, roles and structures which maintain the curriculum cannot be circumvented but must be persuasively engaged. This, of course, makes the task of curriculum development that much more demanding, more frustratingly gradual, at least in its first phase. But such a process hopefully will provide a better basis for development than the short cuts of the past.

The problem of mobilizing goodwill in the cause of education, however, calls for a more comprehensive theory of action than this scattered groundswell of local initiatives provides. The attraction for me of the democratic theory of evaluation and research lies not only in its educative values but in the breadth of its application. I have said enough in the course of this book about how the democratic persuasion offers some negotiable and defensible purchase on techno/bureaucratic cultures that will certainly not disappear overnight, that preceded the Thatcher regime and will no doubt survive her demise. Given present trends it may well be that democratic evaluation becomes non-negotiable currency in terms of bureaucratically determined contracts. In that event we may have to look to elected bodies at both the national and the local level rather than to administrators in order to negotiate reasonable and fair agreements, or at least to their involvement in some way. But at least we can be clear now about what is at risk and what needs to be secured if we are to have public credibility and democratic utility. We must, at all costs, do what we can and what we dare to counter the assumptions of privilege that we can expect to find within the cases we evaluate, assumptions corresponding to positions of power and authority.

Democratic evaluation can also be seen as a challenge to the assumptions of privilege, corresponding to scientific power and intellectual authority, in the research community. It is a challenge in the first place to the minimalist requirement that has stood for so many years as the fieldwork ethic of social science, that it 'do no harm to its subjects'. This is challenged as naive and insufficient as a basis for conduct. It is also a challenge to the somewhat pious hopes of the research community that in some undefined way the publication of academically impressive studies of the disadvantaged will somehow contribute to their welfare. It has never been explained how this process works.

Finally it is an invitation to the research community in education to work more collaboratively with other educational actors in the system, at all levels, in ways that are more responsive to their problems, more commensurate with their language, more directly useful to them. Research should do more, in other words, to empower its subjects.

The terms of this argument were set out by the SAFARI team and their associates a long time ago now, (but the case has perhaps been most fully stated by MacDonald and Norris in their 1981 paper). It is an argument that has not yet been seriously addressed by the educational research community in the UK, but needs to be. That it is not purely a domestic issue is clear from the emergence of parallel concerns in research communities elsewhere. Let me close with a statement which captures an important dimension of the democratic persuasion in another liberal democracy. Interestingly, it comes from the country I left seventeen years ago:

> ... the goal of a different model of research is clear. It should empower the people who are normally just the objects of research, to develop their capacity to research their own situations and evolve their own solutions. It should embody a relationship where expertise is a resource available to all rather than a form of power for a few. In short, social research can become more democratic, and we would suggest that this is the way, rather than funding elite super-scientists, to produce really useful knowledge. (Connell *et al*, 1982, p. 216)

In so far as this advocacy is limited to collaboration between teachers and the relatively powerless in the determination of educational opportunity, it only partially represents the argument of democratic evaluation. We also need to negotiate, with those who control our own economy, terms of service that afford us some emancipatory influence on the management of democracy. Taking sides with democracy will be no better served by sectoral allegiance than it has been by political docility or safe distance from the compromises of effective engagement.

References

ADELMAN, C. (1979) 'Some dilemmas of institutional evaluation and their relationship to preconditions and procedures', paper presented to the Annual Meeting of the American Educational Research Association, San Francisco, *Studies in Educational Evaluation* (1980) 6, 2, Oxford, Pergamon Press, pp. 165–83.

ADELMAN, C. (Ed) (1984) *The Politics and Ethics of Evaluation*, London, Croom Helm.

ADELMAN, C. and ALEXANDER, R.J. (1982) *The Self-Evaluating Institution: Practice and Principles in the Management of Educational Change*, London, Methuen.

ADELMAN, C., KEMMIS, S., and JENKINS, D. (1976) 'Rethinking case study: Notes from the second Cambridge conference', *Cambridge Journal of Education*, 6, 3. Also in SIMONS, H. (Ed) (1980a) *Towards a Science of the Singular: Essays about Case Study in Educational Research and Evaluation*, CARE Occasional Publications No 10, Norwich, Centre for Applied Research in Education, University of East Anglia, pp. 47–61.

APPLE, M.W. (1974) 'The process and ideology of valuing in educational settings', in APPLE, M., SUBKOVIAK, M.G. and LUFLER, H.S. (Eds) *Educational Evaluation: Analysis and Responsibility*, Berkeley, CA, McCutchan, pp. 3–34.

APPLE, M.W. (1979) *Ideology and Curriculum*, London, Routledge and Kegan Paul.

APPLE, M.W. and TEITELBAUM, K. (1986) 'Are teachers losing control of their skills and curriculum?', *Journal of Curriculum Studies*, 18, 2, pp. 177–84.

ASSESSMENT OF PERFORMANCE UNIT (1980) *APU: What It Is, How It Works*, London, Department of Education and Science.

ATKIN, J.M. (1963) 'Some evaluation problems in a course content improvement project', *Journal of Research in Science Teaching*, 1, pp. 129–32.

ATKIN, J.M. (1967–68) 'Research styles in science education', *Journal of Research in Science Teaching*, 5, pp. 338–45.

ATKIN, J.M. (1968) 'Behavioural objectives in curriculum design: A cautionary note', *The Science Teacher*, 35, 5, pp. 27–30.

ATKIN, J.M. (1980) 'The Government in the Classroom', the Ninth Sir John Adams Lecture delivered at the University of London Institute of Education, 6 March 1980, London, University of London Institute of Education.

ATKIN, J.M. and HOUSE, E.R. (1981) 'The federal role in curriculum development, 1950–80', *Educational Evaluation and Policy Analysis*, 3, 5, pp. 5–36.

ATKIN, J.M. and SIMONS, H. (1977) 'Educational policy making in the seventies: A study of informal policy-making processes in the English educational system', London, University of London Institute of Education, mimeo.

ATKINSON, P. and DELAMONT, S. (1985) 'Bread and dreams or bread and circuses? A Critique of "case study" research in education', in SHIPMAN, M. (Ed) *Educational Research: Principles, Policies and Practices*, Lewes, Falmer Press, pp. 26–45.

BARON, S., MILLER, H., WHITFIELD, R. and YATES, C. (1981) 'On the social organization of evaluation: A case study', in SMETHERHAM, D. (Ed) *Practising Evaluation*, Driffield, Nafferton, pp. 89–110.

BECHER, T., ERAUT, M. and KNIGHT, J. (1981) *Policies for Educational Accountability*, London, Heinemann Educational Books.

BECHER, T. and MACLURE, S. (Eds) (1978) *Accountability in Education*, Windsor, National Foundation for Educational Research Publishing Company.

BECKER, H.S. (1967) 'Whose side are we on?', *Social Problems*, 14, 3, pp. 239–47.

BECKER, H.S., GEER, B., HUGHES, E.C. (1968) *Making the Grade*, New York, Wiley.

BELLAH, R.N., MADSEN, R., SULLIVAN, W.M., SWIDLER, A. and TIPTON, S.M. (1985) *Habits of the Heart*, London and New York, Harper and Row.

BENTLEY, H.C. (1982) *An Approach to Professional Development*, Metropolitan Borough of Rochdale, Education Department.

BERGER, J. and MOHR, P. (1976) *A Fortunate Man*, London, Writers and Readers Publishing cooperative (first published in 1967).

BOOS-NUNNING, U., HOHMANN, M., REICH, H.H., WITTECK, F. (1983) *Aufnahmeunterricht, Muttersprachlicher Unterricht, Interkultureller Unterricht: Ergebnisse einer vergleichenden Untersuchung zum Unterrict für ausländische Kinder in Belgien, England, Frankreich und den Neiderlanden*, Publikation Alfa, München, Oldenbourg.

BRAUNER, C.J. (1974) 'The first probe', AERA monograph series No 7: Four evaluation examples, Chicago, Rand McNally, pp. 77–98.

BRIDGES, D. and EYNON, D. (Eds) (1983) *Issues in School Centred In-service Education*, papers prepared by teachers on a Cambridge-based DES

Regional Programme, Cambridge, Cambridge University Press for Cambridge Institute of Education.

BURGESS, R. (1984a) *In The Field: An Introduction to Field Research*, London, George Allen and Unwin.

BURGESS, R. (Ed) (1984b) *The Research Process in Educational Settings: Ten Case Studies*, Lewes, Falmer Press.

BURGESS, R. (Ed) (1985a) *Strategies of Educational Research: Qualitative Methods*, Lewes, Falmer Press.

BURGESS, R. (Ed) (1985b) *Issues in Educational Research: Qualitative Methods*, Lewes, Falmer Press.

CAMBRIDGE ACCOUNTABILITY PROJECT (1981) 'Case studies in school accountability' (three volumes), Cambridge Institute of Education.

CAMPBELL, D.T. (1977) 'Keeping the data honest in the experimenting society', in MELTON, H.W. and WATSON, D.H.G. (Eds) *Interdisciplinary Dimensions of Accounting for Social Goals and Social Organizations*, a conference of the Department of Accountancy, University of Illinois, Urbana-Champaign, Columbus, OH, Grid Inc., pp. 37–76.

CLIFT, P. (1982) 'LEA schemes for school self-evaluation: A critique', *Educational Research*, 24, 4, pp. 262–71.

COOK, T.D. and CAMPBELL, D.T. (1979) *Quasi-Experimentation: Design and Analysis Issues for Field Settings*, Chicago, Rand McNally.

CONNELL, R.W., ASHENDEN, D.H., KESSLER, S., and DOWSETT, W.G. (1982) *Making the Difference: Schools, Families and Social Division*, London and Boston, MA, George Allen and Unwin.

CRONBACH, L.J. (1963) 'Course improvement through evaluation', *Teachers College Record*, 64, 8, pp. 672–83.

CRONBACH, L.J. (1975) 'Beyond the two disciplines of scientific psychology', *American Psychologist*, 30, 2, pp. 116–27.

CRONBACH, L.J. (1982) *Designing Evaluations of Educational and Social Programs*, San Francisco, CA, Jossey Bass.

CRONBACH, L.J. and ASSOCIATES (1980) *Toward Reform of Program Evaluation: Aims, Methods and Institutional Arrangements*, San Francisco, CA, Jossey Bass.

DALIN, P., RUST, V., and SUMNER, R. (1986) '*Starting An Institutional Development Programme*', *Part I School Development Guide*; Part II, (Butler, R.) (Ed) *Operator's Guide to the NFER/IMTEC Programs*, Slough, National Foundation for Education Research.

DAVIES, B. (1983) 'The sociology of education', in Hirst, P.H. (Ed) *Educational Theory and its Foundation Disciplines*, London, Routledge and Kegan Paul, pp. 100–45.

DAVIS, E. (1981) *Teachers as Curriculum Evaluators*, London, George Allen and Unwin.

DAWSON, JEAN (1984) 'The work of the Assessment of Performance Unit', in SKILBECK, M. (Ed) *Evaluating the Curriculum in the Eighties*, London, Hodder and Stoughton.

DAWSON, JUDITH (1977) 'Validity in qualitative enquiry', Urbana-Champaign, Illinois, University of Illinois, mimeo.

DELAMONT, S. (1976) *Interaction in the Classroom*, London, Methuen.

DELVES, A.R. and WATTS, J. (1979) 'A year of evaluation', *Forum*, 22, 1, pp. 27–30.

DENNY, T. (1977) 'Story telling and educational understanding', Urbana-Champaign, Illinois, University of Illinois, mimeo. In Occasional Paper Series No 12, November 1978, The Evaluation Centre, College of Education, Western Michigan University, Kalamazoo, MI.

DENNY, T. (1978) *Some Still Do: River Acres, Texas*, Booklet 1, Case Studies in Science Education, a project for the National Science Foundation conducted by the Centre for Instructional Research and Curriculum Evaluation (CIRCE) and the Commitee on Culture and Cognition (CCC), CIRCE, Urbana-Champaign, Illinois, University of Illinois.

DENZIN, N.K. (1971) 'The logic of naturalistic inquiry' in *Social Forces*, 50, 2.

DEPARTMENT OF EDUCATION AND SCIENCE (1972) *Teacher Education and Training* (The James Report), London, HMSO.

DEPARTMENT OF EDUCATION AND SCIENCE (1976) *School Education in England: Problems and Initiatives* (Yellow Book), London, HMSO.

DEPARTMENT OF EDUCATION AND SCIENCE (1977a) *Education in Schools: A Consultative Document* (Cmnd 6869) (The Green Paper), London, HMSO.

DEPARTMENT OF EDUCATION AND SCIENCE (1977b) *Local Education Authority Arrangements for the School Curriculum* (Circular 14/77), London, HMSO.

DEPARTMENT OF EDUCATION AND SCIENCE (1977c) *A New Partnership for Our Schools* (The Taylor Report), London, HMSO.

DEPARTMENT OF EDUCATION AND SCIENCE (1978) at the request of the Advisory Committee on the Supply and Training of Teachers, *Making INSET Work*, London, HMSO.

DEPARTMENT OF EDUCATION AND SCIENCE (1980) *A Framework for the School Curriculum*, proposals for consultation by the Secretaries of State for Education and for Wales, London, HMSO.

DEPARTMENT OF EDUCATION AND SCIENCE (1981) *The School Curriculum*, London, HMSO.

DEPARTMENT OF EDUCATION AND SCIENCE (1983) *The School Curriculum* (Circular 8/83), London, HMSO.

DEPARTMENT OF EMPLOYMENT (1986) *Working Together: Education and Training*, (Cmnd. 9823) London, HMSO.

EDUCATION BULLETIN 1/82, Cambridge, Shire Hall.

EISNER, E.W. (1975) 'Applying educational connoisseurship and criticism to education settings', unpublished paper, excerpt in HAMILTON, D. *et al.* (Eds) (1977) *Beyond the Numbers game: A Reader in Educational Evaluation*, London, Macmillan, pp. 97–8.

EISNER, E.W. (1981) 'On the differences between scientific and artistic approaches to qualitative research', *Educational Researcher*, 10, 4, pp. 5–9.

EISNER, E.W. (1984) *The Art of Educational Evaluation: A Personal View*, Lewes, Falmer Press.

ELLIOTT, G. (1980) *Self Evaluation and the Teacher*, an annotated bibliography and report on current practice, Part 1, Hull, University of Hull Institute of Education.

ELLIOTT, G. (1981a) *Self Evaluation and the Teacher*, an annotated bibliography and report on current practice, 1980, Part 2, Hull, University of Hull Institute of Education.

ELLIOTT, G. (1981b) *Self Evaluation and the Teacher*, an annotated bibliography and report on current practice, 1980, Part 3, Hull, University of Hull Institute of Education.

ELLIOTT, G. (1982) *Self Evaluation and the Teacher*, an annotated bibliography and report on current practice, 1981, Part 4, Hull, University of Hull Institute of Education.

ELLIOTT, J. (1973) 'Reflecting where the action is: The design of the Ford Teaching Project', *Education for Teaching*, November, pp. 8–20.

ELLIOTT, J. (1976) *Developing Hypotheses about Classrooms from Teachers' Practical Constructs*, an account of the work of the Ford Teaching Project, North Dakota Study Group on Evaluation, Grand Forks, University of North Dakota Press.

ELLIOTT, J. (1977) 'Democratic evaluation as social criticism: Or putting the judgement back into evaluation', in NORRIS, N. (Ed) (1977) *SAFARI 2: Theory in Practice*, CARE Occasional Publications No 4, Norwich, Centre for Applied Research in Education, University of East Anglia.

ELLIOTT, J. (1978) 'Classroom accountability and the self-monitoring teacher', in HARLEN, W. (Ed) (1978) *Evaluation and the Teachers' Role*, London, Methuen.

ELLIOTT, J. (1979a) 'The case for school self-evaluation', *Forum*, 22, 1, pp. 23–25.

ELLIOTT, J. (1979b) 'Curriculum evaluation and the classroom', paper prepared for DES regional course on 'Curriculum and Administration', Cambridge Institute of Education, mimeo.

ELLIOTT, J. (1980a) 'Who should monitor performance in schools?', in SOCKETT, H. (Ed) (1980) *Accountability in the English Educational System*, London, Hodder and Stoughton.

ELLIOTT, J. (1980b) 'Implications of classroom research for professional development', in HOYLE, E.W. and MEGARRY, J. (Eds) *World Yearbook of Education 1980: Professional Development of Teachers*, London, Kogan Page.

ELLIOTT, J. (1981a) 'The Cambridge Accountability Project', *Cambridge Journal of Education*, 11, 2.

ELLIOTT, J. (1981b) 'Educational accountability and evaluation of teaching', in LEWY, A. and NEVO, D. (Eds) (1981) *Evaluation Roles in Education*, London, Gordon and Breach.

ELLIOTT, J. (1982) 'Facilitating action research in schools: Some dilemmas', paper delivered to Social Science Research Council Conference on Qualitative Methodology and the Study of Education, London, Whitelands College, July.

ELLIOTT, J. (1983) 'Self-evaluation, professional development and accountability', in GALTON, M. and MOON, B. (Eds) (1983) *Changing Schools ... Changing Curriculum*, London, Harper and Row, pp. 224–47.

ELLIOTT, J. (1984) 'Methodology and ethics', in ADELMAN, C. (Ed) (1984) *The Politics and Ethics of Evaluation*, London, Croom Helm, pp. 17–25.

ELLIOTT, J. (1985) 'Some key concepts underlying teachers' evaluations of innovations', in TAMIR, P. (Ed) *The Role of Evaluators in Curriculum Development*, Kent, Croom Helm, pp. 142–61.

ELLIOTT, J. and ADELMAN, C. (1976) 'Innovation at the classroom level: A case study of the Ford Teaching Project', in *Curriculum Design and Development*, Course E203, Unit 28, Milton Keynes, Open University Press, pp. 52–64.

ELLIOTT, J., BRIDGES, D., EBBUTT, D., GIBSON, R. and NIAS, J. (1981) *School Accountability*, London, Grant McIntyre.

ERAUT, M. (1976) 'School-based evaluation', in RAGGETT, M. and CLARKSON, M. (Eds) *Teaching the Eight to Thirteen*, Volume 2, London, Ward Lock Education, pp. 240–256.

ERAUT, M. (1978) 'Accountability at school level: Some options and their implications', in BECHER, T. and MACLURE, S. (Eds) pp. 152–99.

ERAUT, M. (1984a) 'Handling value issues', in ADELMAN, C. (Ed) pp. 26–42. Also published in HOUSE, E.R. (Ed) (1982) *Evaluation Studies Review Annual*, 7, Beverly Hills, California, Sage Publications.

ERAUT, M. (1984b) 'Institution-based curriculum evaluation', in SKILBECK, M. (Ed) *Evaluating the Curriculum* in the Eighties, London, Hodder and Stoughton, pp. 54–63.

FOX, T. and STRONACH, I. (1986) 'Raising educational questions', CARE, Norwich, University of East Anglia, mimeo.

FRASER, B.J. (1985) *Case Studies in Curriculum Evaluation*, Bentley, Western Australia, Western Australian Social Science Education Consortium.

FULLAN, M. (1982) *The Meaning of Educational Change*, New York, Teachers College Press.

GALTON, M. and MOON, B. (Eds) (1983) *Changing Schools ... Changing Curriculum*, London, Harper and Row.

GEERTZ, C. (1973) 'Thick description: Toward an interpretive theory of culture', in GEERTZ, C. *The Interpretation of Cultures*, New York, Basic Books.

GIBSON, R. (1986) *Critical Theory and Education*, London, Hodder and Stoughton.

GIPPS, C. and GOLDSTEIN, H. (1983) *Monitoring Children: An Evaluation of the Assessment of Performance Unit*, London, Heinemann Educational Books.

GLASER, B.G. and STRAUSS, A.L. (1973) *The Discovery of Grounded Theory: Strategies for Qualitative Research*, Chicago, Aldine Publishing Company (first published in 1967, London, Weidenfield and Nicolson).

GLASS, G.V. (1972) 'The wisdom of scientific inquiry on education', *Journal of Research in Science Teaching*, 9, 1, pp. 3–18.

GOODLAD, J.I. (1967) 'The reform movement', *Rational Planning in Curriculum and Instruction*, published by the NEA Center for the Study of Instruction.

GOULDNER, A.V. (1973) *For Sociology: Renewal and Critique in Sociology Today*, London, Allen Lane.

GOODSON, I. (1977) 'Evaluation and evolution, in NORRIS, N. (Ed) *SAFARI 2: Theory in Practice*, CARE Occasional Publications No 4, Norwich, Centre for Applied Research in Education, University of East Anglia, pp. 147–62.

GUBA, E.G. (1978) *Toward a Methodology of Naturalistic Inquiry in Educational Evaluation*, Monograph Series in Evaluation 8, Los Angeles, CA, UCLA, Center for the Study of Evaluation.

GUBA, E. (1986) 'The development of parallel criteria for trustworthiness', paper delivered to the annual meeting of the American Educational Research Association in a symposium titled 'Issues of Trustworthiness and Authenticity in New Paradigm Research', San Francisco, April.

GUBA, E.G. and LINCOLN, Y.S. (1981) *Effective Evaluation*, San Francisco, CA, Jossey Bass.

GUBA, E.G. and LINCOLN, Y.S. (1985) *Naturalistic Inquiry*, Beverly Hills, CA, and London, Sage Publications.

GUIDELINES FOR REVIEW AND INTERNAL DEVELOPMENT IN SCHOOLS (GRIDS) (1985) School Curriculum Development Committee, Newcombe House, Notting Hill Gate, London, Wll. See also McMAHON, A. *et al.* (1984) *Guidelines for Review and Internal Development in Schools: Secondary School Handbook*, Schools Council Publications, York, Longman.

HALL, J. (1985) 'The centralist tendency', *Forum*, 28, 1, pp. 4–7.

HAMILTON, D. (1976a) 'Classroom research: A cautionary tale', in WOLFSON, J. (Ed) *Personality and Learning*, London, Open University Press and Hodder and Stoughton.

HAMILTON, D. (1976b) 'Classroom research: A critique and a new approach', in STUBBS, M. and DELAMONT, S. (Eds) (1976) *Explorations in Classroom Observation*, London, Wiley.

HAMILTON, D. (1976c) *Curriculum Evaluation*, London, Open Books.

HAMILTON, D. (1977) 'Making sense of curriculum evaluation: Continuities and discontinuities in an educational idea', University of Glasgow, mimeo., in SHULMAN, L. (Ed) (1978) *Review of Research in Education*, Vol. 5, Itasca, IL, Peacock Press, pp. 318–47.

HAMILTON, D. (1980a) 'Educational research and the shadows of Francis Galton and Ronald Fisher', in DOCKRELL, W.B. and HAMILTON, D. (Eds) (1980) *Rethinking Educational Research*, London, Hodder and Stoughton, pp. 153–68.

HAMILTON, D. (1980b) 'Educational research and the shadow of John Stuart Mill', in HAMILTON, D. and SMITH, J.V. (Eds) (1980) *The Meritocratic Intellect: Studies in the History of Educational Research*, Aberdeen, Aberdeen University Press, pp. 3–14.

HAMILTON, D. (1980c) 'Some contrasting assumptions about case study research and survey analysis', in SIMONS, H. (Ed) (1980) *Towards a Science of the Singular: Essays about Case Study in Educational Research and Evaluation*, CARE Occasional Publications No 10, Norwich, Centre for Applied Research in Education, University of East Anglia, pp. 78–92.

HAMILTON, D., JENKINS, D., KING, C., MacDONALD, B. and PARLETT, M. (Eds) (1977) *Beyond the Numbers Game: A Reader in Educational Evaluation*, London, Macmillan Educational.

HAMINGSON, D. (Ed) (1973) *Towards Judgement*, CARE Occasional Publications No 1, Norwich, Centre for Applied Research in Education, University of East Anglia.

HAMMERSLEY, M. and HARGREAVES, A. (Eds) (1983) *Curriculum Practice: Some Sociological Case Studies*, Lewes, Falmer Press.

HARGREAVES, D.H. (1967) *Social Relations in a Secondary School*, London, Routledge and Kegan Paul.

HARGREAVES, D.H. (1982) *The Challenge for the Comprehensive School: Culture, Community and Curriculum*, London, Routledge and Kegan Paul.

HARLEN, W. (1973) 'Science 5/13 project', in TAWNEY, D. (Ed) *Evaluation in Curriculum Development: Twelve Case Studies*, London, Macmillan Educational, pp. 16–35.

HARLEN, W. (1975) *Science 5/13: A Formative Evaluation*, Schools Council Research Series, London, Macmillan Educational.

HARLEN, W. (1976) 'Evaluation in the context of helping children learn science', *Education 3–13*, 4, 2.

HARLEN, W. (1977a) *Match and Mismatch: Raising Questions*, Topics for In-service Study, Edinburgh, Oliver and Boyd.

HARLEN, W. (1977b) *Match and Mismatch, Finding Answers*, Guide to Diagnosis and Development, Edinburgh, Oliver and Boyd.

HARLEN, W. (1979a) 'School-based evaluation, pupil assessment', *School-based Evaluation*, Classroom Action Research Network Bulletin 3, Cambridge, Cambridge Institute of Education.

HARLEN, W. (1979b) 'Accountability that is of benefit to schools', *Journal of Curriculum Studies*, 11, 4, pp. 287–297.

HASTINGS, J.T. (1969) 'The kith and kin of educational measures', *Journal of Educational Measurement*, 6, 3.

HER MAJESTY'S INSPECTORATE (1977) *Curriculum 11–16*, London, HMSO.

HER MAJESTY'S INSPECTORATE (1978) *Primary Education in England: A Survey by HM Inspectors of Schools*, London, HMSO.

HOLLY, P. (1984) 'The institutionalization of action-research in schools', *Cambridge Journal of Education*, 14, 2, pp. 5–18.

HOLT, M. (1981) *Evaluating the Evaluators*, London, Hodder and Stoughton.

HOPKINS, D. (1983) *School-based Review for School Improvement. A Preliminary State of the Art*, International School Improvement Project, Area, 1, Paris, Centre for Educational Research and Innovation (CERI), Organization for Economic Cooperation and Development (OECD).

HOUSE, E.R. (1972) 'The conscience of educational evaluation', *Teachers College Record*, 73, 3 February, pp. 405–14. Reprinted in HOUSE, E.R. (Ed) (1973a) *School Evaluation: The Politics and Process*, Berkeley, CA, McCutchan, pp. 125–35.

HOUSE, E.R. (Ed) (1973a) *School Evaluation: The Politics and Process*, Berkeley, CA, McCutchan.

HOUSE, E.R. (1973b) 'The price of productivity: who pays?', University of Illinos at Urbana, Champaign, mimeo.

HOUSE, E.R. (1974) *The Politics of Educational Innovation*, Berkeley, CA, McCutchan.

HOUSE, E.R. (1976) 'Justice in evaluation', in GLASS, G.V. (Ed) *Evaluation Studies Annual Review*, Vol 1, Beverly Hills, CA, Sage Publications, pp. 75–100.

HOUSE, E.R. (1977) *The Logic of Evaluative Argument*, CSE Monograph Series in Evaluation, No 7, Los Angeles, CA, Center for the Study of Evaluation, UCLA.

HOUSE, E.R. (1978) 'Assumptions underlying evaluation models', *Educational Researcher* 7, pp. 4–12.

HOUSE, E.R. (1979a) 'The objectivity, fairness and justice of federal evaluation policy as reflected in the follow through evaluation', *Educational Evaluation and Policy Analysis*, 1, 1, pp. 28–42.

HOUSE, E.R. (1979b) 'Coherence and credibility: The aesthetics of evaluation', *Educational Evaluation and Policy Analysis*, 1, 5, pp. 5–17.

HOUSE, E.R. (1980) *Evaluating with Validity*, Beverly Hills, CA, Sage Publications.

HOUSE, E.R. (1986) 'Participatory evaluation: The stakeholder approach', Introduction in HOUSE, E.R. (Ed) *New Directions in Educational Evaluation*, Lewes, Falmer Press, pp. 143–4.

HOUSE, E.R. and GJERDE, C.L. (1973) 'PLATO comes to the community college', Urbana-Champaign, Center for Instructional Research and Curriculum Evaluation, University of Illinois. In HOUSE, E.R. (1974), *The Politics of Educational Innovation*, Berkeley, CA, McCutchan.

HOUSE, E.R., GLASS, G.V., McLEAN, L.D. and WALKER, D. (1978) 'No simple answer: Critique of the follow through evaluation', *Harvard Educational Review*, 48, May, pp. 128–60.

HOUSE, E.R., STEELE, J.M. and KERINS, T. (1971) *The Gifted Classroom*, Urbana-Champaign IL, Center for Instructional Research and Curriculum Evaluation, University of Illinois.

HUGHES, P. (1979) *Curriculum Evaluation in Australia: A new Challenge for Teachers*, Discussion Paper No 1, Canberra, Australia, Teachers as Evaluators Project, Curriculum Development Centre.

HUGHES, P., RUSSELL, N. and McCONACHY, D. (1981) 'A perspective on school-level curriculum evaluation in Australia', *Curriculum Perspectives*, 1, 2, May.

HUGHES, P., RUSSELL, N., McCONACHY, D. and HARLEN, W. (1979) *A Guide to Evaluation*, Canberra, Australia, Teachers as Evaluators Project, Curriculum Development Centre.

HUMANITIES CURRICULUM PROJECT (1970) *The Humanities Curriculum Project*, London, Heinemann Educational Books.

HUMANITIES CURRICULUM PROJECT EVALUATION (1968–72) in VERMA, G.K. (Ed) (1980) *The Impact of Innovation*, Volume 1 of the revised edition of *Towards Judgement*, the publications of the Evaluation Unit of the Humanities Curriculum Project, CARE Occasional Publications No 9, Norwich, Centre for Applied Research in Education, University of East Anglia.

HUMBLE, S. and SIMONS, H. (1978) *From Council to Classroom: An Evaluation of the Diffusion of the Humanities Curriculum Project*, London, Macmillan.

HUTCHINSON, B. and WHITEHOUSE, P. (1986) 'Action research, professional competence and school organization', *British Educational Research Journal*, 12, 1, pp. 85–94.

INNER LONDON EDUCATION AUTHORITY (1977) *Keeping the School Under Review*, a method of self-assessment for schools devised by the ILEA Inspectorate, London, ILEA.

JAMES, M. (1982a) 'School initiated self-evaluation and the improvement of educational practice: Some issues for consideration', in ELLIOTT, J. and WHITEHEAD, D. (Eds) *Action-Research for Professional Development and the Improvement of Schooling*, Curriculum Action Research Network Bulletin No 5, Cambridge, Cambridge Institute of Education.

JAMES, M. (1982b) *A First Review and Register of School and College Initiated Self-Evaluation Activities in the United Kingdom*, Educational Evaluation and Accountability Research Group, Faculty of Educational Studies, Milton Keynes, Open University.

JENKINS, D. (1980) 'An adversary's account of SAFARI's ethics of case study', in SIMONS, H. (Ed) *Towards a Science of the Singular: Essays About Case Study in Educational Research and Evaluation*, CARE Occasional Publications No 10, Norwich, Centre for Applied Research in Education, University of East Anglia, pp. 147–59.

JENKINS, D., KEMMIS, S., MACDONALD, B. and VERMA, G. (1977) 'Racism and educational evaluation', Norwich, Centre for Applied Research in Education, University of East Anglia, mimeo. in VERMA, G. and BAGLEY, C. (Eds) (1979) *Race, Education and Identity*, London, Macmillan.

JENKINS, D. and O'TOOLE, B. (1978) 'Curriculum evaluation, literary criticism, and the para curriculum', in WILLIS, G. (1978) *Qualitative Evaluation: Concepts and Cases in Curriculum Criticism*, Berkeley, CA, McCutchan Publishing Corporation, pp. 524–54.

JENKINS, D., SIMONS, H. and WALKER, R. (1981) 'Thou nature art my goddess: naturalistic inquiry in educational evaluation', reflections from a Nuffield International Workshop held at Girton College, Cambridge, 17–20 December 1979, *Cambridge Journal of Education*, 11, 3, pp. 169–89.

JOURNAL OF EVALUATION IN EDUCATION (n.d.) LONG, R.S. and SLATER, S.M. (Eds), Bromley House, Uttoxeter Road, Abbots Bromley, Staffordshire, England.

KARIER, C., VIOLAS, P. and SPRING, J. (1973) *Roots of Crisis: American Education in the Twentieth Century*, Chicago, Rand McNally.

KELLY, E.F. (1975) 'Curriculum evaluation and literary criticism: comments on the analogy', Curriculum Theory Network 5, pp. 98–106.

KEMMIS, S. (1980) 'The imagination of the case and the invention of the study', in SIMONS, H. (Ed) (1980), *Towards a Science of the Singular: Essays About Case Study in Educational Research and Evaluation*, CARE Occasional Publications No 10, Norwich, Centre for Applied Research in Education, University of East Anglia, pp. 96–142.

KEMMIS, S. and ROBOTTOM, I. (1981) 'Principles of procedure in curriculum evaluation', *Journal of Curriculum Studies*, 13, 2, pp. 151–5.

KERR, J.F. (1968) *Changing the Curriculum*, London, University of London Press.

KINGSTON-UPON-THAMES (1980) *The Evaluation and Monitoring of Secondary Schools*, Royal Borough of Kingston-Upon-Thames.

KOGAN, M. (1978) *The Politics of Educational Change*, London, Fontana.

KUSHNER, S. and LOGAN, T. (1984) *Made in England: An Evaluation of Curriculum in Transition*, CARE Occasional Publications No 14, Norwich, Centre for Applied Research in Education, University of East Anglia.

LACEY, C. (1970) *Hightown Grammar*, Manchester, Manchester University Press.

LACEY, C. and LAWTON, D. (Eds) (1981) *Issues in Accountability and Evaluation*, London, Methuen.

LAKOMSKI, G. (1983) 'Ways of knowing and ways of evaluating: Or how democratic is democratic evaluation?', *Journal of Curriculum Studies*, 15, 3, pp. 265–76.

LANCASHIRE EDUCATION COMMITTEE (1980) *Primary School Evaluation — A Schedule for Self-Appraisal, Spring 1980*, Lancashire, Lancashire Education Committee.

LAWTON, D. (1980) *The Politics of the School Curriculum*, London, Routledge and Kegan Paul.

LINCOLN, Y.S. (1986) 'The development of intrinsic criteria for authenticity', paper delivered to the annual meeting of the American Educational Research Association in a symposium titled 'Issues of Trustworthiness and Authenticity in New Paradigm Research', San Francisco, April.

LINCOLNSHIRE EDUCATION COMMITTEE (1981) *A Discussion Document on School Self-Appraisal for Lincolnshire Schools*, Lincolnshire, Lincolnshire Education Committee.

LINDBLOM, C.E. and COHEN, D.K. (1979) *Usable Knowledge: Social Science and Problem Solving*, New Haven, CT and London, Yale University Press.

McCULLOCH, G. (1986) 'Policy, politics and education: The Technical and Vocational Education Initiative', *Journal of Education Policy*, 1, pp. 35–52.

MacDONALD, B. (1970) 'The evaluation of the Humanities Curriculum Project: A holistic approach', paper presented to the annual meeting of the American Educational Research Association, New York. Published in *Theory into Practice*, June 1971.

MacDONALD, B. (1973) 'Briefing decision-makers', in HOUSE, E.R. (Ed) *School Evaluation: The Politics and Process*, Berkeley, CA, McCutchan, pp. 174–87. Also under the title 'Humanities Curriculum Project', in TAWNEY, D. (Ed) (1973) *Evaluation in Curriculum Development: Twelve Case Studies*, London, Macmillan Educational, pp. 80–90.

MacDONALD, B. (1974) 'Evaluation and the control of education', in MacDONALD, B. and WALKER, R. (Eds) (1974) *SAFARI I: Innovation, Evaluation, Research and the Problem of Control*, Norwich, Centre for Applied Research in Education, University of East Anglia, pp. 9–22. Also in TAWNEY, D. (Ed) (1976) *Curriculum Evaluation Today: Trends and Implications*, Schools Council Research Studies, London, Macmillan Educational.

MacDONALD, B. (1976) 'The portrayal of persons as evaluation data', paper presented at the annual meeting of the American Educational Research Association, San Francisco, April. Also in NORRIS, N. (Ed) (1977) *SAFARI 2: Theory in Practice*, CARE Occasional Publications No 4, Norwich, Centre for Applied Research in Education, University of East Anglia, pp. 50–67.

MacDonald, B. (1978a) *The Experience of Innovation*, CARE Occasional Publications No 6, Norwich, Centre for Applied Research in Education, University of East Anglia.

MacDonald, B. (1978b) 'Accountability, standards and the process of schooling', paper commissioned by the Educational Research Board of the Social Science Research Council, in Becher, T. and Maclure, S. (Eds) (1978) *Accountability in Education*, Windsor, National Foundation for Educational Research Publishing Company, pp. 127–51.

MacDonald, B. (1979) 'Hard times — accountability in England', *Educational Analysis*, 1, 1, summer.

MacDonald, B. (1980a) 'Letters from a headmaster', in Simons, H. (Ed) *Towards a Science of the Singular: Essays About Case Study in Educational Research and Evaluation*, CARE Occasional Publications No 10, Norwich, Centre for Applied Research in Education, University of East Anglia, pp. 17–44.

MacDonald, B. (1980b) 'Barriers to democratic evaluation', paper delivered at the University of Illinois, July, Norwich, University of East Anglia, mimeo.

MacDonald, B. (1981) 'Interviewing in case study evaluation', paper presented at the annual meeting of the American Educational Research Association, Los Angeles, April, in *Phi Delta Kappa CEDR Quarterly*, 14, 4, Bloomington, IND.

MacDonald, B. (1982a) 'Mandarins and lemons — The executive investment in program evaluation', paper presented at the annual meeting of the American Educational Research Association, Los Angeles, April 1981, in *Phi Delta Kappa CEDR* Quarterly, 15, 2, Bloomington, IND.

MacDonald, B. (1982b) 'Educational evaluation in the contemporary world', invited presentation to the Simposium Internacional De Didactica General y Didacticas Especiales, La Manga del Mar Menor, Spain, 27 September–2 October.

MacDonald, B. (1983a) 'Making a difference', presentation to the National Curriculum Conference, Adelaide, 19–22 August 1983. Edited version in Hutchins, G. (Ed) (1984) *Shaping the Curriculum*, Vol. 2, Australian Curriculum Studies Association.

MacDonald, B. (1983b) 'Issues in project evaluation', Meta-Evaluation of the European Community Action Programme: Transition from Education to Working Life, Norwich, Centre for Applied Research in Education, University of East Anglia, mimeo.

MacDonald, B. (1984a) 'Democratic evaluation in practice', paper presented at the Second National Evaluation Conference, 26–27 July, Melbourne, Victoria, Australia.

MacDonald, B. (1984b) 'Teacher education for teacher-led development', key note address to the annual conference of the South Pacific Association for Teacher Education, Canberra, July.

MacDonald, B., Adelman, C., Kushner, S. and Walker, R. (1982) *Bread and Dreams: A Case Study of Bilingual Schooling in the USA*, CARE Occasional Publications No 12, Norwich, Centre for Applied Research in Education, University of East Anglia.

MacDonald, B., Argent, M.J., Elliott, J., May, N., Naylor, J.T., and Norris, N.F.J. (1987) *Police Probationer Training in England and Wales*, London, Home Office.

MacDonald, B. and Jenkins, D. (1980) 'Understanding computer assisted learning', final report of the Evaluation of the National Development Programme in Computer Assisted Learning, Norwich, Centre for Applied Research in Education, University of East Anglia, mimeo.

MacDonald, B., Jenkins, D., Kemmis, S. and Tawney, D. (1975) *The Programme at Two*, an Evaluation Report on the National Development Programme in Computer Assisted Learning, Norwich, Centre for Applied Research in Education, University of East Anglia.

MacDonald, B. with Jenkins, D., Kemmis, S. and Verma, G. (1977) 'Racism and educational evaluation', Norwich, Centre for Applied Research in Education, University of East Anglia, mimeo. In Verma, G. and Bagley, C. (Eds) (1979) *Race, Education and Identity*, London, Macmillan.

MacDonald, B., Jenkins, D., Kushner, S., Logan, T. and Norris, N. (1981) *Evaluators at Work: Report of a Workshop*, report commissioned and published by IFAPLAN, Cologne, West Germany (on behalf of the Commission of the European Communities). (Available in EURYDICE.)

MacDonald, B. and Norris, N. (1981) 'Looking up for a change — Political horizons in policy evaluation', Norwich, Centre for Applied Research in Education, University of East Anglia, mimeo. An earlier version of this paper is published in Popkewitz, T.S. and Tabachnik, B.R. (1981) *The Study of Schooling: Field Based Methodologies in Educational Research and Evaluation*, New York, Praeger, pp. 276–88, under the title 'Twin political horizons in evaluation fieldwork'.

MacDonald, B. and Parlett, M. (1973) 'Rethinking evaluation: Notes from the Cambridge Conference', *Cambridge Journal of Education*, 3, 2, pp. 74–82.

MacDonald, B. and Sanger, J. (1982) 'Just for the record? Notes towards a theory of interviewing in evaluation', in House, E.R. (Ed) *Evaluation Studies Review Annual*, Vol 7, Beverly Hills, CA, Sage Publications, pp. 175–97.

MacDonald, B. and Stake, R.E. (1974) 'Confidentiality: Procedures and principles of the UNCAL evaluation with respect to information about projects in the National Development Programme in Computer Assisted Learning', Norwich, Centre for Applied Research in Education, University of East Anglia, mimeo.

MacDonald, B. and Walker, R. (Eds) (1974) *SAFARI I: Innovation,*

Evaluation, Research and the Problem of Control, Norwich, Centre for Applied Research in Education, University of East Anglia.

MacDonald, B. and Walker, R. (1975) 'Case study and the social philosophy of educational research', *Cambridge Journal of* Education, 5, 1, pp. 2–11.

MacDonald, B. and Walker, R. (1976) *Changing the Curriculum*, London, Open Books.

Maclure, S. (1978) 'Introduction — Background to the accountability debate' in Becher, T. and Maclure, S. (1978) *Accountability in Education*, Windsor, National Foundation for Educational Research Publishing Company, pp. 9–26.

McLaughlin, M.W. (1975) *Education and Reform: The Elementary and Secondary Education Act of 1965 Title 1* (A Rand educational policy study), Cambridge, MA, Ballinger (Lippincott).

McMahon, A., Bolam, R., Abbott, R. and Holly, P. (1984) *Guidelines for Review and Internal Development in schools: Secondary School Handbook*, Schools Council Publications, York, Longman.

McPherson, C. (1973) *Democratic Theory: Essays in Retrieval*, London, Oxford University Press.

Manpower Services Commission (1982) 'New pilot scheme of technical and vocational education', press notice, 1 December.

Manzer, R.A. (1970) *Teachers and Politics*, Manchester, Manchester University Press.

May, N. (1981) 'The teacher as researcher movement in Britain', paper delivered at the annual meeting of the American Educational Research Association, Los Angeles, April. In Schubert, W. and Schubert, A. (Eds)(1982) *Conceptions of Curriculum Knowledge: Focus on Students and Teachers*, College of Education, Pennsylvania State University, pp. 23–30.

Miles, M. (1983) 'Unravelling the mystery of institutionalization', *Educational Leadership*, 41, 3, pp. 14–19.

Mitchell, P. (1984) 'Institutional evaluation: The process within a school', in Skilbeck, M. (Ed) *Evaluating the Curriculum in the Eighties*, London, Hodder and Stoughton, pp. 64–70.

Nash, R. (1973) *Classrooms Observed: The Teacher's Perception and the Pupil's Performance*, London, Routledge and Kegan Paul.

Nias, J. (1981) 'The nature of trust', in Elliott, J. *et al School Accountability*, London, Grant McIntyre, pp. 211–23.

Nilsson, N. and Hogben, D. (1983) 'Metaevaluation', in House, E.R. (Ed) *Philosophy of Evaluation*, New Directions for Program Evaluation, a publication of the Evaluation Research Society, London, San Francisco CA, Jossey-Bass Inc., Publishers, pp. 83–97.

Nisbet, J. (1974) 'Educational research — The state of the art', paper presented at the inaugural meeting of the British Educational Research Association.

NISBET, R. (1976) *Sociology as an Art Form*, London, Heinemann.

NORRIS, N. (Ed) (1977) *SAFARI 2: Theory in Practice*, CARE Occasional Publications No 4, Norwich, Centre for Applied Research in Education, University of East Anglia.

NORRIS, N. (1984) 'The context and tradition of contemporary educational evaluation', Norwich, Centre for Applied Research in Education, University of East Anglia, mimeo.

NUTTALL, D.L. (1981) *School Self-Evaluation: Accountability with a Human Face?*, report and commentary on a Schools Council conference held at Stoke Rochford Hall, 23–26 February, London, Schools Council Publications.

NUTTALL, D.L. (1982a) *Accountability and Evaluation*, Course E364, Block 1, Parts A and B, Educational Studies: A Third Level Course, Curriculum Evaluation and Assessment in Educational Institutions, Milton Keynes, Open University Press.

NUTTALL, D.L. (1982b) 'The person and the process', *Journal of Evaluation in Education*, 2, pp. 2–6.

NUTTALL, D.L., CLIFT, P., TURNER, J. and MCCORMICK, R. (1987) *Studies in School Self-Evaluation*, Lewes, Falmer Press.

OPEN UNIVERSITY (1982) Course E364, *Curriculum Evaluation and Assessment in Educational Institutions*, Block 1, *Accountability and Evaluation*; Block 2, *Approaches to Evaluation* (Part 1, LEA initiated schemes; Part 2, Institutional self-evaluation; Part 3, Inspections; Part 4, Audited self-evaluation); Block 6, *Organization and Use of Evaluation*, Milton Keynes, Open University Press.

OXFORDSHIRE COUNTY COUNCIL (1979) *Starting Points in Self-Evaluation*, Oxford, Oxfordshire Education Department.

PARLETT, M. (1975) 'A descriptive analysis of a liberal arts college: Methods and interpretation in a commissioned case study', paper written for a symposium on 'The Applied Anthropology of School Organization: An International Comparison of Descriptive Methodologies and Utilitarian Objectives', held as part of the 34th annual meeting of the Society for Applied Anthropology, Royal Tropical Institute, Amsterdam, 19–22 March, 1975.

PARLETT, M. (1976) 'Illuminative evaluation and research in education', Slough, National Foundation for Educational Research, mimeo.

PARLETT, M. (1981) 'Illuminative evaluation', in REASON, P. and ROWAN, J. (Eds) (1981) *Human Inquiry: A Sourcebook of New Paradigm Research*, London, Wiley.

PARLETT, M. and DEARDEN, G. (1977) *Introduction to Illuminative Evaluation: Studies in Higher Education*, Cardiff-by-the Sea, CA, Pacific Soundings Press; (1981) London, Society for Research in Higher Education.

PARLETT, M. and HAMILTON, D. (1972) 'Evaluation as illumination: A new approach to the study of innovatory programmes', Occasional Paper 9, Centre for Research in the Educational Sciences, University of Edinburgh. Reprinted in HAMILTON, D. *et al* (Eds) (1977) *Beyond the Numbers game: A Reader in Educational Evaluation*, London, Macmillan, pp. 6–22, and GLASS, G. (Ed) (1976) *Evaluation Studies Review Annual*, 1, Beverly Hills, CA, Sage Publications, pp. 140–57.

PARLETT, M. and SIMONS, H. (1976) *Learning From Learners: A Study Of The Student's Experience of Academic Life*, London, The Nuffield Foundation.

PARSONS, C. (1976) 'The new evaluation: A cautionary note', *Journal of Curriculum Studies*, 8, 2, pp. 125–38.

PATTON, M.W. (1978) *Utilization-Focused Evaluation*, Beverly Hills, CA, Sage Publications.

PATTON, M.W. (1980) *Qualitative Evaluation Methods*, Beverly Hills, CA, Sage Publications.

PICK, C. and WALKER, R. (1976) *Other Rooms, Other Voices*, Ford Safari Project, Norwich, Centre for Applied Research in Education, University of East Anglia.

PLASKOW, M. (Ed) (1985) *Life and Death of the Schools Council*, Lewes, Falmer Press.

POLYANI, M. (1958) *Personal Knowledge: Towards a Post Critical Philosophy*, New York, Harper and Row; London, Routledge and Kegan Paul.

POPKEWITZ, T.S. (1984) *Paradigm and Ideology in Educational Research: The Social Functions of the Intellectual*, Lewes, Falmer Press.

PRING, R. (1984) 'Confidentiality and the right to know', in ADELMAN, C. (Ed) *The Politics and Ethics of Evaluation*, London, Croom Helm, pp. 8–18.

RAWLS, J.A. (1971) *A Theory of Justice*, Cambridge, MA, Harvard University Press.

READ, L.F. (1973) 'An Assessment of the Michigan assessment', in HOUSE, E.R. *School Evaluation: The Politics and Process*, Berkeley, CA, McCutchan, pp. 60–79.

REID, W. and WALKER, D. (Eds) (1975) *Case Studies in Curriculum Change: Great Britain and the United States*, London and Boston, MA, Routledge and Kegan Paul.

RICHARDSON, E. (1973) *The Teacher, the School and the Task of Management*, London, Heinemann Educational Books.

RIPPEY, R.M. (Ed) (1973) *Studies in Transactional Evaluation*, Berkeley, CA, McCutchan.

ROTHSCHILD, LORD (1981) *The Organisation and Management of Government Research and Development* (Cmnd 4814), London, HMSO.

RUDDUCK, J. (1981) *Making the Most of the Short In-Service Course*, Schools Council Working Paper 71, London, Methuen Educational.

RUDDUCK, J. (1985) 'A case for case records?: A discussion of some aspects of Lawrence Stenhouse's work in case study methodology', in BURGESS, R. (Ed) *Strategies of Educational Research: Qualitative Methods*, Lewes, Falmer Press, pp. 101–19.

RUDDUCK, J., HOPKINS, D., GROUNDWATER SMITH, S. and LABBETT, B. (1983) *Library Access and Sixth Form Study, A Report to the British Library Research and Development Department*.

RUNKEL, P. and SCHMUCK, R. (1984) 'The place of organization development (OD) in schools', in HOPKINS, D. and WIDEEN, M. (Eds) *Alternative Perspectives on School Improvement*, Lewes, Falmer Press, pp. 153–63.

SCHOOL IMPROVEMENT PLAN (1983) Ministerial Paper 2, *Ministerial Papers 1–4*, Melbourne, Victoria, Minister for Public Information and Discussion.

SALFORD EDUCATION DEPARTMENT (1982) *Profile 82*, City of Salford, Education Department.

SALTER, B. and TAPPER, T. (1981) *Education, Politics and the State: The Theory and Practice of Educational Change*, London, Grant McIntyre.

SCHATZMAN, L. and STRAUSS, A.L. (1973) *Field Research: Strategies for a Natural Sociology*, Englewood Cliffs, NJ, Prentice Hall.

SCRIVEN, M. (1967) 'The methodology of evaluation', in TYLER, R.W., GAGNE, R.M. and SCRIVEN, M. (1967) *Perspectives of Curriculum Evaluation*, American Educational Research Association Monograph Series on Curriculum Evaluation No 1, Chicago, Rand McNally.

SCRIVEN, M. (1974) 'Evaluation perspectives and procedures', in POPHAM, W.J. (Ed) *Evaluation in Education: Current Applications*, Berkeley, CA, McCutchan.

SHARP, R. and GREEN, A. (1975) *Education and Social Control: A Study in Progressive Primary Education*, London, Routledge and Kegan Paul.

SHIPMAN, M. (1979) *In-School Evaluation*, London, Heinemann Educational Books.

SHIPMAN, M. (1981) 'Parvenu evaluation', in SMETHERHAM, D. (Ed) *Practising Evaluation*, Driffield, Nafferton Books, pp. 111–26.

SHIPMAN, M. (1983) 'Styles of school-based evaluations', in GALTON, M. and MOON, B. (Eds) *Changing Schools ... Changing Curriculum*, London, Harper and Row, pp. 248–54.

SILVERMAN, D. (1985) *Qualitative Methodology and Sociology*, Hants, England and Vermont, USA, Gower Publishing Company.

SIMONS, H. (1971) 'Innovation and the case study of schools', *Cambridge Journal of Education*, 3, pp. 118–23.

SIMONS, H. (1974) 'Reworked essays: An alternative assessment system to examinations', in KLUG, B. (Ed) (1975) *A Question Of Degree: Assorted Papers on Assessment*. London, The Nuffield Foundation.

SIMONS, H. (1975) *Negotiating The Curriculum: A Case Study of Sociology Workshops at Keele University*, London, Nuffield Foundation.

SIMONS, H. (1977a) 'Conversation piece: The practice of interviewing in case study research', in NORRIS, N. (Ed) *SAFARI 2: Theory in Practice,* CARE Occasional Publications No 4, Norwich, Centre for Applied Research in Education, University of East Anglia, pp. 110–135. Also published in ADELMAN, C. (Ed) (1981) *Uttering Muttering,* London, Grant McIntyre, pp. 27–50.

SIMONS, H. (1977b) 'Building a social contract: Negotiation and participation in condensed field research', in NORRIS, N. (Ed) (1977) *SAFARI 2: Theory in Practice,* CARE Occasional Publications No 4, Norwich, Centre for Applied Research in Education, University of East Anglia, pp. 25–46.

SIMONS, H. (1977c) 'Suggestions for a school self-evaluation based on democratic principles', University of London Institute of Education, mimeo. Published under the title 'School-based evaluation on democratic principles', Curriculum Action Research Network Bulletin No 2, January 1978, Cambridge, Cambridge Institute of Education.

SIMONS, H. (1978–79) *EEC Pilot Project Mother Tongue and Culture in Bedfordshire,* first external evaluation report, January-September 1978, Cambridge Institute of Education, mimeo.

SIMONS, H. (Ed) (1980a) *Towards a Science of the Singular: Essays About Case Study in Educational Research and Evaluation,* CARE Occasional Publications No 10, Norwich, Centre for Applied Research in Education, University of East Anglia.

SIMONS, H. (1980b) 'The evaluative school', *Forum,* 22, 2, pp. 55–7.

SIMONS, H. (1981a) 'Process evaluation in schools', in LACEY, C. and LAWTON, D. (Eds) *Issues in Accountability and Evaluation,* London, Methuen, pp. 114–44.

SIMONS, H. (1981b) 'Case-studying superordinates: The power politics of policy evaluation', paper presented at the annual meeting of the American Educational Research Association, Los Angeles, April, in a symposium titled 'Case study in policy evaluation: Paradoxes of popularity, University of London Institute of Education, mimeo.

SIMONS, H. (1983) 'Club rules: The limits of participant evaluation', paper presented to the Social Science Research Council Conference on Qualitative Methodology and the Study of Education, London, Whitelands College, July.

SIMONS, H. (1984a) 'Issues in curriculum evaluation at the local level', in SKILBECK, M. (Ed) *Evaluating the Curriculum in the Eighties,* London, Hodder and Stoughton, pp. 45–53.

SIMONS, H. (1984b) *School Evaluation: The Democratization of Evaluation Processes,* unpublished PhD thesis, University of East Anglia.

SIMONS, H. (1985) Against the rules: Procedural problems in School self evaluation, Curriculum Perspectives, 5, 2, pp. 1–6.

Simons, H. and Parlett, M. (1976) *Up To Expectations: A Study of the Student's First Few Weeks*, London, The Nuffield Foundation.

Skilbeck, M. (1985) 'Purpose in the curriculum', in Day, C.W., Morton, D.J. and Yeoman, G.D. (Eds) *Prospect for Curriculum: Purpose, Provision and Practice*, published by the Association for the Study of the Curriculum, pp. 16–38.

Smith, L.M. (1971) 'Participant observation and evaluation strategies', paper presented to an American Educational Research Association symposium on PARTICIPANT observation and curriculum: Research and evaluation, New York, February.

Smith, L.M. (1978) 'An evolving logic of participant observation, educational ethnography and other case studies', in Shulman, L. (Ed) (1978) *Review of Research in Education*, Chicago, Peacock.

Smith, L.M. (1980) 'Reflecting on Cambridge III', notes arising from discussion at the Cambridge III Conference on Naturalistic Inquiry in Educational Research and Evaluation, Girton College, Cambridge, December 1979, Washington University, mimeo.

Smith, L.M. *et al* (1981) 'Observer role and field study knowledge', *Educational Evaluation and Policy Analysis*, 3, 3, pp. 83–90.

Smith, L.M. and Geoffrey, W. (1968) *The Complexities of an Urban Classroom: An Analysis Toward a General Theory of Teaching*, New York, Holt, Rinehart and Winston.

Smith, L.M. and Keith, P.M. (1971) *Anatomy of Educational Innovation*, New York, John Wiley.

Smith, L.M. and Pohland, P.W. (1974) 'Education, technology, and the rural highlands', in Kraft *et al* (Eds) *Four Evaluation Examples: Anthropological, Economic, Narrative and Portrayal*, AERA Monograph Series on Curriculum Evaluation 7, Chicago, Rand McNally, pp. 5–54.

Smith, L.M. and Schumacher, S. (1972) 'Extended pilot trials of the aesthetic education programme: A qualitative description, analysis and evaluation', St. Ann, Missouri, CEMREL. Extract in Hamilton, D. *et al* (Eds) (1977) *Beyond the Numbers game: A Reader in Educational Evaluation*, London, Macmillan, pp. 311–30.

Sockett, H. (Ed) (1980) *Accountability in the English Educational System*, London, Hodder and Stoughton.

Solihull Education Committee (1979) *Evaluating the School — A Guide for Secondary Schools in the Metropolitan Borough of Solihull*, Solihull, Metropolitan Borough of Solihull Education Committee.

Solihull Education Committee (1980) *Evaluating the Primary School — A Guide for Primary Schools in the Metropolitan Borough of Solihull*, Solihull, Metropolitan Borough of Solihull Education Committee.

Stake, R.E. (1967a) 'Toward a technology for the evaluation of educational programs', in Tyler, R.W. *et al Perspectives of Curriculum Evaluation*,

AERA Monograph Series on Curriculum Evaluation No 1, Chicago, Rand McNally.

STAKE, R.E. (1967b) 'The countenance of educational evaluation', *Teachers College Record*, 68, 7, pp. 523–40. Extracts in HAMILTON, D. *et al* (Eds) (1977) *Beyond the Numbers game: A Reader in Educational Evaluation*, London, Macmillan, pp. 311–30.

STAKE, R.E. (1972a) 'Responsive evaluation', Urbana-Champaign, Illinois, University of Illinois, mimeo. Revised as 'To evaluate an arts program', in STAKE, R.E. (Ed) (1975) *Evaluating the Arts in Education: A Responsive Approach*, Columbus, OH, Charles E Merrill Publishing Company.

STAKE, R.E. (1972b) 'An approach to the evaluation of instructional programs (program portrayal vs analysis)', paper delivered at the annual meeting of the American Educational Research Association, Chicago, April. Extracts (pp. 1–4) reprinted in HAMILTON, D. *et al* (Eds) *Beyond the Numbers game: A Reader in Educational Evaluation*, London, Macmillan, pp. 161–2.

STAKE, R.E. (1973) 'Measuring what learners learn', in HOUSE, E.R. (Ed) *School Evaluation: The Politics and Process*, Berkeley, CA, McCutchan, pp. 193–223.

STAKE, R.E. (1974) 'Legacies and eulogies', in MACDONALD, B. and WALKER, R. (Eds) (1974) *SAFARI I: Innovation, Evaluation, Research and the Problem of Control: Some Interim Papers*, Norwich Centre for Applied Research in Education, University of East Anglia, pp. 134–9.

STAKE, R.E. (Ed) (1975) *Evaluating the Arts in Education: A Responsive Approach*, Columbus, OH, Charles E. Merrill Publishing Company.

STAKE, R.E. (1976) 'Making school evaluations relevant', *North Central Association Quarterly*, 50, 4, pp. 347–52.

STAKE, R.E. (1978) 'The case study method in social inquiry', *Educational Researcher*, 7, pp. 5–8. Also in SIMONS, H. (Ed) (1980) *Towards a Science of the Singular: Essays About Case Study in Educational Research and Evaluation*, CARE Occasional Publications No 10, Norwich, Centre for Applied Research in Education, University of East Anglia, pp. 64–75.

STAKE, R.E. and EASLEY, J. (Eds) (1978) 'Case studies in science education', a project for the National Science Foundation conducted by the Centre for Instructional Research and Curriculum Evaluation (CIRCE) and the Committee on Culture and Cognition (CCC), CIRCE, Urbana-Champaign, IL, University of Illinois.

STAKE, R.E. and GJERDE, C. (1974) 'An evaluation of TCITY, the Twin-City Institute for Talented Youth, 1981', in KRAFT *et al* (Eds) *Four Evaluation Examples: Anthropological, Economic, Narrative and Portrayal*, AERA Monograph Series on Curriculum Evaluation 7, Chicago, Rand McNally, pp. 99–139.

STENHOUSE, L. *et al* (1970) *The Humanities Curriculum Project: An introduction*, London, Heinemann Educational Books.

STENHOUSE, L. (1975) *An Introduction to Curriculum Research and Development*, London, Heinemann Educational Books.

STENHOUSE, L. (1977) 'Exemplary case records: Towards a descriptive educational research tradition grounded in science', a proposal to the Social Science Research Council.

STENHOUSE, L. (1978) 'Case study and case records: Towards a contemporary history of education', *British Educational Research Journal*, 4, 2, pp. 21–39.

STENHOUSE, L. (1984) 'Evaluating curriculum evaluation', in ADELMAN, C. (Ed) *The Politics and Ethics of Evaluation*, London, Croom Helm, pp. 77–86.

STENHOUSE, L., VERMA, G., WILD, R.D. and NIXON, J. (1982) *Teaching About Race Relations: Problems and Effects*, London, Routledge and Kegan Paul.

STUFFLEBEAM, D.L., FOLEY, W.J., GEPHART, W.J., GUBA, E.F., HAMMOND, R.E., MERRIMAN, H.O. and PROVUS, M.M. (1971) (Phi Delta Kappa National Study Committee on Evaluation) *Educational Evaluation and Decision Making*, Itasca, IL F.E. Peacock Publishers Inc.

SUFFOLK EDUCATION COMMITTEE (1981) *Primary Schools Self Appraisal*, Suffolk, Suffolk County Council Education Committee.

TANSLEY, P. (1981) 'EC sponsored mother tongue and culture pilot project', final external evaluation report, September 1979–July 1980, Windsor, National Foundation for Educational Research Publishing Company, mimeo.

TAYLOR, T. (1977) *A New Partnership for our Schools*, Report by a Committee of Enquiry appointed by the Secretary of State for Education and Science and the Secretary of State for Wales, London, HMSO.

TIMES EDUCATIONAL SUPPLEMENT (TES) (1980) 'Immigrants Mother Tongue Costing Too Much?', 23, 8, 1980.

TOSI, A. (1986) 'A new jewel in the crown of the modern prince', in SKUTNABB-KANGAS, T. and CUMMINS, J. (Eds) *Multi-Lingual Matters*,

TYLER, R.W. (1949) *Basic Principles of Curriculum and Instruction*, Chicago, Rand McNally.

WALKER, R. (1974a) 'Classroom research: A view from SAFARI', in MACDONALD, B. and WALKER, R. (Eds) *SAFARI I: Innovation, Evaluation, Research and the Problem of Control*, Norwich, Centre for Applied Research in Education, University of East Anglia, pp. 23–7.

WALKER, R. (1974b) 'The conduct of educational case study: Ethics, theory and procedures', in MACDONALD, B. and WALKER, R. (Eds) *SAFARI I: Innovation, Evaluation, Research and the Problem of Control*, Norwich, Centre for Applied Research in Education, University of East Anglia, pp. 75–114.

WALKER, R. (1982) 'The use of case studies in applied research and evaluation', in HARTNETT, A. (Ed) *The Social Sciences in Educational Studies*, London, Heinemann.

WALKER, R. (1985) *Doing Research: A Handbook for Teachers*, London, Methuen.

WALKER, R. (1986) 'Three good reasons for not doing case studies in curriculum research', in HOUSE, E.R. (Ed) *New Directions in Educational Evaluation*, Lewes, Falmer Press, pp. 103–16. Earlier published in *Journal of Curriculum Studies*, 1983, 15, 2, pp. 155–65.

WALKER, R. and ADELMAN, C. (1975) *A Guide to Classroom Observation*, London, Methuen.

WALKER, R. and MACDONALD, B. (1975) 'The press we deserve', *Times Educational Supplement*, 6 June.

WEISS, C.H. (Ed) (1972) *Evaluating Action Programs: Readings in Social Action and Education*, Boston, MA, Allyn and Bacon.

WEISS, C.H. (1975a) 'Evaluation research in the political context', in STRUENING, E.L. and GUTTENTAG, M. (Eds) *Handbook for Evaluation Research*, Vol. 1, Beverly Hills, CA, Sage Publications, pp. 13–26.

WEISS, C.H. (1975b) 'Interviewing in evaluation research', in STRUENING, E.L. and GUTTENTAG, M. (Eds) *Handbook for Evaluation Research*, Vol. 1, Beverly Hills, CA, Sage Publications, pp. 355–95.

WEISS, C.H. (Ed) (1977) *Using Social Research in Public Policy Making*, Lexington, MA, Lexington Books.

WEISS, C.H. (1986) 'Towards the future of stakeholder approaches in evaluation', in HOUSE, E.R. (Ed) *New Directions in Educational Evaluation*, Lewes, Falmer Press, pp. 186–98.

WHITE PAPER (DOE) (1986) *Working Together: Education and Training*, London, HMSO.

WHITTY, G. (1985) *Sociology and School Knowledge: Curriculum Theory, Research and Politics*, London, Methuen.

WOLCOTT, H. (1973) *The Man in the Principal's Office: An Ethnography*, New York, Holt, Rinehart and Winston.

WOLF, R.L. (1974) 'The use of judicial evaluation methods in the formation of educational policy', *Educational Evaluation and Policy Analysis*, 1, May-June, pp. 19–28.

YOUNG, M.F.D. (Ed) (1971) *Knowledge and Control*, London, Collier-Macmillan.

A Guide to Further Reading

Evaluation is still a relatively new field of enquiry that has developed its central concepts and principles through the publication of seminal papers on the subject. Many of these, such as Stake's (1967) 'Countenance' paper, Scriven's (1967) 'Methodology' paper, MacDonald's (1974) political classification and Parlett and Hamilton's (1972) illuminative evaluation are referenced in this book so there is no need to reproduce them here. This guide to further reading focusses selectively upon a few readings that are particularly relevant to the issues raised in this book. For an annotated bibliography of curriculum evaluation literature more generally, see FRASER, B.J., in collaboration with HOUGHTON, K., (1982) *Annotated Bibliography of Curriculum Evaluation Literature*, Israel Curriculum Centre, Ministry of Education and Culture. Included in this bibliography is a list of the major journals in evaluation that have emerged since 1975 for discussion of new developments and directions in the field.

The Evaluation Studies Review Annual provides a useful source of evaluation papers annually and the American Educational Research Association (AERA) Evaluation Monographs are still an excellent source of seminal papers documenting the early development of and changes in the evaluation field.

For a very useful bibliography on qualitative methodology and field work traditions in general see BURGESS, R.G. (1985) (Ed) *Strategies of Educational Research: Qualitative Methods*, Lewes, Falmer Press, pp. 323–9.

ADELMAN, C. (Ed) (1984) *The Politics and Ethics of Evaluation*, London, Croom Helm.

Written by practising UK evaluators, a very useful book reflecting upon the ethical and political issues evaluators experienced conducting and aspiring to disseminate evaluations. Issues of confidentiality, control and the right to know are discussed in several of the papers. There is an excellent paper by Eraut on 'Handling values issues' in evaluation and two sets of guidelines for the conduct of evaluation, one written by an evaluator, the other by a barrister exploring the legal dimension of evaluation reporting.

ADELMAN, C. and ALEXANDER, R. (1982) *The Self-Evaluating Institution: Practice and Principles in the Management of Educational Change*, London, Methuen.

A book examining the nature of institutional self-evaluation with particular reference to higher education. The description and analysis of two case studies illustrating different processes of managing educational change is set within a helpful discussion of the major issues and problems of evaluation in relation to curriculum development, curriculum decision-making, accountability and the management of change.

CRONBACH, L.J. and ASSOCIATES (1980) *Toward Reform of Program Evaluation: Aims, Methods and Institutional Arrangements*, San Francisco, CA, Jossey Bass.

A reconceptualization of the field of evaluation as a gradual educative process of change. The book examines the deficiencies of the experimental approach towards evaluating educational programmes and argues a persuasive case for evaluation to take a long term service educative role in shaping and influencing policy.

GUBA, E.G. and LINCOLN, Y.S. (1981) *Effective Evaluation: Improving the Usefulness of Evaluation Results Through Responsive and Naturalistic Approaches*, San Francisco, CA, Jossey Bass.

An extremely useful book making the case for naturalistic inquiry in evaluation from both a theoretical and methodological standpoint. Part 1 traces the emergence of the 'new approach' providing a succinct comparison of evaluation models which challenged traditional assumptions and an extensive discussion of Stake's responsive evaluation. Part 2 details the advantages and problems of the naturalistic method of inquiry. In Part 3, devoted primarily to methods of collecting and reporting data, there is an interesting discussion of the self as the major instrument of research in this form of inquiry.

HAMILTON, D. (1976c) *Curriculum Evaluation*, London, Open Books.

An historical review of curriculum evaluation that documents the development and deficiencies of early forms of evaluation, such as the classical experimental comparative model and the objectives model before comparing them with the more natur-alistic forms of evaluation which developed in the seventies.

HAMILTON, D., JENKINS, D., KING, C., MACDONALD, B., PARLETT, M. (Eds) (1977) *Beyond the Numbers Game: A reader in Educational Evaluation*, London, Macmillan.

Stemming from the first Cambridge conference on alternative styles of evaluation, a collection of readings documenting the emerging trend in evaluation towards qualitative forms of in-quiry. It includes an analysis of the work of key theorists influential in this change, such as Atkin, Scriven, Stake, Eisner, Stenhouse, and the identification of major issues, approaches and examples of evaluation more qualitative in kind. While many of the excerpts are irritatingly short, the book is worth reading alone for the illuminating and often witty introductions to the major sections.

HOUSE, E.R. (1980) *Evaluating With Validity*, Beverly Hills, CA, Sage Publications.

An excellent book on evaluation theory that brings together epistemological, political and ethical issues and addresses the central question of validity in different models of evaluation. It includes several of House's earlier key papers on justice in evaluation, the logic of evaluative argument and assumptions underlying evaluation models.

MCCORMICK, R. and JAMES, M. (1983) *Curriculum Evaluation in Schools*, London and Canberra, Croom Helm.

An extensive book setting out the main arguments for school curriculum evaluation in terms of accountability, professional development and curriculum review, and comparing strategies for development by insiders and outsiders. The second part is a review of approaches, techniques and issues in reporting that may prove helpful in conducting school evaluations. It contains a useful bibliography.

MACDONALD, B. and WALKER, R. (Eds) (1974) *SAFARI: Innovation, Evaluation, and the Problem of Control, Some Interim Papers*, Norwich, Centre for Applied Research in Education, University of East Anglia.

A collection of papers examining the democratic case-study research approach to the SAFARI (Success and Failure and Recent Innovation) Project. It includes MacDonald's political classification of evaluation paper, and a long paper by Walker examining inspirations for, and problems of, educational case study.

MCLAUGHLIN, M.W. (1975) *Education and Reform*, The Elementary and Secondary Education Act of 1965, Title I (A Rand educational policy study), Cambridge, MA, Ballinger (Lippincott).

An excellent study of the aspirations and effects of the evaluation of the Elementary and Secondary Education Act of 1965, Title I in the USA. A very useful context study for understanding the growth of mandatory reporting in the USA, it also illustrates the difficulties and shortfalls of evaluations conducted in a multi-level government structure.

NORRIS, N. (Ed) (1977) *SAFARI II: Theory in Practice*, CARE Occasional Publications, No. 4, Norwich, Centre for Applied Research in Education, University of East Anglia.

An extremely useful set of papers drawing on the experience of the SAFARI and UNCAL (Understanding Computer Assisted Learning) evaluation studies in the UK, examining the implications of democratic evaluation in practice. It includes both methodological and theoretical reflections on the process and an internal critique.

PATTON, M.Q. (1978) *Utilization-focused Evaluation*, Beverly Hills, CA, Sage Publications.

A very useful book exposing the rational decision-making model of evaluation and offering an approach to evaluation that is realistically based upon how decisions are made and how evaluations could be more useful.

PATTON, M.Q. (1980) *Qualitative Evaluation Methods*, Beverly Hills, CA, Sage Publications.

A book that presents the case for qualitative methods in evaluation and offers practical guidance in each of the qualitative methods discussed — interviewing, observing, documentary materials. Introduced with not a little humour, each section is eminently readable and accessible as a guide to evaluation design, collection of data, analysis and interpretation.

SIMONS, H. (Ed) (1980a) *Towards a Science of the Singular: Essays About Case Study in Educational Research and Evaluation*, CARE Occasional Publications No. 10, Norwich, Centre for Applied Research in Education, University of East Anglia.

Arising out of the second Cambridge conference on alternative styles of evaluation a selection of essays arguing the case for case study in evaluation and educational research and exploring related ethical issues in fieldwork and reporting. Papers by Stake, Hamilton and Kemmis examine the theoretical case for case study; MacDonald and Smith focus on ethical issues while there are interesting papers by Graef and Wilby respectively on related ethical issues in documentary film-making and journalism.

Index

For Product Safety Concerns and Information please contact our EU
representative GPSR@taylorandfrancis.com Taylor & Francis Verlag GmbH,
Kaufingerstraße 24, 80331 München, Germany

Batch number: 08158359

Printed by Printforce, the Netherlands